THEATRE IN THE THIRD REICH, THE PREWAR YEARS

Recent Titles in
Contributions to the Study of World History

Families in Context: A World History of Population
G. Robina Quale

Waiting for Jerusalem: Surviving the Holocaust in Romania
I. C. Butnaru

Israel's Leadership: From Utopia to Crisis
Jacob Abadi

Christopher Columbus and the Portuguese, 1476–1498
Rebecca Catz

Clinging to Grandeur: British Attitudes and Foreign Policy in the Aftermath of the Second World War
Michael Blackwell

The Legend of the Mutilated Victory: Italy, the Great War, and the Paris Peace Conference, 1915–1919
H. James Burgwyn

Spain in the Nineteenth-Century World: Essays on Spanish Diplomacy, 1789–1898
James W. Cortada, editor

The Entangling Alliance: The United States and European Security, 1950–1993
Ronald E. Powaski

Kings of Celtic Scotland
Benjamin T. Hudson

America's Feeble Weapon: Funding the Marshall Plan in France and Italy, 1948–1950
Chiarella Esposito

The Jews of Medieval France: The Community of Champagne
Emily Taitz

Royalist Political Thought During the French Revolution
James L. Osen

Theatre in the Third Reich, the Prewar Years

Essays on Theatre in Nazi Germany

Edited by Glen W. Gadberry

Contributions to the Study of World History, *Number 49*

Greenwood Press
Westport, Connecticut • London

Library of Congress Cataloging-in-Publication Data

Theatre in the Third Reich, the prewar years : essays on theatre in
  Nazi Germany / edited by Glen W. Gadberry.
      p.   cm. — (Contributions to the study of world history, ISSN
  0885-9159 ; no. 49)
    Includes bibliographical references and index.
    ISBN 0-313-29516-6 (alk. paper)
    1. Theater—Germany—History—20th century. 2. German drama—20th
  century—History and criticism. I. Gadberry, Glen W. II. Series :
  Contributions to the study of world history ; no. 49.
  PN2654.T55 1995
  792'.0943'09043—dc20   94-36642

British Library Cataloguing in Publication Data is available.

Copyright © 1995 by Glen W. Gadberry

All rights reserved. No portion of this book may be
reproduced, by any process or technique, without the
express written consent of the publisher.

Library of Congress Catalog Card Number: 94-36642
ISBN: 0-313-29516-6
ISSN: 0885-9159

First published in 1995

Greenwood Press, 88 Post Road West, Westport, CT 06881
An imprint of Greenwood Publishing Group, Inc.

Printed in the United States of America

The paper used in this book complies with the
Permanent Paper Standard issued by the National
Information Standards Organization (Z39.48-1984).

10 9 8 7 6 5 4 3 2

Lo, where the Stage, the poor, degraded Stage,
Holds its warped mirror to a gaping age!
—Charles Sprague, *Curiosity*

Die Kunst ist keine Dienerin der Menge
—August von Platen, *Die verhängnisvolle Gabel*

Contents

1. Introduction: The Year of Power—1933
   Glen W. Gadberry — 1

2. The National Socialist *Volksgemeinschaft* Fantasy and the Drama of National Rebirth
   Robert A. Pois — 17

3. Theatre in Detmold 1933–1939: A Case Study of Provincial Theatre During the Nazi Prewar Era
   Ron Engle — 33

4. Theatre of the Front: Sigmund Graff and *Die endlose Straße*
   William Sonnega — 47

5. Eberhard Wolfgang Möller: Politically Correct Playwright of the Third Reich
   Rufus J. Cadigan — 65

6. Ordained Hands on the Altar of Art: Gründgens, Hilpert, and Fehling in Berlin
   William Grange — 75

7. Werner Krauß and the Third Reich
   William R. Elwood — 91

8.	Nazi Berlin and the Großes Schauspielhaus *Yvonne Shafer*	103
9.	The First National Socialist Theatre Festival—Dresden 1934 *Glen W. Gadberry*	121
10.	Collaboration or Survival, 1933–1938: Reassessing the Role of the *Jüdischer Kulturbund* *Rebecca Rovit*	141
11.	The Final Chapter: Theatre in the Concentration Camps of Nazi Germany *Michael Patterson, with material by Louise Stafford-Charles*	157

Bibliography	167
Index	179
About the Editor and Contributors	185

THEATRE IN THE THIRD REICH,
THE PREWAR YEARS

1

Introduction: The Year of Power—1933

Glen W. Gadberry

Adolf Hitler was named German Chancellor by aging President Paul von Hindenburg on 30 January 1933. The event was subsequently glorified as the *Machtergreifung* (seizure of power or power grab), although absolute power would not be taken until later in the year. On the night of the thirtieth, thousands of Berlin SS, SA, and *Stahlhelm* (Steel Helmet, a right-wing veterans organization) formed a torchlit parade that snaked its way up Wilhelmstraße to Unter den Linden. The column turned left to pass through the Brandenburg Gate and then left again on its way to the Chancellory. The "Thousand-Year" Reich began with this impressive celebration of fire and order and military precision, enthusiastically received by a large portion of Berlin's population. It would end twelve years later, in fire, destruction, and military invasion, to the dismay or relief of a population repeatedly decimated by unprecedented horrors, acts of terror, and a bloody war of liberation.

Hitler, the swastika, and the gas chamber are perhaps the most powerful icons of twentieth-century European history, and they dominated the theatre space as completely as they did every other aspect of German life. During the two decades that National Socialism sought and exercised state power, the German theatre continued to function and, when it complied with the directives of the state, to flourish. The National Socialist leadership was vitally interested in the arts, and through its prejudice, largesse, and regulation, it changed the face of German theatre in gross and subtle ways.

The stage was systematically purged and replenished. New faces and forms sought to satisfy the major arts policies, coming from competing cultural bureaucracies. Theatre underwent a *"braun* shift": staff, repertoire, aesthetics, and audiences were politicized and colorized by the dominant ideologic hue of National Socialism, the pervasive *braun* of its Munich headquarters (the *Braun* House) and of its brown-shirted Storm Troopers, the SA bully boys at the Party precinct level. The theatre was to acknowledge the red-white-black of the Nazi flag, designed by Hitler himself.[1] There was to be no sympathy for the red-gold-pink of the victims of fascism: Communists, Jews, and gays, murdered in back streets, "re-education" camps, and gas chambers. Under this barbaric regime, where even aesthetic decisions might carry life-or-death consequences, there were tens of thousands of performance events. There are examples of fanatic reverence for Nazi ideology, abject compliance, and careful (sometimes careless) subversion.

Seldom has theatre operated under such conditions, and seldom with so much scholarly neglect.[2] This volume is intended to explore some of this theatre in extremis. The essays that follow treat select topics of Third Reich theatre during the prewar years—that is, during those aggressive years of political power and national expansion prior to the 1939 invasion of Poland. It was an era that mixed heady exhilaration with persuasion and coercion. These are the years of greatest cultural upheaval and innovation. By World War II, national ideology had changed the German production staff, new stages had been built, narrowly creative programs and ventures had been attempted. Many projects failed and the legitimate stage settled into a sort of normalcy. After 1939, government and national interest shifted to the war effort. Restricted repertoire, the aesthetic and physical demands of the military, and ultimately the closure or destruction of German stages reconfigured the Third Reich theatre. The period after 1939 deserves a volume in its own right.

The present collection includes essays on performers, ideology, specialized theatres, national theatre events, dramatic types, and to help balance the image an essay on theatre in the concentration camps as a kind of grotesque postscript. Their diversity is to suggest something of the range of subjects available in this period. There is no one critical approach, except that contributors were encouraged to concentrate upon this neglected period rather than theorizing methodology. The focus is the functioning theatre during the Third Reich, not contemporary critical or historiographic discourse. The Third Reich began officially that 30th of January 1933. While the Nazi faithful celebrated their triumph, Germans of other political, racial, artistic, and sexual persuasions reviewed what had been spelled out for their future. The Nazi agenda was readily available, even to the most casual observer. Most of Third Reich ideology derived from Hitler's *Mein Kampf*, which was itself derivative of right-wing and nationalist thought of the nineteenth century.[3] Although dictated back in 1924, Hitler's credo continued to set the goals and justifications for the Party and Nazi state, virtually unchanged, until that state was forced out of existence. Hitler's principal remarks on the arts are found in two chapters, "The Causes of the Collapse" of the Second German Reich in 1918 and "*Volk* and Race," which develops his assumptions about the larger causes of cultural decay.[4]

Hitler argued that there had been a radical decline in German culture after the turn of the century. This "bolshevism of art" had produced the likes of cubism, dada, and expressionism, those "sickly aberrations of the insane or depraved." That such abominations had found their way into galleries and museums, paid for with public funds, was a sign of "spiritual lunacy" and "a slowly rotting world."[5] Hitler's aversion to the avant-garde may be understood by looking at his own work and the reactions of his contemporaries: his realistic postcard drawings, romantic landscapes, or sentimental portraits could be sold on the streets of Imperial Vienna, but were dismissed by established critics and galleries.[6] Anxious for revenge, access, and national rebirth, Hitler demanded a strong government to purge the arts, for the sake of Germany itself.

As deplorable as conditions were in the studio arts, it was theatre that had abused German culture the most:

> The theatre in particular "had sunk deep" into this abyss. With but a few exceptions, German theatres had become places for good Germans to avoid: it was a tragic sign of this inner decay that the young could no longer be sent into any of these so-called "abodes of art." This was openly admitted without shame: "Children not admitted!," just like the warnings at side-shows.[7]

Not only had the theatre exhibited the aberrant avant-garde, but it had also degraded the cultural monuments of the past—Schiller, Goethe, and Shakespeare. "For it was typical of this time: not only did the theatre continue to show filth, but worse, it dirtied everything truly great in the past."[8]

Theatre's decline had been abetted by producers who blocked "true nationalist art" and by "Bolshevist" critics who attacked anything but their preferred drama. In the early 1920s, "real" German drama had been kept from the stage by critically praised expressionist "hallucinations."[9] Hitler's scenario of conspiracy and exclusion may have been suggested by the career of his friend and racial mentor, Dietrich Eckart (1868–1923), who had died only months before (Hitler dedicated the first book of *Mein Kampf* to Eckart). Except for a popular adaptation of Ibsen's *Peer Gynt*, Eckart had been rejected by the pre-Nazi German stage. His plays would only come into their own with the Machtergreifung: four received posthumous premieres during the first full Nazi season. Because so many of their braun artists had suffered this kind of neglect, the Nazis would restaff theatres, museums, and galleries to empower their own and to avenge rejected "geniuses" such as Dietrich Eckart. "Proper art" would again fill the halls of German culture.

In "*Volk* and Race," Hitler outlined the cause for artistic decline: German art had been dominated by racial aliens, by Jews. Like his mentors, Eckart and Vienna Mayor Karl Lüger, Hitler could find an "international Jewish conspiracy" behind any social or historic phenomenon that blocked nationalist interests. Somewhat grudgingly, he tells us, he came to believe that Jews had no culture of their own, and worse, were cultural destroyers. They pulled down superior peoples of "host" countries to their own level through a variety of methodologies and ideologies, ancient and modern: Judeo-Christian brotherhood, eighteenth-century *fraternité*, nineteenth-century capitalism, and twentieth-century Communism. Hitler's fantasies of cultural spoilation were made the more rabid and lurid by nightmare images of rape and miscegenation; he pictured the "black-haired Jew boy, with Satanic joy in his face," lying in wait to ambush the "unsuspecting [blond] girl whom he defiles with his blood and steals from her people."[10] Jewish spoilation of race was paralleled by Jewish destruction of culture.

Hitler felt the stage particularly prone to Jewish cultural assault because Jews were used to role playing in their "host" countries: acting was a learned survival skill. This proficiency at deception allowed easy entry to theatre, because, he assumed, most stage acting was merely imitation, without real invention. Acting was an ideal craft for a race without artistic talent.

> But here, too, he's really only the "buffoon," or, to put it better: the ape. Here, too, he lacks the ultimate touch of real greatness; here, too, he's not an original creator, but a surface imitator. But his turns and tricks cannot deceive us: there is no inner life to his impersonations. It's now that the Jewish press comes lovingly to his aid. It raises such a racket of hosannas about every new actor, even the most mediocre incompetent, provided he's a Jew, that our contemporaries finally believe they see a real artist before them. But in truth he's just a lame stooge.[11]

Empowered by Hitler's artistic view, the Third Reich would discredit contributions of Jews to German theatre history and purge the living stage. The Nazis tried to rewrite the past and discredit memory. The task was formidable, because so many brilliant Jewish actors and directors were etched in German theatre history. Although it took over two years, it proved easier to strip the stage of its Jews, as well as its Communists and aesthetic decadents, than to make the Volk forget the artistry of Otto Brahm, Max Reinhardt, or Elizabeth Bergner. Hitler and his cultural minions were only too clear about their opinions and plans: their hate-filled commentaries filled specialty bookshops and the Party newspaper. The general media carried countless interviews and feature stories on the Nazis and what might be expected under Hitler as Chancellor. Hitler promised that heads would roll, and many Germans gave him support for his program and for his honesty.

The first evening of the Third Reich, Berlin's twenty-nine theatres continued their regular schedules. Berliners could forgo the Nazi torch parade for the likes of Goethe's *Faust I* at the Staatliches Schauspielhaus or Kleist's *Prinz von Homburg* at the Deutsches Theater. Thornton Wilder's *Glückliche Reise (Happy Journey to Trenton and Camden)* was playing at the Theater am Kurfürstendamm and Carl Zuckmayer's *Schinderhannes* at the Volksbühne. There was *Madame Butterfly* at the Städtische Oper, Johann Strauß's *Eine Nacht in Venedig* at the Staatsoper and Franz Léhar's *Zarewitsch* at the Metropol. There was also the typical slate of light dramatic fare, including the revue *Männer sind mal so* ("Men Are Like That") at the Schiller Theater, *Achtung, frisch Gestrichen* ("Careful, Wet Paint") by René Fauchois at the Komödienhaus, and *Terzett* ("Trio") by Marcel Achard at the Theater in der Stresemannstraße (the street and theatre were subsequently rechristened "Saarlandstraße" by the Nazis, who reviled the liberal former Chancellor and Foreign Minister Gustav Stresemann). Additionally there was *Ein Mädel ohne Mann* ("A Girl Without a Man") at the Komödie, Erich Ebermayer and Franz Cammerlohr's *Bargeld lacht* ("Cash Talks") at the Theater in der Behrenstraße, *Mutter muß heiraten* ("Mother Must Marry") by English playwright Neil Forbes Grant at the Renaissance-Theater, Anna Gmeyner's *Das Automatenbüfett* ("The Automat Buffet") at the Theater am Schiffbauerdamm, Paul Abraham's operetta *Ball im Savoy* at the Großes Schauspielhaus, and Kalman's *Zirkusprinzessin* ("The Circus Princess") at the Rose-Theater. Less major theatres offered even more minor entertainments.

On this night of power, Berlin theatre did not offer much to tempt National Socialists or their sympathizers. *Faust* or *Prinz von Homburg* were acceptable expressions of German stage genius, but Goethe and Kleist were compromised in theatres with recent Jewish associations—Leopold Jessner at the Staatliches Schauspielhaus and Max Reinhardt at the Deutsches Theater. The Berlin schedule reinforced Hitler's complaints about the German stage: foreign domination, entertainments of limited political or cultural value, and nothing to speak to the new "racial heroism" that had won the struggle for power.

National Socialist works had been produced prior to the Machtergreifung, but typically far from Berlin. This is not surprising, because the strength of the Party would first express itself in regional *Gaue* (districts) such as Thüringen (Weimar), Weser-Ems (Oldenburg), or München-Oberbayern (Munich) and because "cultural bolshevists" were supposedly too entrenched in the theatres of the capital to allow access. It was the Cologne Schauspielhaus which produced Germany's first National Socialist premiere back in 1927: Hanns Johst's *Thomas Paine*. This inventive stage biography of Paine as American nationalist revolutionary, forgotten by his country while he sits in a French Republican prison, was called "the first political drama of the New Germany."[12] Until the Machtergreifung, there had been a gradual increase in nationalist production in Germany. During January 1933, the last month of the Weimar Republic, ten of the twenty-two premieres in Germany's two hundred legitimate theatres were by playwrights who would subsequently hold membership in the Third Reich writers union, the *Reichsverband Deutscher Schriftsteller* (National Association of German Authors).[13]

Three of those ten playwrights had prominent careers in the Third Reich, and their January premieres illustrate subjects of recurring interest to nationalists. Paul Joseph Cremers's *Marneschlacht* ("Battle of the Marne") premiered at Mannheim on 14 January. It is one of many dramas about World War I, that geo-political event which had humiliated Germany and helped bring Hitler to power. *Aufbruch aus Österreich* ("Departure from Austria," Munich, 18 January) by Eugen Ortner is set in Hitler's homeland, which had been, like Germany, stripped of immediate significance by the foreign powers dictating the Versailles Treaty. Based upon postwar history, the play shows a group of religious zealots who plan to flee Europe and its recurring disasters to found a colony in Africa. Flight is prevented and, to the new nationalists, is undesirable: the Greater German Fatherland ought not be deserted, especially in times of need. Austrian Richard Billinger's comedy *Lob des Landes* ("Land's Praise") premiered in Leipzig, 25 January. Its dominant theme is that urban life upsets the inherent purity and strength nurtured by national soil. The play is an example of *Blut und Boden* (Blood and Soil): nationalists believed that genetics and geography provided one's own people with a distinct advantage in human development and world culture. The privileged mixture of heredity and environment, nature and nurture, honed by generations of hardship and sacrifice, authorized the emergence of a triumphant people—once its enemies were overcome. Cremers, Ortner, and Billinger reinforced National Socialist interpretations of past and present, and their careers had marked advance after 1933 in and out of Berlin.

Only three works premiered in the "cosmopolitan" capital in January, but they typically had no appeal to the emerging nationalist ideology. Although Karl von Mühlfeldt would be admitted to the Nazi writers union, he was uncomfortable with the new Germany: he emigrated to Vienna in 1936 and at the Anschluß moved on to the Philippines. His *Was uns fehlt? Arbeit!* ("What Do we Need? Work!," Tribüne, 23 January) might have treated the powerful social issue of postwar and post-Crash unemployment in ways to appeal to the far right—or to the far left. But his sentimental play was merely "banal and trivial." Unemployment was the dramaturgic crisis to force family reconciliation.[14] The second Berlin premiere was by "Alfred Kallir"—a pseudonym for Ernst Lach. It appears that Lach was Jewish and had no significant career, in Germany or elsewhere. His artists' comedy *Nr. 51 "Badendes Mädchen"* ("Number 51 'Bathing Beauty'") premiered at the Kleines Theater on the eighteenth. Published in 1932 by Samuel Fischer, it was an entertaining but innocuous "racketeer comedy" in the artists' milieu—a typical "dilettante work."[15] Similarly forgotten was Karl Külb's comedy, *Narren des Ruhms* ("Fools' Glory," premiere at the Zentral-Theater on the twentieth); the play was dropped from the repertoire after a few performances and went unreviewed and unpublished. These last premieres of the Weimar Republic in Germany's cultural capital did little to reinforce the singular place Berlin held in German and European theatre history.[16]

A fourth premiere had been scheduled, Polish playwright László Fodor's *Kuß vor dem Spiegel* ("Kiss Before the Mirror"), but the play was postponed when the management of the Lessing-Theater went bankrupt. The theatre had been overseen by enterpreneurs Alfred and Fritz Rotter, along with the Metropol, Theater in der Stresemannstraße, Lustspielhaus, Großes Schauspielhaus, Theater des Westens, and minor revue houses. The brothers bought and sold theatre spaces and leases, and, according to general complaint, flooded their variously important theatres with innocuous fare and erotic revues. By mid-January, the Rotters had overextended and were unable to meet loan payments, rents, and salaries. Their whole enterprise collapsed. While banks and actors scrambled to save what they could, the Rotters fled to Liechtenstein to avoid arrest—bankruptcy carried legal consequences in Weimar Germany. Because the Rotters were Jewish, their financial manipulations and swift flight fueled anti-Semitic assaults on Weimar theatre during its last weeks.[17] The Nazis complained that there had been no twentieth century German theatre, rather one "of the Jewish nation" which was destroying German culture.[18]

After the Machtergreifung, the Nazis intended to set all "right." As they consolidated political power and eliminated opposition, they did not neglect the arts in their year of power. A chronology of dates and events of importance to the German theatre might be helpful, to position the essays that follow. Government regulation and emerging cultural bureaucracies demonstrate the complexity of theatre in the Third Reich. Nazi cultural order was swiftly imposed and curiously disordered.

> *4 February 1933:* As one of his first acts as Chancellor, Hitler issued the *Verordnung zum Schutz des deutschen Volkes* ("Decree for the Protection of the German People"). One paragraph directly affected the arts: police were given virtually unlimited power to confiscate or ban literature that might "endanger public order."[19] Subsequent refinements put the police and immediate censorship at the discretion of Nazi cultural offices.
>
> *27–28 February 1933:* the Reichstag was burned and Hitler used this all-too-convenient "act of Communist terrorism" to demand and

receive unlimited power to deal with the "national crisis." Germany was now a dictatorship under the Führer.

13 March 1933: Hitler created the *Reichsministerium für Propaganda und Volksaufklärung* (Reich Ministry of Propaganda and Popular Enlightenment). The *Gauleiter*, or district leader, for Greater Berlin since 1926 and Party propagandist since 1929, Dr. Joseph Goebbels (1897–1945, suicide) was named Reichsminister. Goebbels preferred the more positive term *culture* to *propaganda* for the title and tried to change it in 1934, but was overruled by Hitler, who had a special affection for *propaganda*.[20] Goebbels nonetheless tried to dominate all cultural activity in the Third Reich.

15 March 1933: The new Propaganda Minister addressed the press. He told Germans their Ministry was a populist organization: "It arose out of the people and will always execute the will of the people. I reject most passionately the idea that this government stands for reactionary aims, that we are reactionaries." He promised close coordination of national and state policy with the aim of winning the people to heartfelt approval of their state philosophy: "It is not enough for people to be more or less reconciled to our regime, to be persuaded to adopt a neutral attitude towards us, rather we want to work on people until they have capitulated to us, until they grasp ideologically that what is happening in Germany today not only *must* be accepted but also *can* be accepted." He intended to bring all propaganda and "institutions of public information" into one hand.[21]

7 April 1933: The *Gesetz zur Wiederherstellung des Berufsbeamtentums* (Law for the Restoration of the Career Civil Service) was signed by Hitler and Minister of Interior Wilhelm Frick (1877–1946, executed at Nürnberg). Unless they had a significant war record—a clause added to satisfy President Hindenberg, and revoked when he died—non-Aryan civil servants were "retired" from public life. This law removed Jews from theatres and other arts institutions with national, state, or city subsidy.

11 April 1933: With Hitler/Hess approval, Alfred Rosenberg, head of the *Kampfbund deutscher Kultur* (Militant League for German Culture, formed 1927–28) created the *Reichsverband Deutsche Bühne* (National German Stage Alliance). The Reichsverband was an audience organization offering group-rate tickets to events approved by Rosenberg (1893–1946, executed at Nürnberg). The Union was an effective means to further Rosenberg's more radical Nazi aesthetics, and to sidestep Goebbels. Both organizations were given special authority within the Party by Hitler through his deputy, Rudolf Hess. The "Office Rosenberg" constituted a second, competing cultural level in Nazi Germany.

11 April 1933: Newspapers published an exchange of letters of Berlin Symphony conductor Wilhelm Furtwängler and Goebbels. Furtwängler had complained about the loss of so many artists due to the Civil Service Law of 7 April and how this would hurt German art. Goebbels responded that only non-Germans had been retired. He noted that foreign interests had dominated the arts for too long, and German art could only benefit from their replacement. The exchange received international coverage.

6 May 1933: As Minister President of the huge state of Prussia, Hermann Göring took personal control of Prussian state and city theatres, including major theatres in Berlin. Contracts, hiring, and repertoire were to be handled by or cleared through Göring himself or by the Prussian Offices of Interior or Culture. Goebbels's Theatre Division of the Propaganda Ministry was merely to establish the "general directions" for theatre in Prussia.[22] Thereafter, there would be a third theatre milieu for Nazi theatre, under the aegis of Field Marshall Göring (1893–1946, suicide, facing execution at Nürnberg).

8 May 1933: No doubt with Göring's challenge in mind, Goebbels addressed theatre producers at the Hotel Kaiserhof in Berlin, on *Die Aufgaben des deutschen Theaters* (tasks of the German theatre). The Minister reiterated his new "general directions": outmoded artistic forms would be eliminated in favor of the new Volk art. Third Reich art was to be political, patriotic, and consistent with the philosophy of the ruling Party. "German art of the next decade will be heroic; it will be like steel; it will be romantic, non-sentimental, factual; it will be national with great pathos and at once obligatory and binding, or it will be nothing." He recalled the Furtwängler dialogue by admonishing those who complained that Jews had been removed from the arts, "here and there." Producers should remember the fourteen years of the Weimar Republic when "real Germans" went unemployed because their posts were held by Jews.[23]

10 May 1933: Some 20,000 proscribed books by 160 authors were burned in Berlin and other cities—"The old is in flames. The new will rise up out of the flame in our own hearts." Goebbels praised the "spontaneous" participants for "entrusting to the flames the nonsense of the past"; "the age of exaggerated Jewish intellectuality is at an end."[24] As "fire incantations" were recited, the works of Marx, Freud, Remarque, Kerr, Tucholsky, and others were added to the smoking pyres. Ever expanding lists of forbidden literature were regularly published by the Propaganda Ministry. Rosenberg's office maintained its own lists of forbidden and preferred literature.

16 June 1933: In an open letter to "The National Socialist Administration of Germany," Max Reinhardt surrendered ownership of his Berlin theatres: "I have only one choice remaining, to offer to Germany the possession of my life's work.... The decision to sever myself conclusively from the Deutsches Theater does not come easily for me. With this possession I lose not only the fruit of a 37-year career; more important, I lose the place that I have built up for a lifetime and in which I myself have grown. I lose my home."[25] Reinhardt was able to continue his career elsewhere, unlike thousands of others "retired" from German culture.

21 August 1933: As the 1933/34 season was announced and as plays were in rehearsal, Goebbels created the office of *Reichsdramaturg* (National Dramaturg) to advise the Propaganda Ministry, to assist dramatists, dramaturgs, and critics, and to help shape the German repertoire. The office was empowered to "realize the cultural principles of National Socialism in the world of German Theatre." Critic and dramaturg Dr. Rainer Schlösser (1899–1945) was named to the position.

1 September 1933: Hitler delivered his first Party Congress address on culture at Nürnberg. He reiterated positions found in *Mein Kampf*: "National Socialism recognizes the heroic teaching of the value of blood, race, personality, as well as the eternal laws of selection [which had allowed for the appearance of the German Volk]. It consequently stands absolutely opposed to the world view of international-pacifist democracy and its products." Once again he stressed the racial dimension—"each well-defined race has left its own signature in the book of art, except for those like the Jews who are without any productive artistic ability of their own." Even though there were enormous economic problems to overcome, he promised arts support: "It is important especially in a time of economic need and trouble to make clear to everyone, that a nation too has higher tasks than to bow to mutual economic egoism. The artistic monuments of humankind have always been the altars of awareness of higher mission and greater worth." Hitler recharged the German arts scene and promised support for those who supported the government.[26]

22 September 1933: Goebbels created the *Kulturkammern* (Culture Chambers) within the Propaganda Ministry, to shape the seven arts and media: theatre, literature, press, radio, music, fine arts, and film. Art could be created, shown, or published by members only;

membership was restricted by heritage, political affiliation, and artistry. Theatre people had to hold memberships in one of the offices of the Theatre Chamber; playwrights and critics had to belong to the Literature Chamber. Actor Otto Laubinger (1892–1935) was named head of the Theatre Chamber; Reichsdramaturg Rainer Schlösser succeeded him in 1935. Playwright Hans Friedrich Blunck (1888–1961) was named President of the Literature Chamber and was succeeded by Hanns Johst in 1935.

1 October 1933: Gotthold Lessing's Enlightenment drama of religious tolerance, *Nathan der Weise*, began a series of closed performances in Berlin. It was the first production of the theatre division of the *Kulturbund Deutscher Juden* (Cultural Union of German Jewry). This state-approved Jewish organization provided employment for artists "retired" by civil service laws and unable to emigrate; it also provided entertainment for Jewish audiences. A national organization, the *Reichsverband der Jüdischen Kulturbünde in Deutschland* (National Alliance of the Jewish Cultural Unions in Germany), received a government charter at the end of 1936.[27]

1 November 1933: Supplemental regulations were issued for the Culture Chambers. The police, and hence the powers of swift arts censorship, were placed at the disposal of the Chambers. By December, over one thousands works—some "collected works"—were on lists of forbidden literature.

27 November 1933: The National Socialist workers organization, *Kraft durch Freude* (Strength Through Joy), was created within and for the Labor Front. Workers were to be assured access to German culture. Labor Head Dr. Robert Ley (1890–1945, suicide) proclaimed, "The basic principle must be: the right to enjoy our culture is not for someone who has money or can call a home his own, but for someone who has an inner need. It matters not whether fate has blessed him with earthly goods or not."[28] With the approval of Goebbels's Propaganda Ministry, the Großes Schauspielhaus was redesigned as the first "KdF" theatre: the "Theater des Volkes" (opened 18 January 1934, with Schiller's *Die Räuber*). Similar KdF theatres opened in other major cities. These theatres represented an additional theatrical environment, competing with the Prussian theatres of Göring, the ideologic theatres of Rosenberg, and the national theatres of Goebbels.

This "Year of Power" ended with New Year's messages from the Führer to his trusted aides. Published in the *Völkischer Beobachter*, and other national newspapers, the first round of greetings were directed to the "Seven Pillars of the Party": Deputy Führer Rudolf Hess, Party Treasurer Franz Xaver

Schwarz, publisher Max Amann (subsequent President of the Press Chamber), SA-Leader Ernst Röhm (murdered in the 1934 purge of the SA, the "Night of Long Knives"), SS-Leader Heinrich Himmler, and the cultural rivals Goebbels and Rosenberg. Hitler congratulated them all for their individual efforts winning national power, and he promised new triumphs to follow.[29]

In 1934, Germany's commercial theatres, the remaining twenty percent of all German professional houses, were put under the same controls as subsidized state and local theatres. On 3 September 1935, Hans Hinkel (1901–1960), a leading arts fuctionary in Prussia and the Propaganda Ministry and overseer of the Jewish Theatre, announced that all Jews had been cleared from the public German arts.[30] On 1 September 1939, Hitler's armies invaded Poland; Polish, English, and French plays slipped from the repertoire. Five years later, 1 September 1944, all German theatres were closed to meet the fanatic and futile demands of "total war." The euphoria of 1933 Machtergreifung became 1945 *Götterdämmerung* (twilight of the gods), or perhaps more accurately, *Teufeldämmerung* (twilight of the demons). Hitler's visions of national and artistic triumph would leave mountains of rubble—*Teufelsberge*—at the outskirts of bombed-out cities. The German theatre, purged in 1933, and thereafter an often willing contributor to Hitler's National Socialist ideology, would also be left in ruins.

NOTES

1. Cf. Hitler, *Mein Kampf*, 123–124th ed. (Munich, 1935): 554–57 on that process and the symbolism of the colors.

2. See my IFTR conference paper attempting to address the issue of neglect, suggesting some of the central topics of the period: Glen W. Gadberry, "The Theatre of the Third Reich: Issues and Concerns," in *Nordic Theatre Studies*—Special International Issue: New Directions in Theatre Research. Proceedings of the XIth FIRT/IFTR Congress, Stockholm, 1989, ed. Willmar Sauter (Copenhagen, 1990): 75–78.

3. For example, see George Mosse, *The Crisis of German Ideology: Intellectual Origins of the Third Reich* (New York, 1964).

4. Hitler, *Mein Kampf*, Book I, Chapter 10, 245–310, and Chapter 11, 311–62.

5. Ibid., 283–84.

6. See Henry Grosshans, *Hitler and the Artists* (New York, 1983). Grosshans paints a convincing portrait of the cultural milieu at the time Hitler tried to enter the National Academy and thereafter, as he tried to live as a local artist.

7. Hitler, *Mein Kampf*, 284.

8. Ibid., 285.

9. Ibid., 287–88. Hitler overstates the situation, of course: in Berlin, the radical dramas of German Expressionism were typically produced in closed performances by theatre clubs, such as Heinz Herald's "Junges Deutschland" or Moriz Seeler's "Junge Bühne." Expressionist plays probably accounted for no more than 1 per-

cent of all Berlin production during the years of German Expressionism (1912–1925).

10. Ibid., 357. In a 1953 essay, "Der Führer persönlich," Herbert Lüthy wrote vividly of this aspect of Hitler's fantasies: Hitler imagined

> an insane world in which history, politics and the "life struggle of the peoples" are pictured solely in terms of coupling, fornication, pollution of the blood, selective breeding, hybridisation, generation in the primeval slime which will improve or mar the race, violation, rape and harassment of the woman—world history as an orgy of rut, in which dissolute and devilish submen lie in wait for the golden-haired female.

Quoted in Joachim C. Fest, *The Face of the Third Reich: Portraits of the Nazi Leadership*, tr. Michael Bullock (New York, 1970): 12. Racists of every hue, it seems, ultimately resort to this incendiary justification: they take violent action to protect their women from the sexual advances of variously defined "submen."

11. Hitler, *Mein Kampf*, 332. In his 1930 *Myth of the 20th Century*, radical Party theoretician Alfred Rosenberg recast Hitler's artistic and racial prejudices into even more explicit language. As he dealt with Weimar theatre and art, Rosenberg wrote,

> These last songsters for democracy and Marxism have neither belief in others nor any values in themselves. Klabund, Hofmannsthal, Hasenclever, Reinhardt exhume and dress up figures from Chinese, Greek, Indian literature or they bring in Niggers from Timbuktu to give their select audience "new beauty," a "new life rhythm."
>
> *That* is the essence of the spirituality of today, that is modern drama, modern theatre, modern music! A stench of corpses exudes from Paris, Vienna, Moscow and New York. The Jewish stink [*foetor judaicus*] mixes in with the scum of all peoples. Bastards are the "heroes" of the age, the Nigger-directed whore's or nude dance revues were the art form of the November Democracy. The result—the soul's plague seems to be reached.

Rosenberg, *Mythus des 20. Jahrhunderts*, 87–90 ed. (Munich, 1935): 446–47.

12. Hermann Wanderscheck, *Deutsche Dramatik der Gegenwart* (Berlin, 1938): 93. See Glen W. Gadberry, "Dramatic Contraries: The Paine Histories of Hanns Johst and Howard Fast," *Text and Presentation* 9 (1989): 61–72.

13. Membership did not necessarily mean the writer was a committed Nazi, but that he or she was acceptable to the Propaganda Ministry in terms of race, ideology and artistry; that is, he or she was not Jewish, Communist, or aesthetically radical.

14. F. [Emil Fechter], "Kleines Volksstück," *Deutsche Allgemeine Zeitung* (Berlin), 25 Jan. 1933: 4.

15. Ernst Heilborn, "Schieberkomödie," *Frankfurter Zeitung* (Reichsausgabe), 2 Feb. 1933: 10.

16. Ironically, *Wer ist der Dümmste?* ("Who Is the Stupidest?") was the first work to premiere in the capital after Machtergreifung, at the Kleines Theater, 4 February 1933. The revue was produced by Truppe 31, an agit-prop theatre collective formed in 1931 and headed by Gustav von Wangenheim, a Communist who had acted for Reinhardt. His 1933 agit-prop revue was an assault upon the basic

principles of capitalism; the factory owner is supposedly the cleverest person in this "money-possessed world order, while the stupidest can only be the man who lets himself be exploited the most" (Bernhard Diebold, "Dreierlei Kunst. Drei dramatische Beispiele," *Frankfurter Zeitung* [Reichsausgabe], 11 Feb. 1933: 9). *Wer ist der Dümmste?* was the kind of leftist provocation that soon disappeared from the German stage. Truppe 31 was forbidden 4 March 1933, and Wangenheim emigrated to the Soviet Union. His plays were subsequently banned 27 November 1934.

17. In April, six Berlin youths, "ardent Nazis," tried to force the Rotters back to Germany for trial. Alfred and his wife died trying to escape and Fritz was hospitalized. The attempted kidnapping received international coverage.

18. Hans Severus Ziegler (1937) in Josef Wulf, *Theater und Film im Dritten Reich; Eine Dokumentation* (Gütersloh, 1966): 234. The charges were supported by statistics: 80 percent of Berlin Intendants in 1919 and 67 percent (72 of 108) of the drama publishers in 1924 were Jewish. Of 260 German premieres in 1925, 95 had been written by Jews; in 1932, 85 of 280 premieres were by Jews. "These were certainly shameful numbers," according to critic Hans Knudsen (1940), in Wulf: 235.

19. Noted in Manfred Overesch, ed., "Das Dritte Reich, 1933–1939," Part I of *Chronik deutscher Zeitgeschichte: Politik—Wirtschaft—Kultur*, vol. 2 (Düsseldorf: 1982): 13.

20. Hitler's objections, as well as those of the Minister of Education and Science, Bernhard Rust, are cited in J. Noakes and G. Pridham, eds., *Nazism 1919–1945*, vol. 2 (State, Economy and Society 1933–1939, a Documentary Reader) (Exeter, 1984): 380. Cf. Hitler, *Mein Kampf*, 649–69 (Book 2, Chapter 11, "Propaganda and Organization").

21. Noakes and Pridham eds., *Nazism 1919–1945*, 380–81. The full speech is in Axel Friedrichs, ed., *Die nationalsozialistische Revolution 1933* (Berlin: 1937): 262–71.

22. Reported in "Die preußische Theater," *Frankfurter Zeitung* (Reichsausgabe), 8 May 1933: 2.

23. The speech is reprinted in Friedrichs, ed., *Die nationalsozialistische Revolution 1933*, 286–300.

24. "Rede Goebbels' bei der Verbrennung undeutschen Schrifttums am 10. Mai 1933," in Axel Friedrichs, ed., *Die nationalsozialistische Revolution 1933* (Berlin: 1935): 277–79.

25. Cited in Wayne Kvam, "The Nazification of Max Reinhardt's Deutsches Theater Berlin," *Theatre Journal* 40, no. 3 (Oct. 1988): 367.

26. "Adolf Hitlers Rede auf der Kulturtagung der NSDAP. am 1. September," Friedrichs ed., *Die nationalsozialistische Revolution 1933* (Berlin: 1935): 281–90. The speech was dropped from the 1937 edition.

27. The Nazi-approved Jewish cultural organizations would ultimately have offices in over 100 German cities, with full theatre companies in Berlin, Hamburg, and Cologne. These societies continued to operate under gradually deteriorating conditions until September 1941. See Chapter 10 in this book; Herbert Freeden (as Herbert Friedenthal he was an administrator and play adaptor for the Berlin association), *Jüdisches Theater in Nazideutschland* (Tübingen, 1964); and Glen W. Gadberry, "Nazi Germany's Jewish Theatre," *Theatre Survey* 21, no. 1 (May 1980): 15–32.

28. "'Kampf durch Freude!' Die große Kundgebung der Deutschen Arbeitsfront," *Der völkische Beobachter* (Berlin), 29 Nov. 1933: 2.

29. "Der Führer dankt seinen hervorragendsten Mitkämpfern," *Der völkische Beobachter* (Berlin), 2 Jan. 1934: 2. A second round of telegrams was reported on the third, directed to Hermann Göring, Robert Ley (as Leader of Party Organization), Youth Leader Baldur von Schirach, Party Arbitrator Walter Buch, and, as Head of the *Stahlhelm*, Franz Seldte; "Weitere Briefe des Führers an alte Mitkämpfer," *Der völkische Beobachter* (Berlin), 3 Jan. 1934: 1.

30. "Culture Chamber Ousts Jews," *New York Times*, 4 Sept. 1935: 14. In 1934, Goebbels had complained that "retired" Jews "again are appearing in German theatres, variety shows and cabarets." He instructed German states to enforce the anti-Jewish arts legislation; "Nazis Order Jews Ousted from Stage," *New York Times*, 6 March 1934: 28.

2

The National Socialist *Volksgemeinschaft* Fantasy and the Drama of National Rebirth

Robert A. Pois

In a nation first unified in 1871 and sharply divided along regional and class lines, the term *Volksgemeinschaft* (folk community) came to have an almost magical pull to it. This was particularly the case in conservative bourgeois circles, but even political liberals, just as eager as more right-wing countrymen to avoid the travails of class and interest politics, often found the notion of a putatively non-divisive folk community very enticing. After the World War I disaster, Germany, in the eyes of many, was burdened with a republic and the unfamiliar trappings of political pluralism, both understandably associated with defeat. Thus, the magical attraction of some sort of folk community, immune to the traumas associated with republican political life, was greater than ever before. In any case, nearly about every political party or organization to the right of the socialists declared itself to be in favor of it.[1] Not unexpectedly, the newly formed National Socialists, probably for the most part genuinely, saw themselves embodying the Volksgemeinschaft principle more consistently, and to a far greater degree, than other political organizations. Their self-conscious adherence to blood-racism certainly gave them the right to do so.

However chimerical the folk community ideal proved to be once the Nazis came to power, there can be no question that many in the movement believed in it and that, for many Germans, National Socialist claims to best represent this time-honored ideal were of crucial importance in causing them to lend support to the movement, if not in fact to join it.[2] Even for those Germans whose support of the Nazis was not motivated by anti-Semitism, the idea of a class- and interest-free community from which only a generally disliked portion of the population was excluded enabled many of them to back a group widely recognized as being stridently racist.[3]

Many historians of Nazi Germany have pointed out that the Volksgemeinschaft ideal was informed by middle-class values. Here, emphasis upon traditional roles for women, well-scrubbed youth, traditional (as opposed to "degenerate" modern) art forms, various small town and bucolic usages, and, of course, nationalism is most often noted as important.[4] Of course, not a few of the goals of the National Socialist leadership went considerably beyond average middle-class spiritual horizons, but most Germans either did not know of them or chose not to. Nonetheless, even if one sees German National Socialism as a kind of secular religion that, in the final analysis, had to challenge those established Judeo-Christian usages central to German bourgeois life, it is plain that many Germans, both outside and within the movement, saw it as being, in effect, rooted in some sort of mythical "better" German past. The most noble elements of this would attain more complete amplification within a Volksgemeinschaft now in the process of being attained.

As in the case of most right-wing political movements, a crucial appeal of Nazism was its call upon a form of idealism. It would not do to proclaim proudly that it was standing only for a restoration, or preservation, of traditional values. As far as the average German was concerned, at least with regard to truly revolutionary social change, such might have been the case. It is plain, however, that in its particular call for the establishment of the folk community—something that other Weimar-period German political parties raised as well—the National Socialists emphasized a "revolution of spirit," something that would take the form of what Adolf Hitler called the "nationalization of the masses."[5] The German people was to become aware of itself not as a collection of individuals divided along class and political lines, but as unified "Volk" tied together by traditions sanctified by blood. To take part in the "National Socialist revolution" one need not—in fact, one ought not—feel constrained to engage in activities consonant with revolution in the traditional sense; that is, some form of radical social upheaval. Rather, one should feel oneself part of a community informed by eternal values sanctified by nature. Inasmuch as the values publicly extolled by the National Socialist movement were, in essence, middle class, the average German was being extolled to feel idealistic simply by adhering to exaggerated versions of what he or she believed in the first place. To make matters yet more enticing, the most obviously banal beliefs were now declared to be central to a natural order, gratuitously declared eternal.

If, as has been suggested, all ideologies—or, if one wishes, secular religions—are death-defying attempts at rebirth, then National Socialism provided that this in the end chimerical existential project was a relatively painless one for most Germans (provided, of course, that they did nothing to impede the implementation of larger projects crucial to the new national leadership).[6] One could participate in national rebirth by, spiritually speaking, standing still. In the end, even apart from the hideous atrocities necessitated by the translation of naturalistic "laws of life" into reality, the National Socialist claim upon authenticity demanded that bad faith be exorcised on all levels of national life. An area in which this was immediately obvious was that of culture.

Even though Nazism was able to attract support, at least at first, from an impressive number of intellectuals, scientists, and artists, it was, at its core, anti-intellectual.[7] Indeed, having established a regime that, as they saw it, was or soon would be ruling in accordance to nature's eternal laws, not merely criticism but any form of expression that could in any way be deemed critical had to be seen as constituting a form of blasphemy. A logical corollary of this was the paradox of an essentially elitist movement being able to articulate itself in egalitarian terms. One could not rely upon perpetually uncertain, brooding, yet critical minds to serve the needs of the emerging new Volksgemeinschaft. No, in the end it was the *Volk*, the people, who would provide the spiritual raw material essential for its construction. This view was best articulated by Hitler in a speech of 10 May 1933:

> I know this broad mass of my Volk and would like to say only one thing to our intellectuals: any Reich built only upon the classes of intellect is a weak construction!
> I know this intellect: perpetually brooding, perpetually inquiring, but also perpetually uncertain, perpetually hesitating, vacillating, never firm! He who would construct a Reich on these intellectual classes alone will find that he is building on sand. It is no accident that religions are more stable than the various forms of government. They generally tend to sink their roots deeper into the earth; they would be inconceivable without this broad mass of people. . . . This broad mass of people is certainly often dull and certainly backward in some respects, not as nimble, not as witty, not as intellectual. But it does have one thing: it has faith, it has persistence, it has stability.[8]

In this long quotation, the words *religion, faith,* and *stability* are of crucial importance. While Hitler sometimes denied being concerned with establishing a new religious order, any movement that claimed to be ruling in accordance with eternal laws of life was making claims more religious than political. At the same time, however, a crucial aspect of at least the Judeo-Christian tradition, transcendence, had to be denied, and thus the National Socialist revolution of spirit necessarily demanded that the people in whose name this "revolution" was putatively carried out show its faith through stability—in the end, by rejecting criticism or inquiry in any form.[9] While it can certainly be argued that dictatorship in any form had to reject critical thinking or expression, National Socialism, in claiming to represent a new but eternal natural order, was uniquely able to cast this rejection in terms of authenticity.

A Volksgemeinschaft that was, by definition, authentic demanded that art in all forms also be authentic, and this meant that it had to embody those *völkische* values that the regime, with some justification, perceived as widely held by the public, values that neatly dovetailed with its own. A public that, as Hitler saw it, was somewhat "dull" and valued stability could be counted on to reject any art—literary, plastic, or dramatic—that by its very nature was probing or critical. At the same time, it would accept, even admire, art forms that, in their uncritical or static qualities, proffered a soothing sense of stability. In a well-known decree of November 1936, Minister of Propaganda and Public Enlightenment Paul Josef Goebbels forbade any form of art criticism, something that he said "dates from the time of the Jewish domination of art. The critic is to be superseded by the art editor. The reporting of art should not be concerned with its values, but should confine itself to description. Such reporting should give the public a chance to make its own judgments, should stimulate it to form an opinion about artistic achievements through its own attitude and feelings."[10] Obviously, Dr. Goebbels thought, the German public, very much on its own, could be counted on to treasure aesthetic values consonant with the development of a Volksgemeinschaft ipso facto "healthy" in nature.

Of course, the regime, even if forbidding conventional forms of art criticism, certainly saw itself as having a role in assisting the public in determining what art was acceptable and what was not. Some general guidelines were laid down early in 1933 by the *Führerrat der Vereinigten Deutsche Kultur und Kunst Verbände* (Führer's Council of United German Culture and Art Organizations), and these would inform the activities of the *Reichskulturkammern* (Reich Culture Chambers), which came into existence later that year. Very cleverly, these were presented as requests for guidance posed by artists eager to participate in the drama of national rebirth. The guideline demanded by artists was to be informed by "a philosophy drawn from a passionate national and state consciousness anchored in the realities of blood and history! Art shall serve the growth and strengthening of this folkish community. . . . " After calling upon the regime actively to persecute materialistic Marxist influences in all areas, the *Führerrat* declared that it was "the sacred duty of the state to place in the front lines those soldiers who have already proved their mettle in cultural battle."[11] As one might expect of a movement that saw all aspects of life, but particularly those concerning the establishment of the Volksgemeinschaft, in terms of struggle, military analogies were much favored. In the 1933 *Frankfurter Theater Almanach*, which was almost entirely devoted to the establishment of a new national theatre, the role of the theatre producer (*Generalintendant*) was described as the "commanding general of the fine arts," someone who "gathers the nine muses to the attack." The "goal and object of his strategic operations is the people, to whom he brings art. Or in the words of Herr Prussian Minister President Goering—'Art to the people in order that the people will again come to art!' "[12]

In *Mein Kampf*, Hitler had decried manifestations of what he called "Art Bolshevism" (he was particularly hard on Futurists, Cubists, and Dadaists) and what he saw as the degradation of the German stage: "It was a sad sign of inner decay that the youth could no longer be sent into most of these so-called 'abodes of art'—a fact which was admitted with shameless frankness by a general display of the penny-arcade warning: 'Young people are not admitted.' "[13] Now, with the coming to power of National Socialism, all art would be rendered accessible to every German. Wilhelm Müller-Scheld, Propaganda Director of *Gau* Hesse-Nassau, emphasized the role of National Socialism in engendering "healthy strengths" in the German people. As if in response to the admonitions presented in *Mein Kampf*, Müller-Scheld declared that, instead of works produced by "aesthetes estranged from reality or speculating sexual psychologists," the new theatre would be both accessible and accountable to every member of the folk community. "Just as in the meeting halls," he proclaimed, "the only questions which will be dealt with on the stage [will be] those which are important for the *entire* German people."[14] For art in general, and the theatre in particular, the issues of importance would be precisely the same as those emphasized in political rallies. In an emerging folk community, the nationalization of aesthetics was not only necessary but virtually demanded by the laws of life in which such a community was grounded.

The theatre pieces rejected by Hitler and his supporters were mostly late nineteenth- and twentieth-century ones. In issues such as sexuality (here Frank Wedekind comes to mind), these works were and are considered representative of modernity. For the Nazis, ever so modern in matters of war and annihilation, the modern critical spirit was degenerate through and through. To be sure, for a while there was a lively debate in Party circles over the possibility of integrating at least some aspects of German Expressionism into those plastic arts deemed fit to be seen by members of the emerging folk community. By 1934, however, the issue had been settled pretty much in favor of the Führer's petit-bourgeois tastes.[15] In any event, in keeping with the guidelines laid down by the *Führerrat* pronouncement, exhibitions of "degenerate art" were underway in order to familiarize the German public with the aesthetic forms in which enemies of folkish wholeness articulated themselves. This process was finalized by the infamous "Exhibition of Degenerate Art," held in Munich in July 1937.[16]

Certainly, from the point of view of adherents to what has to be seen as a naturalistic, secular religion, an approach to art that rejected criticism or anything critical at all in any variety of art, was understandable, even logical. After all, as with cultural life in general, the critical, probing aesthetic imagination had to be perceived as inimical to the interests of a folk community that being natural and thus conforming to the "laws of life," could not tolerate individuals whose imaginations compelled them to depict blue cows or non-Aryan human forms. In any event, the masses in whom Hitler had so much faith could be trusted to recognize the degenerate dribblings of deracinated intellects for what they were and reject them with alacrity; although, to be sure, the National Socialist movement was duty-bound to lend a hand.

Again, it is necessary to point out that, for the average German, there was an important dividend in giving vent to commonly held feelings about divisive or critical intellectuals and artists or, at the very least, acquiescing in their persecution. By so doing, one was acting (even if not doing anything at all) as an idealistic builder of the Volksgemeinschaft. As for the artists and intellectuals themselves, what gave them whatever vitality or value was the blood and soil in which they were grounded. In fact, if one were not grounded in the soil of the nature-hallowed folk community, as evidenced by the perverse nature of works produced, then one was really not an artist at all. This was, of course, a stridently political definition of art, but, as Goebbels put it, this was perfectly correct. In a speech delivered 17 June 1935, upon the occasion of the second annual Reich Theatre Festival Week, he declared, "It is not true that the artist is unpolitical, for political means nothing else but to serve the public with understanding."[17] Such a politicization of art was certainly understandable when bearing in mind the implications involved if one accepts the Volksgemeinschaft as not only a fact of life, but the highest form of life. In such a context, Alfred Rosenberg (an individual held in contempt by Goebbels) was being quite consistent when he declared that he "believe[d] that *any* healthy SA man could . . . arrive at the same judgement as a conscious artist."[18] Certainly, this had to have been the case if a "conscious artist" by definition had to share the same values as an SA man in order to be one in the first case.

Thus, what Hitler called "the nationalization of the masses" ultimately had to involve the politicization of culture. Again, it is obvious that such has to occur when any ideologically informed movement assumes power. It is important to emphasize, however, that the National Socialist ideology allowed for an extraordinary consistency in this regard. Bringing together, as it did, elements of political mysticism and supposedly "well-established scientific truths" into a unique synthesis (dubbed "biological mysticism" by Hermann Rauschning, a one-time companion and later critic of Hitler), National Socialist leaders had created an ideology that could represent itself as embodying natural, eternal truths. Thus—and here National Socialist "idealism" could articulate itself in very pragmatic terms—any act undertaken or attitude expressed by the movement was correct, particularly in view of the presumed fact that such was done in order to establish and strengthen the sacred folk community.[19] In these circumstances, it was quite logical (if not exactly rational) that art—which, in order to be art, had to express the nature-bound values of the folk community—be seen as inherently political. Indeed, if one assumed that creativity was, as such, representative, or an embodiment, of the folk spirit central to national community, then aesthetics in particular was *more* political than other aspects of national life.

Naturally, under Nazi rule, there was no Volksgemeinschaft. Economic and social realities, which became ever more pressing as Hitler pushed the country toward war, assured that this was the case. Certainly, by the time Germany actually became involved in war, the average German had become aware that many old social inequities remained and that, in fact, rather than creating a Volksgemeinschaft, National Socialism had had the effect of atomizing the German people.[20] Yet the National Socialist call for the establishment of a true folk community, for a national rebirth, had been one of the most crucial elements in gaining support for the movement. Moreover, after Germany went to war the tantalizing possibility that such could be actualized once total military victory had been achieved and presumed enemies of the "laws of life" eliminated (although the average German was not to know how this was being done) served to sustain public faith in the individual who remained most associated with this ideal, Adolf Hitler.[21] In any event, if National Socialist Germany had triumphed there can be little doubt, judging from what we know of artistic expression in the Third Reich and from architectural planning for the postwar Thousand-Year Reich, that Western culture would have been stamped with that combination of bucolic sentimentalism and neo-classical grandeur that so often appeals to middle-class tastes. Whether or not there would have been significant social changes—a "leveling" of sorts associated with the Volksgemeinschaft—in the new Germany is a matter of debate.[22] That aesthetic values consonant with such a community would have prevailed is not. Thus, in a community in which political life in the conventional sense would have ended, aesthetics would have been an area in which political action could have taken place.

In his writings on aesthetics, G. W. F. Hegel (1770–1831) declared that, at some point in the not-too-distant future, art as an autonomous sphere of human spiritual endeavor would disappear, absorbed by philosophy. If one views Nazism as a secular religion, informed by a genuine *Weltanschauung* or world view, then perhaps one can say that, in a general sense, Hegel had been prescient. Bearing in mind salient characteristics of the National Socialist movement, however, we can suggest that while art, at least as defined by that vital human characteristic, creativity, disappeared into politics, conventional political life had been transformed into aesthetics, theatre in particular.[23]

In his 1977 work, *An Anatomy of a Drama*, Martin Esslin has pointed out several characteristics of drama:

1. Emphasis on response, leading to action or at least the planning of action.
2. A happening in the "eternal present tense" . . . in the "here and now."
3. The simulation of reality . . . "play."[24]

While Esslin's hypotheses have not gone unchallenged, these characteristics can be seen as having been central to the political culture of National Socialism, which, seeing itself as a secular religion of nature, was in a singular position to embody them.

First of all, there is general agreement among all who have commented upon the National Socialist ideology that it, along with other movements deemed fascist, was action-oriented. In fact, this emphasis upon action was something that attracted support from many young people, overwhelmingly male, of course. Nazi Party rallies and important addresses by major National Socialist figures before and after seizure of power in 1933 were characterized by an extraordinary dynamism, an emphasis upon heroic events that were about to unfold. That often extremely perceptive observer of Hitlerian Germany, William L. Schirer, has described Party rallies, particularly those at which Hitler himself spoke, as being occasions of high drama, infused with suspense and sense of expectation. Often, he said, the appearance of the Führer himself would be accompanied by the playing of the especially rousing *Badenweiler* march. Just before he spoke, an orchestra would play Beethoven's *Egmont* overture, an unusually stirring piece that, introducing a play concerned with the Dutch (i.e., Nordic) patriotic struggle against Spanish tyranny, summons forth both dramatic tension and images of heroic action to come.[25] The addresses that followed usually emphasized Germany's "rebirth," and those extraordinary events attached to it. A common theme was "We are strong, and will become stronger!"[26] something which could be expected since, according to the laws of nature, the nation was witnessing the emergence of "a new German man."[27]

Of course, appeals to a heroic future are inherent not only to ideologies but to political movements in general. In a word, that quality ascribed by Esslin to drama, "action" or the "planning of action," is crucial to any form of political life. National Socialism, however, in its biological mysticism, was unique in its ability to see whatever action it declared or undertook as being in conformity with the laws of nature, thus endowing it with a sort of dramatic necessity and, at the same time, almost superhuman mystery. Nature, after all, has an elusive quality to it, something that defies human understanding. It was this quality which, above all, was ascribed to Hitler by the German population as a whole. It is a curious fact that, while he and a variety of National Socialist leaders often appealed to a mythic, "better" German past, both the content of the National Socialist ideology and the idiom in which it was articulated were ahistorical, perhaps even antihistorical. After all, policies concerned with the establishment and defense of the Volksgemeinschaft, including, of course "the final solution," were taking place in the eternal realm of nature and thus removed from mundane historical scrutiny.[28] In National Socialism, the claim of translating "scientific" understanding of the natural order of things had been brought together with a sense of mystery, endowing the movement with the qualities of a religion that, while in some part a product of history, nonetheless stood outside of it. This leads us to another quality ascribed by Esslin to drama.

Virtually everyone who has described a Nazi rally, particularly one at which Hitler himself spoke, has emphasized the almost hysterical sense of enthusiasm that prevailed. Individual judgment, indeed any sense of individuality at all, was swept away. In its place, there emerged a sense of participating in something that was enormous, larger than life, and almost sacred in nature. In *Deutschland Erwacht* ("Germany Awakened," 1933), a popular, well-illustrated study of the National Socialist struggle for and seizure of power, there is a description of a gathering at which Hitler, along with President Hindenburg, laid wreaths at a memorial to Germany's war dead. In concluding its description of the events of 12 March 1933, the country's memorial day, we find the following:

> Hit-ler, Hit-ler, Hit-ler, feet hammer the rhythm, heavy boots thunder on the earth.
> The flags flutter . . . in their spirit . . . in their spirit.
> The sun shines. . . .
> Now, they have not fallen in vain, the two million.
> Now, everything is good.
> Now, we can again think of them without shame, and of their victories and deaths.
> Now, their spirit lives again, now Germany is again
> a Reich. . . . It is a truly healing spring which has broken out.[29]

Probably the best summary of such events has been provided by J. P. Stern: "What is enacted here is a situation of total immanence, where nobody believes in anything; or rather, where few if any believe in the man before them but all, including Hitler himself, fully believe in the image they have created."[30] What is being described is an "eternal present" within which past and future (however ill-defined) are somehow brought together in the solvent of immanency. The dead of the Great War have not died in vain, a new yet old Reich has been founded, and a "healing spring" beckons seductively toward a glorious future. Again, some of the symbolism and rhetoric was and is generic to other ideologies and, indeed, to political life in general. National Socialism, however, with its emphasis upon history-defying naturalism, was singularly endowed—at least from the point of view of those staging dramas such as the one described above—to infuse political activism with the authenticity of nature itself. The Volksgemeinschaft would find spiritual articulation in numberless, history-defying "eternal presents," embodiments of the "laws of life."

Another important characteristic of drama provided by Martin Esslin was the simulation of reality observable in play. Having presented this, we must now see what exactly is meant by *play*. Several commentaries on the interaction of art and psychology have focused upon the notion of *play* proffered by the psychoanalyst D. W. Winnicott. What he was referring to was a pattern of interaction that he saw as taking place between mother and child:

> Baby and object are merged in with one another. Baby's view of the object is subjective and the mother is oriented towards the making actual of what the baby is ready to find. . . . The object is repudiated, reaccepted, and perceived objectively. . . . This complex process is highly dependent on there being a mother or mother-figure prepared to participate and to give back what is handed out. This means that the mother (or part of mother) is in a "to and fro" between there being that which the baby has a capacity to find and (alternatively) being herself waiting to be found.[31]

A mother figure exists to be found by a child who wants, in finding her as an objective being, apart from itself, to experience a form of self-discovery. At the same time, the mother herself wants to be discovered. People who have commented upon Hitler's fabled oratory have pointed out that the primary reason for his success was that he was able to tell the Germans what they wanted to hear all along. In a word, he existed to be discovered by them, even as those who listened to him saw themselves embodied in an individual who, while objectively apart, became a vehicle for a form of self-discovery. "At such moments Hitler made 'the collective neurosis the echo of his own obsession.' "[32]

Of course, it is quite plain that any successful politician is that way because he or she is able to tell people what they want to hear. Rarely, however, is this done in the context of that seemingly sanctified immanency provided by a movement that saw itself as not merely representing but embodying eternal natural truths. In his singular ability to achieve what has to be described as a kind of spiritual synergy with the German people, Hitler also went well beyond the realm of conventional politics and even beyond ideology as the word is usually used. Indeed, as a canny analyst of the Nazi phenomenon put it, "Hitler operated more on the metaphysical than the ideological plane. His success with the masses was above all a phenomenon of the psychology of religion. He spoke less to people's political convictions than to their spiritual state."[33] Hitler, who has been described not only as a father figure but as a great nurturer, particularly for young people literally starved by the Allied hunger blockade and spiritually starved by a lack of parenting during the war, was engaged in spiritual play with his audiences.[34] To paraphrase Winnicott, he was there to be discovered by the German people, who were constrained to do so in a bizarre but nonetheless real journey of self-discovery.

Thus, in its affective articulation of a singular variety of secular religiosity, Nazism exhibited at least three of the leading characteristics ascribed by Martin Esslin to theatre. There was always action, real or proposed. All was to unfold in an "eternal present" rendered sacred by the natural truths articulated in the name of the folk-community. Finally, Hitler was engaged in the kind of "giving and getting" play seen by Winnicott as having its roots in the interaction between mother and child. Of course, not all Nazi gatherings, most of which were characterized by very dull speech making, could be described in these terms, and not even the Führer himself provided this sort of show all the time. At crucial times, however, when it was deemed important that, in well-nigh religious terms, symbols became real, indeed greater than reality itself, then these three characteristics crucial to theatre were certainly present.[35] Again, each of these elements can be observed as crucial in other ideologies or even more mundane "ordinary" political movements. However, the National Socialist emphasis upon acting in keeping with a presumed natural order, of which the Volksgemeinschaft was the highest representative, provided for an affective environment at times qualitatively different than that generated by any other political movement up to this time. In point of fact, at least as they saw it, the Nazis had moved out of and beyond politics into an awesome realm in which metaphysics and presumed scientific principles came together.

Of course, we know—and, in unguarded moments, the leaders did as well—that, as a movement concerned with taking and holding on to power, National Socialism was to no small degree political in nature. Hitler was a master politician, and has been described as such. Yet, at the core of National Socialism there was a nexus of beliefs that, if they were to attain even partial articulation in a public setting, could do so only in an idiom seemingly more religious than political. In the non-transcendent world of the (to be sure, non-existent) Volksgemeinschaft, the three characteristics ascribed by Esslin to theatre were important, indeed, necessary, in rendering accessible to the folk-community as a whole those aspects of Nazism which the leadership deemed appropriate for public consumption.

Of course, as will all areas of aesthetics, the Nazis had certain concerns and goals (if not always a coherent or consistent policy), and the chapters that follow will be concerned with these and with theatre-life in National

Socialist Germany. There was, after all, a concern to provide theatre deemed appropriate for a folk community. There were efforts to encourage the writing and production of "folkish" plays, accessible to people whom Hitler himself deemed "dull," and an excursion into exotica in early attempts to revive what was seen as a genuine, old Nordic theatre-form, the outdoor *Thing*, with chorus recitations of hoary themes generic to a healthy, natural "new order." And, as will be seen, the regime encouraged the production of plays written either by more established sorts such as Shakespeare and Schiller, or by less gifted purveyors of melodrama or light comedy. Hitler himself, for all of his oft-proclaimed love of Wagner, seemed particularly to enjoy the latter, as well as movies of a child-like or spectacular nature—*Snow White and the Seven Dwarfs*, *King Kong*, and *Gone With the Wind* were three of his favorites.[36] In any event, in an atmosphere in which art was by its very nature political, anything performed had, hypothetically at least, to nurture the spiritual well-being of the Volksgemeinschaft.

As art, including theatre, was seen as political, however, politics itself assumed the form of art, the most critical affective form of which was theatre. It was in this context that Hitler was able to achieve synergy with the German people. This was real even if the folk community in whose service this was supposedly occurring proved, in the end, to be an elusive fiction in whose interests and defense millions were slaughtered nonetheless. The Nazis saw that, to the greatest extent possible, their victims were done to death in an "eternal present" rendered perversely sacred by those same "laws of life" that demanded a sanctification of national life, itself a blasphemous, if baldly fictive, enterprise. In the process, all the world—or at least all of it that eventually mattered—had to become a stage.

NOTES

1. For the hold that the Volksgemeinschaft fantasy held on German bourgeois politics in general, see Robert A. Pois, "Jewish Treason Against the Laws of Life: Nazi Religiosity and Bourgeois Fantasy," in *Towards the Holocaust: The Social and Economic Collapse of the Weimar Republic*, ed. Michael N. Dobkowski and Isidor Wallimann (Westport, CT, 1983): 343–376.

2. Richard F. Hamilton, *Who Voted for Hitler?* (Princeton, NJ, 1982): 367.

3. On the role of a sort of "abstract" anti-Semitism in German political decision making, see William S. Allen, *The Nazi Seizure of Power: The Experience of a Single German Town, 1922–1945*, rev. ed. (New York, 1984): 84. His student, Sarah Gordon, has made much use of this concept throughout her work, *Hitler, Germans and the "Jewish Question"* (Princeton, NJ, 1984).

4. For summaries of the bourgeois nature of National Socialism, see George Mosse, *The Nationalization of the Masses* (New York, 1975): Chapter 8 in particular, and his *Nazism: A Historical and Comparative Analysis of National Socialism* (New Brunswick, NJ, 1978): 43–44, 61. Cf. Robert A. Pois, *National Socialism and the Religion of Nature* (New York, 1968): 82, 89.

5. This phrase, taken from *Mein Kampf*, provided the title for Mosse's book, cited above. See Adolf Hitler, *Mein Kampf*, tr. Ralph Mannheim (Boston, 1962): 337.

6. For an interesting and disturbing discussion of the role of rebirth in political ideologies, see Ernest Becker, *The Denial of Death* (New York and London, 1973): 133–134, 140.

7. The attraction held out by Nazism for those in the sciences, particularly medicine, has been the subject for Robert N. Proctor's *Racial Hygiene: Medicine Under the Nazis* (Cambridge, MA, 1988). The attraction of the movement for the aging playwright Gerhart Hauptmann, the Expressionist poet Gottfried Benn, the Expressionist painter Emil Nolde, and the existentialist philosopher Martin Heidegger is well known.

8. Adolf Hitler, *Hitler: Speeches and Proclamations 1932–1945, The Chronicle of a Dictatorship*, vol. 1, 1932–1934, ed. Max Domarus, tr. Mary Fran Gilbert (Wauconda, IL, 1990): 321.

9. Rejection of transcendence as a leading characteristic of fascism in general was first considered by Ernst Nolte, *Three Faces of Fascism*, tr. Leila Vennewitz (New York, 1969). Cf. Jean-Pierre Sironneau, *Sécularisation et religions politiques* (The Hague, Paris and New York, 1982): 545; and Pois, *National Socialism*: 3, 144–46.

10. George L. Mosse, ed., *Nazi Culture* (New York, 1966): 162–63.

11. Berthold Hinz, *Art in the Third Reich*, tr. Robert and Rita Kimber (New York, 1979): 28.

12. H. Th. Wüst, "Ein Nationaltheater in Frankfurt," in *Frankfurter Theater Almanach*, vol. 17 (Frankfurt/Main, 1933): 35. I am deeply indebted to Mark and Kellie Matthews-Simmons for making this almanac available to me.

13. Hitler, *Mein Kampf*, 259.

14. Wilhelm Müller-Scheld, "Der Nationale Aufbruch," in *Frankfurter Theater Almanach*, vol. 17 (Frankfurt/Main, 1933): 18–19.

15. Goebbels had evidenced interest in having at least some German Expressionist artists accepted by the movement. He saw their art as representative of a powerful German artistic spirit. Many inside and outside the National Socialist Party supported him, but he was opposed by the official ideologist Alfred Rosenberg, who saw Expressionism as evidence of cultural decay. Eventually, Hitler took a position closer to Rosenberg's. For a study of the debate over Expressionism, see Robert A. Pois, "German Expressionism in the Plastic Arts and Naziism: A Confrontation of Idealists," *German Life and Letters* 21, no. 3 (April 1968): 204–14.

16. Probably the best description of National Socialist art policy can still be found in Hildegard Brenner, *Die Kunstpolitik des Nationalsozialismus* (Hamburg, 1963). (For an account of the various "degenerate" art shows, see. Stephanie Barron, ed., *"Degenerate Art:" The Fate of the Avant-Garde in Nazi Germany* (New York, 1991).—*Ed.*)

17. Joseph Goebbels, *Goebbels-Reden*, vol. 1, ed. Helmut Heiber (Düsseldorf, 1971): 219.

18. Alfred Rosenberg, *Selected Writings*, ed. Robert Pois (London, 1970): 161. The emphasis is Rosenberg's.

19. The National Socialist fusion of idealism and pragmatism is considered in detail in Pois, *National Socialism*, Chapter 4.

20. For consideration of the promise and reality of the Nazi Revolution in social terms, see David Schoenbaum, *Hitler's Social Revolution: Class and Status in*

Nazi Germany, 1933–1939 (New York, 1967). On the atomizing effect of the National Socialist dictatorship, see Detlev J. K. Peukert, *Inside Nazi Germany: Conformity, Opposition, and Racism in Everyday Life*, tr. Richard Deveson (New Haven, CT, 1987): 236–42.

21. Ian Kershaw, *Der Hitler-Mythus: Volksmeinung und Propaganda im Dritten Reich* (Stuttgart, 1980): 63, 150. Peukert, *Inside Nazi Germany*, 72–76.

22. As early as the 1930s, Walter Benjamin of the "Frankfurt School" declared that fascism had succeeded in turning art into aesthetics. See Walter Benjamin, "The Work of Art in the Era of Mechanical Reproduction," in *Illuminations: Essays and Reflections*, ed. Hannah Arendt, tr. Harry Zohn (New York, 1968): 244. The issue of aesthetization of politics is raised throughout Mosse, *The Nationalization of the Masses*.

23. For Henry Ashby Turner, Jr., Hitler's interest in vastly altering the German economy once the war had been won was obvious. See his *German Big Business and the Rise of Hitler* (New York, 1985): 338–39. For an interesting study of an important Nazi who took the notion of social change very seriously, see Ronald Smelser, *Robert Ley: Hitler's Labor Front Leader* (New York, 1988).

24. Martin Esslin, *Anatomy of Drama* (New York, 1977): 14–20, 43–46.

25. William L. Shirer, *Berlin Diary: The Journal of a Foreign Correspondent* (New York, 1979): 18–19.

26. Shirer, *Berlin Diary*, 21.

27. Adolf Hitler, *Hitler: Reden und Proklamationen 1932–1945*, vol. 1, part 2, ed. Max Domarus (Munich, 1965): 642.

28. For a discussion of the "timeless" quality of National Socialist actions, see Pois, *National Socialism*, 144–45.

29. *Deutschland Erwacht. Werden, Kampf und Sieg der NSDAP* (Hamburg-Bahrenfeld, 1933): 85.

30. J. P. Stern, *Hitler: The Führer and the People* (Berkeley, 1975): 89.

31. D. W. Winnicott's notion of *play*, put forth in his *Playing and Reality* (London, 1971), has been of interest to those concerned with the psychological aspects of art. This lengthy quotation is from Annie Herschkowitz, "Symbiosis as a Driving Force in the Creative Process," in *Pictures at an Exhibition: Selected Essays on Art and Art Therapy*, ed. Andrea Gilroy and Tessa Dalley (London and New York, 1989): 59. For a more general discussion of the impact of Winnicott's ideas and their influences, see Chapter 1 of that work, Peter Fuller's "Mother and Child in Henry Moore and Winnicott." Chapter 16 of the work, Rosemary Gordon's "The Psychic Roots of Drama," focuses on Esslin's work and, ties his notion of *play* to Winnicott's.

32. Such was the description offered by the American journalist H. R. Knickerbocker. See Joachim C. Fest, *Hitler*, tr. Richard and Clara Winston (New York, 1975): 327.

33. Fest, *Hitler*, 328–29.

34. For a brilliant and insightful analysis of this doleful topic, see Peter Loewenberg, "The Psychohistorical Origins of the Nazi Youth Cohort," in his *Decoding the Past: The Psychohistorical Approach* (New York, 1983): 240–83.

35. Of course, as collective experiences, religion and theatre have much in common. See Esslin, *Anatomy of Drama*, 26–28.

36. On his admiration for the first two, see Robert G. L. Waite, *The Psychopathic God: Adolf Hitler* (New York, 1977): 8, 289. On *Gone With the Wind*, see Shirer, *Berlin Diary*, 588. Hitler was also particularly fond of the nearly pathological works of the Munich artist Franz von Stuck, who depicted women as threatening, sensually overpowering figures. See Waite, *Psychopathic God*, 79–81. This particular interest, while known by several of Hitler's colleagues, was not public knowledge.

3

Theatre in Detmold 1933–1939: A Case Study of Provincial Theatre During the Nazi Prewar Era

Ron Engle

Little has been written about National Socialism and its effects on theatre activity in provincial centers of culture in Germany during the prewar period between 1933 and 1939. The Landestheater located in Detmold, the provincial capital of the former Free State of Lippe, may serve as an example for an analysis of how the policies of National Socialism affected theatre activity in a provincial city with a population of approximately 20,000 people and the cultural life of the surrounding area. Detmold serves as an excellent example because of its geographic location, its long-standing theatre tradition, its significance as the cultural center of Lippe, and the rather independent spirit of Detmold citizens.

Detmold, situated in north-central Germany in the rolling hills of the Teutoburger Forest, just south of Bielefeld, north of Paderborn, and 100 km from Hannover to the northeast and Münster to the northwest, became the official residence of the Count of Lippe in 1501. The Principality of Lippe became the Free State of Lippe in 1918 and lasted until 1945, when it was incorporated into the Federal State of North Rhine Westphalia in the Federal Republic of Germany.

Theatre activity in Detmold can be traced back to traveling troupes in the sixteenth century. The first theatre structure (Komödienhaus) was erected in 1778, and in 1825, on the site of the present theatre directly across from the Palace Gardens, the Court Theatre (Hochfürstlich-Lippisches Hoftheater) was built by Prince Leopold II. The theatre engaged prominent

German actor Ludwig Devrient and the actor and musician Albert Lortzing between 1826 and 1833. Detmold was the birthplace of playwright Christian Dietrich Grabbe (1801–1836), whose *Don Juan und Faust* premiered in the Hoftheater in 1829. Grabbe also served as resident critic for the Court Theatre from 1827 to 1829.[1] In 1912 the theatre was totally destroyed by fire, and in 1919 it was rebuilt by Prince Leopold IV and renamed the Lippisches Landestheater. The same basic structure is in use today with an addition and several renovations having been made in recent years.

From 1921 until his death in 1934, Emil Becker served as *Intendant* (artistic manager) of the Landestheater. During this period, Becker had to contend with the inflationary economy of the Weimar Republic and a shrinking budget. Becker was well respected by his colleagues, and even though the number of new productions dwindled in number each season during his twelve-year reign, critics pointed out that he brought an impressive list of contemporary plays into the repertory. They included plays by Ibsen, Strindberg, Gorky, Tolstoy, Wedekind, Expressionist works by Franz Werfel, Georg Kaiser's *Gas* (1923), Georg Büchner's *Woyzeck* (1924), Carl Zuckmayer's latest works, and many German classics, as well as Shakespeare and others. The repertory was representative of the plays being produced in the theatres of Berlin, Hamburg, Dresden, and Munich.[2] The 1931–32 season included the following productions:

> *Judith*, Friedrich Hebbel
>
> *Kean*, Alexandre Dumas *père*
>
> *Othello*, William Shakespeare
>
> *Hamlet*, William Shakespeare
>
> *Emilia Galotti*, Gotthold Ephraim Lessing
>
> *Egmont*, Johann Wolfgang von Goethe
>
> *Hauptmann von Köpenick*, Carl Zuckmayer
>
> *Der goldene Anker*, Marcel Pagnol
>
> *Der Mann, den sein Gewissen trieb*, Edmond Rostand
>
> *Staps, ein Held aus napoleonischer Zeit*, Walter von Molo
>
> *Kollege Crampton*, Gerhart Hauptmann
>
> *Katharina Knie* (revival), Carl Zuckmayer[3]

Certainly this 1931–32 season could hardly be considered a lightweight production schedule. The productions not only reflected the current trends in major theatre centers, such as Zuckmayer's popularity, but also included a substantial number of today's classics, with surprisingly few farces, which might otherwise be expected in a provincial theatre company. The only outright oddity was perhaps Molo's *Staps*, a folk play from 1918.

On 27 September 1933, the organization and repertory of the Landestheater entered a new era. At a meeting of the management, staff, and company members, it was announced that "everything which has disgraced the German theatre in the past is being erased," and that which would remain would be pure German *Wollen* (will).[4] This proclamation was the first official announcement at the Landestheater of the new direction set by National Socialism for unification of artistic and political interests of the party and state. With a clean slate and a new beginning, the 1933–34 season was to be the "attack" of the Landestheater that would prove to be a *kulturelle Entscheidungsschlacht* (culturally decisive battle). The three leading Detmold newspapers, the *Lippische Landes-Zeitung*, the *Lippische Tages-Zeitung*, and the official organ of the National Socialists, the *Lippische Staatszeitung*, carried a press release of the *Generalangriff des Landestheaters* ("General Attack of the Landestheater"). Citizens in Detmold and Lippe were reminded that they had a duty to defend German culture just as Hermann with sword uplifted stood in defense of Germanic tribes and German heritage. (The reference is to Hermann [Arminius], who defended the Germanic tribes in a decisive battle against the Romans in A.D. 9. The *Hermannsdenkmal*, a 26-meter-tall monument of Hermann, is located on a hilltop near Detmold.) The highly nationalistic tone of the story reminds the *Volk* that it has no reason to feel guilty for its cultural past and that, in fact, it has a "holy duty" to protect the "spiritual sovereignty" of German soil and culture. It was a call to arms: "Every Lipper at least once a month into the Landestheater!" In addition to the rhetoric, an ambitious promotional campaign provided further enticement. Prizes donated by local merchants could be won by lucky season ticket holders in a drawing. Items listed included a complete kitchen, a crystal bowl, a clock, a flower vase, four meters of silk, a man's coat, and so on.[5]

The death of Intendant Emil Becker in January 1934 could not have been more timely for the National Socialists. It was announced in late January that Becker on his death bed recommended thirty-three-year-old Otto Will-Rasing to succeed him as Intendant. There was little doubt that Becker's reasons were politically and not artistically motivated. Will-Rasing had become a member of the Landestheater company in 1924 and had played primarily minor character roles. As a director, his background was inconsequential. But obviously the National Socialists recognized his organizational and managerial abilities and believed that in matters of play selection and propaganda Will-Rasing would serve the state well.[6]

The National Socialists had already established strong political support in Lippe and Detmold. This mostly Protestant area of northern Germany provided a high percentage of Nazi votes for Adolf Hitler in the July 1932 and the January 1933 elections. Dr. Alfred Meyer, *Gauleiter*, or area commander, for North Rhine Westphalia (which included Detmold), led the election campaign in 1933 and won a clear majority for the National Socialists.[7]

Following Hitler's rise to power, the reorganization of theatre activity and all cultural activity throughout Germany was swift and centralized through Joseph Goebbels's Ministry of Propaganda, the *Reichstheaterkammer*—a union for theatre employees—and other control efforts such as the creation of a special post for a *Reichsdramaturg*.[8] The Landestheater's fall line-up of new productions in October 1933 clearly reflected the result of a calculated and well organized effort to launch a cultural revolution. Opening the season on 1 October was Hanns Johst's *Schlageter*. Johst's play had premiered on 20 April 1933, Hitler's birthday, in the Staatliches Schauspielhaus in Berlin with prominent actors Lothar Müthel, Albert Bassermann, and Emmy Sonnemann, Hermann Göring's bride-to-be, in the lead roles. Johst, who was highly supportive of National Socialism, wrote the play in 1930–32 and dedicated it *"für Adolf Hitler in liebender Verehrung und unwandelbarer Treue"* (for Adolf Hitler in loving veneration and immutable loyalty). Johst became a darling of the National Socialists and was appointed President of the *Reichschriftumskammer*, the writers union, in 1935.[9]

The play focuses on the real-life character of Albert Schlageter, who during the French occupation of the Ruhr District in 1923 led terrorist attacks against the occupation troops. He was finally apprehended and executed. Schlageter became a hero figure and martyr for the National Socialist cause. Johst's play aroused national sentiments against the Versailles Treaty and proved to be a propaganda success, with at least forty productions throughout Germany during the 1933–34 season.[10]

After heavy promotion of the new season, the premiere of *Schlageter* was poorly attended but well received by the three daily newspapers. The critic of the *Lippische Tages-Zeitung* blamed the thin crowd on the Harvest Festival being celebrated in nearby Bückeburg.[11] Otto Gilbert of the *Lippische Landes-Zeitung* noted that the source of the play was actually *Mein Kampf* and the secret hero of the play was, in fact, Adolf Hitler. Gilbert noted the sudden transition of Schlageter into a herald of a new age and found the melodramatic execution scene at the end of the play lacking in substance. "The play is thus only half a drama, the other half explanation and secret prophecy . . . of the Third Reich."[12] As might be expected, Ernst Heiß, the critic of the National Socialist paper, the *Lippische Staatszeitung*, failed to mention the poor attendance but praised the play and the production, expounded on the martyrdom of Schlageter, the "first soldier" of the Third Reich, at great length, and finally, with great enthusiasm, proclaimed the artistic achievement of the evening in the service of the "new art" of the Third Reich.[13]

Schlageter was followed by a lighthearted work about a wayward pig, *Krach um Iolanthe* ("Much Ado About Iolanthe," 1930), by the popular writer of folk farces and outdoor pageants, August Hinrichs, who in 1939 was awarded the Goethe Medallion in recognition of his writing achievements and dedication to the state (Johst received the prize in 1940).[14] Hinrichs's farces were innocuous German folk plays, written mostly in German dialect (*Platt Deutsch*), in which true-blooded northern German farmers and peasants outwitted tax collectors and pompous officials. Hinrichs was immensely popular and among the most-produced playwrights in Germany in both 1933 and 1934.[15]

A new production of Shakespeare's *Merchant of Venice* followed *Iolanthe* on 14 October 1933. Otto Gilbert from the *Lippische Landes-Zeitung* praised Alois Herrmann's Shylock as a "demon of revenge," albeit rather one-dimensional, while the critic of the *Lippische Tages-Zeitung* found a "deliberate" interpretation in many places, which one could perhaps understand from "the spirit of our time" but had no justification in the classic comedy.[16] The critic of the National Socialist *Lippische Staatszeitung*, Ernst Heiß, was pleased that Shylock was "correctly" interpreted, and that the actor emphasized the dominant "Jewish" characteristics of "cunning, craftiness, hate, wrath, and destruction." Heiß also pointed out that Shakespeare was no friend of the Jews and that, seen in the light of 1933, Shakespeare had a definite feeling for "racial purity." This fact, he explained, was the real reason Shakespeare meant so much "to us" and why he was performed more in Germany than in England. "Belonging to the same—in this case Nordic—race causes the same racial awareness."[17]

Shakespeare was followed on 27 October by Hans Kyser's anti-Polish play, *Es brennt an der Grenze* ("Fires Along the Border," 1931). Kyser's play, recommended by the Reichsdramaturg, focused on the plight of a "noble people" along the Weichsel River (Vistula in Polish) fighting for their homeland along the Polish-German border.[18] The plight of the German inhabitants had been created by the Versailles Treaty, which had assigned the land to Poland and forced migration. The season of new productions continued on 3 November with Charles Andermanns's *Des Königs jüngster Rekrut* ("The King's Youngest Recruit"), a clumsy adaptation of Karl Gutzkow's nineteenth-century comedy *Zopf und Schwert* ("Pigtail and Sword").[19] On 10 November, Austrian playwright Karl Schönherr's 1910 realistic drama concerning the plight of Tyrolian farmers during the Counter-Reformation, *Glaube und Heimat* ("Faith and the Homeland"), failed to arouse the interest of Detmold critics, and even Heiß of the *Staatszeitung* had to admit that, although the performance was convincing, the play suffered from structural weaknesses and the hero was not as heroic as national heroes should be (e.g., Michael Kohlhaas, Götz von Berlichingen, or Wilhelm Tell).[20] In 1937, Schönherr was the recipient of the Goethe Medallion, one year before Hitler's *Anschluß* with his native Austria.[21]

Documentation of attendance figures for the 1933–34 season at the Landestheater has disappeared, but the tone of the critics leaves the impression that a decline in attendance occurred, especially for the propaganda plays. However, attendance quickly increased during the 1934–35 season with the introduction of special performances for National Socialist organizations such as *Kraft durch Freude* (Strength Through Joy) and various workers unions. Not only was the number of performances in Detmold increased, but the Landestheater initiated a touring program in 1934–35 that took the company to the nearby towns of Bad Salzuflen, Lemgo, Blomberg, Lage, Paderborn, Bad Lippspringe, Höxter, Steinheim, and other smaller communities without civic theatres of their own. Touring was steadily increased and by the 1936–37 season included twenty-two towns.[22] Over the years the touring program of the Landestheater became vital in the cultural life of Lippe, and the Third Reich cultural hierarchy encouraged this kind of outreach, especially to bring the new propaganda plays to as much of the populace as possible.

The number of new productions mounted at the Landestheater increased substantially during the following two seasons:

The 1934–35 Season

Der Vetter aus Dingsda, Eduard Künneke

Die Heimkehr des Matthias Bruck, Sigmund Graff

Alle gegen einen—einer für alle, Friedrich Forster

Katte, Hermann Klasing

Maria Stuart, J. Friedrich von Schiller

Elga, Gerhart Hauptmann

Pygmalion, George Bernard Shaw

Peer Gynt, Henrik Ibsen (adaptation by Dietrich Eckart)

Wenn der Hahn kräht, August Hinrichs

Krach im Hinterhaus, Maximilian Böttcher

Wintermärchen (Winter's Tale), William Shakespeare

Don Carlos, J. Friedrich von Schiller

Die lange Jule, Carl Hauptmann

The 1935–36 Season

Der Freischütz, Carl Maria von Weber

Zigeunerbaron, Johann Strauß

Rothschild siegt bei Waterloo, Eberhard Wolfgang Möller

Judas von Tirol, Karl Schönherr

Totila, Wilhelm Kube

Kronprätendenten (The Pretenders) Henrik Ibsen

Minna von Barnhelm, Gotthold Ephraim Lessing

Was ihr wollt (Twelfth Night), William Shakespeare

Götz von Berlichingen, Johann Wolfgang von Goethe
Deutsche Kleinstädter, August von Kotzebue
Der Mustergatte, Avery Hopwood
Die Fledermaus, Johann Strauß
Madame Butterfly, Giacomo Puccini[23]

Propaganda plays usually had their premieres at the beginning of the season and often were performed concurrently at many theatres throughout Germany. They were "highly recommended" by the Reichsdramaturg, and the individual theatres had little choice but to include them in their repertory. Most popular, and seemingly harmless, were the *Heimkehr* (homecoming) plays, which focused on soldiers returning home in despair after World War I and facing the indignities of German defeat. Sigmund Graff's *Die Heimkehr des Matthias Bruck* (1933), which opened in the fall of 1934, was typical of this dramatic form. Young Bruck returns from the war to find his wife has remarried and hangs himself.[24]

Friedrich Forster's *Alle gegen einen—einer für alle* ("All Against One—One For All," 1933), which followed Graff in the Landestheater's fall season, represented the dramatic form preferred by the National Socialists. This was a play in which the hero, usually Germanic, leads a tragic struggle to free a people or a country from opposing forces. Essentially, the hero served as a symbol for Adolf Hitler and the struggle a symbol of Hitler's struggle to free the German people.[25] In Forster's work, the Swedish hero, Gustav Wasa, liberates the Swedish people from the rule of Denmark. Initially, only the simple farmers had faith in him, but in the end, he triumphed through the power of faith of the people. The critic of the *Staatszeitung* hailed the play as a drama of the Führer and of the Volk.[26] The critic's words echoed the sentiments of Goebbels's Memorial Address given the day before in Weimar in memory of Friedrich Schiller, whose dramatic works, Goebbels emphasized, embodied the ideals of the Fatherland and a united people.[27]

For the first time in ten years, operetta was introduced into the repertory of the Landestheater in the 1934–35 season with a production of Eduard Künneke's *Der Vetter aus Dingsda* ("The Cousin from Anyville"). And in the 1935–36 season, a production of Carl Maria von Weber's *Der Freischütz* reintroduced opera production to the Detmold audiences. The most striking development was the introduction of the Richard Wagner Festival in July 1935. Gauleiter Dr. Meyer engaged Detmold music teacher Otto Daube to organize the event. Originally conceived as a performance of a few staged scenes from Wagner's works in order to prepare audiences for a visit to the Bayreuth Festival, the Wagner Festival soon developed into a major event, with guest artists, conductors, scenery, and musicians from Berlin, Bayreuth, and throughout Germany.[28] In 1937, the Bochum Civic Orchestra appeared, with Gustav Wünsche as Siegfried, Vilma Fichtmüller as

Brünnhilde, and Lotte Schrader as Isolde.[29] In 1938, an entire Bayreuth original cast performed in Detmold. Although much of the scenery was provided by the Landestheater, on occasion entire sets from other German theatres were used.

The event was heartily welcomed by Detmold music lovers, and the festival concept proved to be an ideal vehicle for the promotion of National Socialist ideology, a celebration of Wagner and Germanic mythology. Wagner was viewed by Hitler and the National Socialists as a spiritual father of German music in the Third Reich.[30] An examination of the ninety-six-page official guide to the festival reveals the political nature of the festival. An obligatory photograph of Adolf Hitler taken by Winifred Wagner and excerpts from *Mein Kampf* occupy the first few pages, followed by Gauleiter Dr. Meyer's Party rhetoric, quotes from Friedrich Nietzsche, and another essay by Dr. Meyer in which he praises the Detmold theatre for serving the will of Adolf Hitler by educating the German people with "heroic" German art and the struggle of German artists. This is followed by a lengthy historical essay by Daube on Wagner, followed by an essay on *Volk und Kunst* (People and Art) with excerpts from Alfred Rosenberg's *Mythus des 20. Jahrhunderts* ("The Myth of the Twentieth Century," 1930) and other writings by disciples of National Socialism. Special events were organized for each day, including special events for Strength Through Joy members and a celebration by the Hitler Youth scheduled for Sunday morning.[31]

Following on the heels of the success of the Wagner Festival in 1935, Gauleiter Dr. Meyer hit upon another opportunity for propaganda and cultural enlightenment in 1936. Originally planned as a one-time event to celebrate the centennial of Christian Dietrich Grabbe's death, "Grabbe Days" featured lectures and performances of Grabbe's plays in Detmold, his birthplace. Grabbe's epic plays, rarely performed outside Germany, portrayed German heroism and soon became a symbol for historical folk drama. Invited productions from theatres in Düsseldorf, Münster, Bochum, Kassel, and Bielefeld brought national attention to Detmold. Grabbe's plays *Don Juan und Faust; Napoleon, oder die Hundert Tage; Hannibal;* and *Hermannsschlacht*, were easily assimilated into the dogma of National Socialism, and Grabbe soon became fashionable in theatres throughout Germany. The first Grabbe Days, held from 26 September to 3 October, featured a lecture by the President of the Grabbe Society, who coincidentally was the Reichsdramaturg, Dr. Rainer Schlösser, who lauded Grabbe as the "single *Volk* visionary of his time."[32]

Propaganda plays in the 1935–36 season included Eberhard Wolfgang Möller's racial history, *Rothschild siegt bei Waterloo* ("Rothschild is the Victor at Waterloo," 1934). The National Socialists praised Möller's playwriting skill in advancing Party ideology.[33] A curious play, *Totila (1933)*, written in 1920 by party functionary Richard Paul Wilhelm Kube, opened on 12 November with great fanfare. Kube's "primitive" play celebrated the

Gothic King Totila's sixth-century victory in Italy. The *Staatszeitung* heralded the play as the "first great dramatic *Gestaltung* of the National Socialist *Weltanschauung*."[34] The accolades, nationalist rhetoric, and hyperbole in the review describe a folk tragedy of such intensity that Greek catharsis is but a whimper in comparison. The *Landes-Zeitung* review is brief but to the point—Totila is a Siegfried and his rhetoric is well known to us today.[35] The premiere took place on November Memorial Day, and Kube, along with other Nazi Party officials, attended the performance. The interior of the theatre was decked out with swastika banners and flags, and the Opera Orchestra played Beethoven's Overture to *Coriolanus*. Following the performance, Kube, honored with stormy applause, spoke to the audience, reminding the spectators of the mission of theatre and art in the new Germany and of their allegiance to the Führer. He ended his speech with *Sieg-Heil*. It was a special occasion, to be sure, but descriptive of at least some theatre events in Detmold during the Third Reich.

The 1936–37 season introduced to Detmold audiences two additional plays by Hanns Johst. *Der Einsame* ("The Lonely One," 1917), based on the life of Grabbe, was well received in the city of Grabbe's birth. The second piece, *Thomas Paine* (1927), had recently been produced in a much-touted revival under the direction of Jürgen Fehling in Hamburg in the spring of 1936. It premiered at the Landestheater on 30 January 1937 to a small audience. *Thomas Paine*, one of the most produced plays that season in Germany, stood high on the list of recommended plays of the Reichsdramaturg. Paine was an "American Horst Wessel," a patriot, a soldier for freedom who united a people and enriched it with a national spirit of unity for its fatherland—ready to sacrifice blood for freedom.[36] As Detmold critic Joachim Graber of the *Tages-Zeitung* pointed out, "The nationality of Paine is of little consequence, what matters is his meaning for us today, for all defenders of their fatherland."[37] Erich Meinhard of the *Staatszeitung* was equally enthusiastic.[38]

By the 1938–39 season, the Landestheater had shifted its production schedule more in the direction of opera and operetta.

The 1938–39 Season

Egmont, Johann Wolfgang von Goethe

Maß für Maß (*Measure for Measure*), William Shakespeare

Dollars, Hjalmar Bergman

Die Insel, Harald Bratt

Ein ganzer Kerl, Fritz Peter Buch

Richelieu, Paul Joseph Cremers

Uta von Naumburg, Felix Dhünen

Bengalische Zukunft, Gesell-Martin

Parkstraße 13, Axel Ivers

Die Brücke, Erwin Kolbenheyer

Hochverräter, Curt Langenbeck

Der Weibsteufel, Karl Schönherr

Das Prinzip, Hermann Bahr

Doktor und Apotheker, Karl Ditters von Dittersdorf

Pilger von Mekka, Christoph W. Gluck

Così fan tutte, Wolfgang Amadeus Mozart

Der Maskenball, Giuseppi Verdi

Die schalkhafte Witwe, Ermanno Wolf-Ferrari

Paganini, Franz Lehár

Der Bettelstudent, Karl Millöcker

Korsika, Hans Moltkau

Der Zigeunerbaron, Johann Strauß

Die Fledermaus, Johann Strauß

Der Vogelhändler, Karl Zeller

Only Goethe's *Egmont* and Shakespeare's *Measure for Measure* could be considered classics, while the majority of productions were opera, operetta, and *Unterhaltungsstücke,* or light entertainment pieces, interspersed with at least three political plays by popular National Socialist playwrights. They included Curt Langenbeck's curious tragedy *Hochverräter* ("The Traitor"), which was lauded as a prime example of National Socialist tragedy in a new form at its premiere in Düsseldorf (15 March 1938) but later became the topic for controversy and angered Party dogmatists.[39] The play, written in verse, focuses on Jacob Leisler, a German by descent who led a revolt in the colony of New York in 1689 and assumed power but eventually was overthrown and executed in 1691. The play ends with Leisler shouting, "Heil New York!" before his execution by hanging. Some objected that the farmers and others who supported Leisler were "criminals" and therefore not pure Volk worthy of a tragic hero.[40] But in Detmold, critic Erich Meinhard of the *Staatszeitung* hailed the play as a breakthrough in the development of a new form of modern tragedy. Meinhard especially praised as innovative Langenbeck's use of the city elders as chorus.[41]

Erwin Kolbenheyer's 1929 philosophical play *Die Brücke* ("The Bridge") was performed on the author's sixtieth birthday. Although not necessarily a play with a political message, Kolbenheyer's philosophical ideas concerning metaphysical and biological traits in the development of mankind were promoted by the National Socialists in support of their ideology.[42] Finally, Cremers' anti-French history play, *Richelieu* (1934), rounded out the propaganda repertory for the 1938–39 season. The play features the cardinal as a "God-sent Führer, whose highest ethic is the well-being of the *Volk*." His political decisions are made from arch-nationalist sympathies and despite the "weak and decadent King Louis XIII."[43]

By 1936, freedom of the press in Detmold was reduced to one independent newspaper. Shortly after reducing its format size, the National Socialists forced the *Landes-Zeitung* to cease publication, and its theatre critic, Otto Gilbert, the last voice to "appeal to reason and defend the right of the critic," was silenced.[44] Although Gilbert had not been outspoken in his criticism, he could distinguish propaganda from art and used understatement as a technique to support his views. In 1938, the last Detmold independent newspaper, the *Tages-Zeitung* was shut down, leaving the Party newspaper, the *Staatszeitung*, and the rather formal criticism of Erich Meinhard as the sole guardian of critical commentary.

During the years 1934 to 1939, the Landestheater developed a new audience (some of whom most assuredly attended the theatre as a political rather than artistic event), which was created through the promotion of cultural awareness and civic duty, organized theatre visits, and an outreach program of scheduled tours to smaller towns in the Lippe region. Although productions increased substantially during this period, objectionable playwrights, such as Zuckmayer, were banned from the stage. Fewer classics were performed while lighter entertainments, farces, operas, and operettas increasingly filled the season. Didactic political plays became obligatory, and historical pieces were reinterpreted to support the dogma of the Third Reich. Most notably, the regional touring program, the introduction of the Wagner Festival, and the Grabbe Days theatre festival stand out as ambitious and commendable developments, in spite of their politically motivated origins.

Detmold, a city with agriculture and small industry as its economic base, far away from the climate of the big city demonstrations, street fighting, and political agitation that preceded Hitler's rise to power, swiftly and seemingly without serious objection or defiance, acquiesced to the new order and structure of the Third Reich's cultural agenda. During these years, theatre institutions in Berlin, Hamburg, and other major theatre centers in Germany could do little to stem the tide of censorship, reorganization, and propaganda plays, and the Detmold Landestheater followed the same course of history.

NOTES

The author would like to thank Mr. Wassermann and the staff of the Lippische Landesbibliothek in Detmold, Dr. Julius Graefe, and Barbara Engle for their research assistance.

1. See Hans Georg Peters, *Vom Hoftheater zum Landestheater: Die Detmolder Bühne von 1825 bis 1969* (Detmold, 1972): 53. Peters's work is the most exhaustive history of the Landestheater to date. The least informative section is on the theatre from 1933 to 1945, which Peters dismissed as artistically the "low point" in the history of the theatre and which he therefore summarized in brief (pages 206–7). See also *Zum Jubiläum des Landestheaters: 150 Jahre Theater in Detmold* (Detmold, 1975).

2. Peters, *Vom Hoftheater*, 192.

3. Lists were compiled from information provided in Peters, *Vom Hoftheater*; newspapers; and programs. Unfortunately, there are no records from the period 1933–45 in the archives of the Landestheater. Most of the material used in this study is located in the Lippische Landesbibliothek and Stadtarchiv. Some promptbooks are housed in the Theatermuseum der Universität zu Köln in Schloß Wahn.

4. Peters, *Vom Hoftheater*, 196–97.

5. The identical news release appeared prominently in all three newspapers on 1 October 1933. The *Lippische Landes-Zeitung* featured a full page with photos of the lead company members.

6. Peters, *Vom Hoftheater*, 205. Will-Rasing served as Indendant from 1934 to 1945 and again from 1949 to 1969. Hajo Hinrichs, son of August Hinrichs, was opera director from 1949 to 1951.

7. Alfred Meyer, "Das Kampfjahr 1932 und der Landtagswahlkampf in Lippe im Januar 1933," in *Hitler kämpft und siegt in Lippe 1933* (Detmold, 1934). This booklet was issued for the victory celebration to be held 13–14 January 1934.

8. See Boguslaw Drewniak, *Das Theater im NS-Staat: Szenarium deutscher Zeitgeschichte, 1933–1945* (Düsseldorf, 1983): 18–19.

9. See Günther Rühle, *Zeit und Theater: 1933–1945*, vol. 6 (Frankfurt, 1980): 729–41. The play is in Volume 5 of this excellent series on National Socialist theatre.

10. Bertolt Brecht parodied Johst's *Der Einsame* in his 1927 version of *Baal*.

11. *Lippische Tages-Zeitung*, 3 Oct. 1933.

12. *Lippische Landes-Zeitung*, 2 Oct. 1933.

13. *Lippische Tages-Zeitung*, 2 Oct. 1933.

14. See Drewniak, *Theater*, 221–22. Cf. Glen W. Gadberry, "The *Stedingers*: Nazi Festival Drama of the Destruction of a People," *Theatre History Studies* 10 (1990): 105–26.

15. See Drewniak, *Theater*, 222.

16. *Lippische Landes-Zeitung*, 17 Oct. 1933, and 18 Oct. 1933.

17. *Lippische Staatszeitung*, 17 Oct. 1933. (In a 1940 speech, Nazi author Hermann Burte noted, "Shakespeare belongs as much to us as he does to the English; indeed, we know him and perform his plays better than they do. And we boldly assert that as Germans of 1940 we in truth are closer to the spirit of the Elizabethan English and their genius William than the Englishmen of today, behind whose throne lurks and rules that Shylock whom Shakespeare recognized and rejected." George. Mosse, ed., *Nazi Culture* (New York, 1966): 143–44. Cf. Drewniak, *Theater*, 253, for the performance statistics for Shakespeare in German theatres, 1936–40. (*Merchant of Venice* was not produced as frequently as one might suppose, with only five productions in 1936 and three in 1939, compared, for example, to *Taming of the Shrew*'s twenty-six and twenty, respectively.—Ed.)

18. Drewniak, *Theater*, 236.

19. Peters, *Vom Hoftheater*, 197.
20. *Lippische Staatszeitung*, 11 Nov. 1933.
21. See Drewniak, *Theater*, 189.
22. Peters, *Vom Hoftheater*, 206.
23. This is a representative list only and may include some plays from a previous season that are not documented in programs from the period.
24. Peters, *Vom Hoftheater*, 210.
25. See Günther Rühle, *Zeit und Theater*, Introduction.
26. *Lippische Staatszeitung*, 11 Nov. 1934.
27. "Die Gedächtnisrede Dr. Goebbels," *Lippische Staatszeitung*, 11 Nov. 1934.
28. Peters, *Vom Hoftheater*, 207–8.
29. See Otto Daube, ed., *Amtlicher Führer durch die Richard-Wagner-Festwoche, Detmold 1937* (Detmold, 1937).
30. See Drewniak, *Theater*, 286–89.
31. Daube, *Amtlicher Führer*, 12.
32. Drewniak, *Theater*, 174–75. Cf. Peters, *Vom Hoftheater*, 208–9. The Grabbe Days aroused new local and national interest in Grabbe. This interest gave birth to the Grabbe Society and the Grabbe Archives, founded by Professor Dr. Alfred Bergmann in 1938 in Detmold.
33. Drewniak, *Theater*, 220–21. Also see Chapter 5 of this book.
34. *Lippische Staatszeitung*, 13 Nov. 1935.
35. Ibid.
36. Drewniak, *Theater*, 183–84. Cf. Rühle, *Zeit und Theater*, 19–20.
37. *Lippische Tages-Zeitung*, 31 Jan. 1937.
38. *Lippische Staatszeitung*, 31 Jan. 1937.
39. The play is included in Rühle's *Zeit und Theater*, with an analysis on pp. 794–807.
40. See Drewniak, *Theater*, 218–20.
41. *Lippische Staatszeitung*, 30 Oct. 1938.
42. See Rühle, *Zeit und Theater*, 766–76, and Peters, *Vom Hoftheater*, 211.
43. Hermann Wanderscheck, *Deutsche Dramatik der Gegenwart* (Berlin, 1938): 129.
44. Peters, *Vom Hoftheater*, 213.

4

Theatre of the Front: Sigmund Graff and *Die endlose Straße*

William Sonnega

> Where man stands against man, courage against courage, the final glimmer of "Romanticism" shimmers over the wretched, gas-impregnated vacuum and desolation of the modern mechanized war.
>
> —Sigmund Graff (1936)[1]

For the common soldier, the First World War was unique among modern wars. On one hand, military strategies of both the German and Allied armies generally remained focused on nineteenth-century notions of victory as it was ultimately achieved via man-to-man combat. On the other hand, soldiers had access to an expanding array of efficient new weapons, including the gas cannister, the hand grenade, the flamethrower, the trench mortar, the telescopic sight, the tank, and the submarine, all of which rendered the process of killing less personal. As a result, few men who served on either side of the Western Front between 1914 and 1918 fully understood the nature of their roles in the theatre of war. Entrenched in foreign soil, beneath a canopy of bullets and bombs, they were forced to pit themselves in mortal combat against an often unseen enemy in order to advance the front, a spatial demarcation between good and evil, right and wrong, self and other. In victory, they lived to dig yet another trench and resume their primordial struggle for territory. In defeat, they were either maimed, killed, or captured to be abused at the hands of their opponents. Faceless pawns on a board larger than many of them were ever aware of, they sacrificed their lives simply because they were expected to, because they had been drafted. In most cases, ideological ambitions had little to do with their immediate experiences of the front.

In the early 1930s, a half dozen plays that addressed the experiences of front soldiers in the First World War premiered in Germany—more than in any other nation that had been directly or indirectly involved in the war.[2] This sudden proliferation of front plays, or *Frontstücke*, was linked in part to the rise of National Socialism in the tumultuous period prior to Hitler's seizure of power in 1933. Whereas creating new weapons for retaliatory purposes was, at least temporarily, out of the question (in that the Versailles Treaty had expressly forbidden it and international opinion weighed heavily against allowing the Germans the unlimited right to rearm themselves), the staging of soldiers in a revisionist, dramatized history of the nation's role in the war held some potential. The theatre, in this sense, could be utilized as an effective tool for the dissemination of National Socialist propaganda that concerned itself with the identity of the First World War German soldier. The goal of such propaganda was to stage the soldier as neither a victim nor a hero of the war, but a man whose identity had been politically or even mythically transformed in the context of a network of comradely relations. In view of this goal, the mass circulation of war memories among German veterans of the Western Front in the early 1930s represented a significant source of inspiration for the soldier turned playwright.

Friedrich Bethge's *Reims* (1934), for example, examined how a soldier's relationship to his country could be constructively crystallized by *das Fronterlebnis* (the front experience). In *Reims*, Sergeant Franz Jarkusch deserts from his regiment when he learns that his wife is having an affair with a Russian prisoner of war. Captured en route to his home, he is brought before a court martial. When he learns that during his absence his regiment has been annihilated at the front, Jarkusch assumes responsibility for their deaths: "If I had stayed, maybe they would still be alive!" Though he is acquitted, a newly and fervently nationalistic Jarkusch volunteers for duty at the front in order to atone for his guilt. As neither victim nor hero, but simply a soldier who has confronted his ultimate dependence on his comrades, he is killed at Reims while fighting alongside the few remaining survivors of his regiment.[3]

In *Weg in den Morgen* ("Road in the Morning," 1934), Otto Paust similarly staged the comradeship of front soldiers in political terms. Set on "the world front" in 1918, the play depicts a heated debate among the members of a battalion over how prosperity should be restored to Germany following its imminent defeat. As they struggle to adopt a unified *Weltanschauung*, the soldiers divide themselves into competing ideological camps, including anarchist, communist, and Nazi. The play concludes in Berlin, in January 1933, on the eve of the Nazis' seizure of power. The National Socialist revolution has prevailed and Germany is soon to be unified beneath the banner of the Nazi party. In this context, the battalion's front-line debate represents the fractured political environment out of which National Socialism emerged as a catalyst for revolution. *Weg in den Morgen* therefore indicated to 1930s German audiences that the First World War need not evoke solely their nation's devastating loss to the Allies. Rather, a soldier's memories of comradeship at the front, for example, could also be construed as the historical antecedents of the Third Reich. In 1938, Hermann Wanderscheck summarized the political significance of these memories for Reich dramatists: "The front experience is the dramatic confession underlying the new Germany."[4]

Memories of front comradeship were similarly exalted in *Einsidel* (1934), by Walther Gottfried Klucke, though in mythic rather than political terms. In the play, Einsidel, "an unknown, badly wounded soldier" in the First World War, is employed as a gardener's assistant in a small graveyard. Ten years after the war, the ghosts of Einsidel's front-line comrades suddenly appear to him one day at work. In reminding him that they sacrificed their lives in order for the new Reich to thrive, they instruct Einsidel that "the youth have the legacy of the unknown soldiers to carry on." In the scope of the play's evocative recollections of the front experience, this prophetic admonition was perhaps directed by Klucke toward younger playwrights of the period who had not experienced the heroism—and horrors—of the front firsthand.[5]

I

As one of the most popularly and critically acclaimed *Frontstücke* of late Weimar Germany, *Die endlose Straße* ("The Endless Road," 1929), by Sigmund Graff and Carl Ernst Hintze, staged soldiers whose bodies and minds had been graphically marked by war. Its cast is comprised of the twenty soldiers of a German battalion, the Eleventh Company, half of whom are officers and half privates. Set in 1917 on the front in northern France, roughly six months after the battle of Verdun, the play chronicles a twenty-four-hour period in which the Eleventh's defense of the front temporarily falters under heavy artillery fire from the French. Forced into retreat at dawn, the surviving members of the company attend to their wounded and attempt to bolster their spirits by drinking and singing. The following morning, a war-weary yet determined Eleventh then returns to the front in order to repair the hole punched in it by the French. In the knowledge that their ranks will inevitably be further diminished, the company's march back to the front is construed, in this instance, as a march without end—a journey into the maw of death. Private Richter, for example, considers how the endless road is an appropriate metaphor for the experience that awaits them:

> I only wish we could start! There's nothing to think about then. All you can see is your front rank man. Helmet and pack. Then, suddenly, you find he's gone. But you'll see another helmet and pack there all the same. And he'll be your front rank man then. That's how it's been going for three years—always the same thing.[6]

The action of *Die endlose Straße* is confined to a single day, a day, as Richter indicates, not unlike most at the front. Within this compressed time and space, a haunting inertia dominates the Eleventh's soldiers. In a structural illustration of this inertia, the four acts of the play do not record a series of heroic actions in the heat of battle, but the mundane conversations of those who have either just returned from the front or are preparing to return to it again. Accompanied by the sounds of exploding enemy shells, the soldiers play an ongoing game of cards in order to preserve the fragile continuity of their lives. Unlike Paust's soldiers in *Weg in den Morgen*, Graff's soldiers— who similarly occupy the final trenches of the First World War—seldom question the greater ideological arena in which their presence on the front has been deemed necessary. Graff, perhaps assuming that his audience would be sufficiently aware of this arena already, employs the First World War as a backdrop rather than foreground for his play. The Eleventh's unchallenged acceptance of its predicament thus powerfully focuses *Die endlose Straße* on existential rather than ideological subtexts of the front experience; on how the space of the front itself rather than nationalist rhetoric determined the actual staging of soldiers.

In the interwar period, the play's uncanny representation of the actualities of war was necessarily perplexing. As the critic Alfred Kerr summarized in his review of a February 1932 staging of *Die endlose Straße* at Berlin's Schiller-Theater, "That is not a war play; that is the war."[7] Herbert Ihering similarly observed of the same production:

> One must search to come to terms with it. The play places some other task before the critic. *Die endlose Straße* can be appraised as neither theater piece nor ideological treatise. In no work for the stage does the experience of war speak so directly—without translation into overtly dramatic or political terms. It describes the passion of a company which has just been relieved from the foremost trench at Lille, yet must immediately return to the front. Communal destiny. Resignation. No exit. The endless road.[8]

Sentiments such as these had not always accompanied the play, however. When Graff initially submitted *Die endlose Straße* to a variety of German state theatres in 1926—including those in Dresden, Munich, Stuttgart, and Berlin, as well as the Nationaltheater at Mannheim and Deutsches Schauspielhaus in Hamburg—it was rejected for production. Three years later, when it was first published in Germany, it had still not appeared on the German stage. As Graff later recounted, when in 1929 the play's publisher had written to 198 German theatres requesting a production, he received only three replies, all of which expressed rejection. The following year, the publisher sent an identical letter to 336 German theatres and gathered 48 rejections and two offers of acceptance.[9]

Ironically, *Die endlose Straße* first appeared on stage in London, in 1929 at the Gate Theatre, where it was produced in an English version entitled *The Endless Road*, by Graham Rawson. Apart from the designation of act 1 as "Prologue," Rawson's version of *Die endlose Straße* was essentially a line-by-line translation of Graff and Hintze's original; in a footnote to his text, however, Rawson noted "certain differences between English and German army practice" that informed his translation of the play.[10] Due in part to successful reviews in England, which were reprinted shortly thereafter in Indian and Australian newspapers, *Die endlose Straße* eventually received its German premiere at the Stadttheater in Aachen on 19 November 1930. It did not reappear on the German stage until nearly a year later when it was offered for three performances at the Nationaltheater at Weimar, then a popular theatrical forum for the elucidation of proto-Nazi ideas. Here the play was so well received that its run was extended to include over twenty performances.[11] Following its triumph at politically conservative Weimar, *Die endlose Straße* subsequently became the most frequently produced *Kriegsstück* (war play) of the 1930s, receiving over five thousand performances, in Germany as well as in Rio de Janeiro, Buenos Aires, São Paulo, Santiago de Chile, Valparaiso, Riga, and Basel.[12]

Formal accolades soon followed. Local officials in Hamburg acknowledged the play's inspirational portrayal of the front experience for soldiers of the Third Reich by awarding it the first Dietrich-Eckart Prize on 19 December 1933. The following year, the play appeared at the first annual Reichstheaterfestwoche in Dresden.[13] In 1935, however, as the popularity of *Die endlose Straße* peaked in Germany and with a variety of audiences abroad, the office of the Reichsdramaturg, under the direction of Dr. Rainer Schlösser, requested that Graff make several changes in the text. (Ironically, Graff may have been employed by Schlösser at the time. In May 1933, he had worked for Dr. Joseph Goebbels in the Theater Division of the Reich Ministry of Popular Enlightenment and Propaganda, first under Otto Laubinger, and later under Schlösser. Given that Wanderscheck noted in 1938 that Graff was "currently employed" by Schlösser, the playwright appears to have worked for the Propaganda Ministry at the time the Reichsdramaturg requested that changes be made to his play.[14]) On 5 April 1934, the following announcement issued by Schlösser indicated that performances of all front plays in Germany required special sanctions:

> The Reichsdramaturg hereby informs theatre management that, for considerations of fundamental interest to the state, all performances of plays which represent the front experience and that of the military base camp, respectively, will until further notice be mounted only given the prior approval of the Reichsdramaturg.[15]

Ultimately, Graff suggested to Schlösser that it was better to withdraw *Die endlose Straße* from production rather than make the desired changes to it, and the play was removed from the canon of plays officially sanctioned for production in the Third Reich.

The play's initial difficulty in finding its way to the stage suggests that its reputation, at least among German theatre professionals, had always been controversial. Wanderscheck, for example, writing in Germany on the eve of the Second World War, cited Jewish domination of the German theatre prior to 1933 for preventing the play's immediate production. Such an analysis of the production history of *Die endlose Straße*, however, was likely informed by Wanderscheck's personal alignment with Third Reich ideology. More generally, however, even Graff observed that various elements of *Die endlose Straße*, while reflective of the period in which the play was written, were subject to reinterpretation during the Third Reich. Of a November 1933 production at the Plaza Theatre in Berlin he noted:

> In this production you will also hear a couple of sentences, which were written in 1926, though which in 1932 neither in Charlottenburg [Schiller-Theater] nor in Gendarmenmarkt [Staatstheater] could be heard (though they were heard everywhere throughout the Reich): because in the Reich's capital these lines for self-evident, purely dramaturgical reasons had to be removed from the play.[16]

While Graff declined to note the specific lines deemed inappropriate for presentation on the prominent Berlin stages, it is likely that the "dramaturgical" reasons for censorship he cited were in fact political reasons pertaining to the provocative vision of war at the core of the play.

In act 2, for example, Lieutenant Schroeder expresses his desire to take leave from the front in order to visit French prostitutes at Lille (724). For an audience heavily populated with Reich dignitaries and authorities, the suggestion of a German officer abandoning his post to cavort with the enemy in this manner may have been regarded as offensive. Furthermore, it uncomfortably linked a sexual liaison with a woman to the primordial acts of aggression required of soliders who would thrive at the front. In this respect, even the fantasized presence of a female among the front ranks may have been understood to diminish the German soldier's nationalistic ardor, transforming his desire for killing into an equal and opposite desire for sex or even love. Other moments in *Die endlose Straße* indicate tensions between what the front soldier was required to do and what he perhaps really wanted. In the final act, for example, three badly wounded men who have just returned from the front recount their experiences for those who are about to do battle:

> *First Wounded*: As for the men on the front, we never saw any of them again.
> *Third Wounded*: No jerk could have lived through it. (Long Pause)
> . . . .
> *First Wounded*: Nothing to be done.
> *Second Wounded*: They dropped a half dozen big ones on every inch of the line.
> *First Wounded*: And then came over us with their tanks.
> *Second Wounded*: And then hit us with an artillery barrage.
> *First Wounded*: And then they attacked us again.
> . . . .
> *First Wounded*: No, there's nothing to be done. [760]

While it is possible that in 1935 some Reich authorities read a moment such as this as an evocation of the heroic qualities of ideal National Socialist or "Nordic" soldiers, men who would selflessly lay down their lives in the name of revolution, it is likely that more saw in it a dark pacifistic glimpse of the resignation and despair of men whose lives had been brutally stripped of meaning.[17] With the establishment of compulsory military service for German men in 1935, it is further possible that the title of the play, insofar as it conjured a Sisyphean existential dilemma, contained too few allusions to an ultimate (Nazi) victory, a final destination along "the endless road" of war, to warrant the play's inclusion in the Reich's restricted canon. Graff's soldiers, whose presence on the front was not explicitly motivated by Nazi or any other ideology, likely embodied an overly universalized vision of the warrior for Reich authorities. Pressured by Goebbels to rid German art of its ideological impurities, the Reichsdramaturg may have thus construed the absence of a pro-Nazi discourse in the play as an inherently subversive omission.

The official withdrawal of *Die endlose Straße* from production by the Reichsdramaturg was largely symptomatic of a concerted effort on the part of the Nazis to re-interpret and control the political function of art in general. Playwrights, and all artists, were to make manifest in their work the unique racial and historical characteristics that Hitler had decreed to be fundamental to German superiority. This meant that images of decadence and weakness—as exemplified by the Lieutenant's desire for prostitutes and the wounded soldiers' lack of stamina at the front, for example—were strictly forbidden. At the 1935 Nürnberg Party Rally, Hitler declared, "It is not the function of art to wallow in dirt for dirt's sake, never its task to paint men in the state of decomposition, to draw cretins as the symbol of motherhood, to picture hunchbacked idiots as representative of manly strength."[18] The pressure to work within an increasingly limited aesthetic framework, in concert with Hitler's massive reinforcement of the German military, thus quickly removed a large number of artists and would-be artists from the cultural mainstream in the early 1930s. An equal number of artists, however, were ready to take their place.

Graff, for one, continued to write, though it is not surprising that one of his best-known plays of the 1930s, *Die Heimkehr des Matthias Bruck* ("The Return of Matthias Bruck," 1933) was a nationalistic treatise of the *Heimkehrer* (homecoming) genre. Like similar works of its type, the play glorified the return to the simple values of peasant life as a basis for national regeneration. In the play, a German front soldier returns to his home after spending seventeen years in Siberia after the war. Working unrecognized as a farmhand on his own farm, he realizes that life has gone on in his absence, and that he has no right to reclaim his wife, who has married again. Despite the lack of fanfare that attended his homecoming, the soldier becomes a hero via his quiet determination to finally be reunited with the fatherland.[19]

The brief production history of *Die endlose Straße* reveals, in this instance, how dramatic texts and their creators were opportunistically exploited by the Reich to serve its ideological imperatives of the moment. In the early 1930s, for example, the play gave dramatic support to the Reich's underlying racial and historical values on both theoretical and practical levels. On one hand, the rugged comradeship and perseverance of the Eleventh at the front could be construed as the consummate manifestation of a fervent German nationalism. On the other hand, the fictive company could be heralded as a pragmatic model to be emulated by actual Nazi military units. As Hitler fortified his ranks during the mid-1930s, however, the battlefield quickly replaced the stage as the primary arena of German political action. It therefore followed that, with Germany's invasion of Poland on 1 September 1939, soldiers had replaced playwrights as the best-equipped members of the *Volk* to stage the values of the Reich in the theatre of war.

II

In tracing the movement of Graff's personal memories of the front from the text of *Die endlose Straße* to Third Reich stages, seldom has theatre history provided a narrative in which the disparate roles of playwright and soldier are as inextricably interwoven. Three months after the onset of the First World War in August 1914, Graff, at age sixteen-and-a-half, enlisted in the German army. As a cadet in a machine gun battalion in the Alpine Corps, he served for two years on all fronts with the exception of Russia, including the bloody 1916 Verdun offensive. Returning from the war unwounded, Graff studied economics and journalism until completing *Die endlose Straße* with Hintze in 1926. While Graff both conceived the idea for and wrote the script, Hintze, a features editor for the *Magdeburgische Zeitung*, apparently functioned as his impassioned and inspirational collaborator. As Graff noted in a letter to a friend, in which he ironically referred to himself in the third person:

> Hintze had no special dramatic abilities, but he was nevertheless heads and shoulders above Graff with regard to story-telling and editorial talent. They had both powerfully and deeply experienced the war on the front, however, and they had both roughly the same instincts for observation, the same will for objective renderings.[20]

Hintze, who had been badly wounded in the war, also brought to the project the corporeal urgency of the front-line soldier's predicament, a point not lost on Graff, who populated each act of the play with the disquieting presence of wounded soldiers. Hintze died on 13 December 1931. Two years later, Graff commemorated his comrade by linking his death to the play they had written together. He wrote: "When [*Die endlose Straße*] opened in an outstanding production on 1 December 1931, in Leipzig, Hintze lay deathly ill in a hospital in Halle. Twelve days later, he died."[21] The subtext of this brief acknowledgement implied that Hintze had triumphed over adversity by living to see the success of the play that had been based so completely on the circumstances of his death.

While Graff had fortunately escaped being physically maimed as a soldier, the war nonetheless left a permanent scar on his psyche and forcefully configured his work as a playwright. Of his personal *Fronterlebnis* and its relation to *Die endlose Straße*, for example, Graff once recalled,

> Prior to Verdun, on a steep embankment near Douaumont, I lay for two days in a narrow ditch with an old brave and faithful rifleman, Rickl, from the First Company. While above us bullets hissed of our death, we spoke barely 20 sentences to each other in the two whole days, because when you can die at any moment, all words are banal and the only possible thing to do is hold your tongue. However, the few words which this "old man" of about 40 in these two days did say to me—an innocent little guy of 18—formed within me the unforgettable and unmistakable mental picture of the world-weary front-line combatant, of the simple man, who could not and would not let his

life be snuffed out.... Ten years later, as I wrote *Die endlose Straße*, this man stood again before me.²²

Shortly after his entrenchment at Douaumont, Graff was sent to Verdun, where, as he later reported, "the longest, most horrible, most wretched battle that world history has ever known" took place.²³ Though *Die endlose Straße* is not set precisely in Verdun, the text does describe a battle in a remote pasture in northern France, near the town of Lille, located roughly one hundred miles northwest of Verdun. In 1917, when the battle depicted in the text ostensibly took place, Lille and Verdun lay along the same front, an ideological boundary constituted by German troops to the north and French and British troops to the south.²⁴ In this respect, while Graff repeatedly acknowledged the personal significance of the 1916 Verdun offensive in his life, his strategy in writing about a lesser-known if not imaginary battle reflected a dramaturgical shift away from the type of war play that sought to reconstruct theatrically the experience of actual soldiers, battles, and battlefields via their well-documented histories. In *Die endlose Straße*, Graff appears more concerned with how the experience of war penetrates the collective unconscious of a group of unknown individuals than the individual conscience of a well-known politician or general.

The characters of *Die endlose Straße* comprise, by contrast, a forgotten community, the reality of their predicament, and its attendant heroism and horrors known only to themselves. Positioned midway between the Tenth and Twelfth companies along an ever-shifting front, the Eleventh is nonetheless removed from the larger German war apparatus (its wire contact with headquarters is severed in the first act). By focusing within the Eleventh on the everyday rather than extraordinary or heroic activities of a group of front soldiers, Graff facilitates a micro- rather than macrocosmic representation of the front experience. As he once reflected, his goal in developing *Die endlose Straße* was determined by a desire to refocus history's lens on the mundane rather than the mythic:

> The evidence I was compelled to file was not of an isolated experience in the monstrous four years [of the First World War], rather it was the experience of the four years themselves. The average. The trivial. In what happened everyday—not in the so-called peak moments, which the army reports named and the command notices celebrated—lay the true magnitude of the war and its warriors. The war—its universal core, as it were—can only be represented in art through the universal, in which every exceptional case disintegrates and is reconstituted as a symbol. So it developed slowly—in seven long years—but always clearly before me the picture or even more the vision of a company, in which no one, whether captain or rifleman, played a specific "role," in which a single unbreakable unity was depicted, the most difficult

task to conquer, what a company in the war had conquered a hundredfold: to be released in the hellfire of the largest battle, and afterwards, in the briefest quiet pause in the midst of this hell, to be forced to return.[25]

In de-romanticizing the front experience in drama, Graff perhaps ironically nurtured a romantic perception of the Nordic man as a primordial warrior willing to die to preserve the sanctity of his *Blut und Boden* (blood and soil), that is, with some sense of *völkisch* heroism. In 1930, as the National Socialists consolidated power and prepared to take control of the German state, the soldiers of Graff's Eleventh Company, like outstanding members of the Volk, could conceivably be regarded as intuitive, non-intellectual "workers" who performed the brutal duties of battle with an obedient vigor. Just as easily, however, they could be understood on a human scale. When the Eleventh is under heavy fire from the enemy, class distinctions and military rank within it cease to exist (just as they do in Allied and perhaps all armies under siege). On receiving marching orders to return to the front, for example, Lieutenant Schroeder implores Captain Reutlinger to remain behind, arguing that a captain is "too good to be turned into dirt." The captain, however, assures the lieutenant that a captain's life is no more valuable than his, nor any soldier's for that matter. "No, Schroeder," he replies, "all men are too good for the dirt" (765).

The constructive relationship of the front experience to the myth of a devoutly selfless *Volk* was also articulated by Goebbels, in his 1929 novel *Michael*. Goebbels's central character, Michael, a young German, reflects with his friend Matthias on the nature of their involvement in the First World War:

> During the war we wrested even more from our bodies and our defiance and we didn't even go to ruin.
> But we suffered grievously in body and soul.
> True, Matthias, it was not easy to overcome it all. But see here, we did it together, worker and master.
> We lay together in the trenches, he who came from a palace and he who hailed from a miner's cottage.
> We clung together, became friends, and for the first time knew each other.
> But when the war was over, the unholy cleavage opened up again.[26]

As Matthias infers, the "cleavage" between ruling and working classes was judged "unholy" by the quasi-religious dictates of National Socialism, an unnatural separation defying the providence of both God and Führer. Like Graff, Goebbels viewed the front as a communal crucible in which arbitrary class distinctions dissolved in the face of adversity. As soldiers clung to one another in the trenches, their identities were titrated to a nationalistic essence—they became purely German men. Bonds formed under these circumstances necessarily constituted life-long relationships. As Ernst Röhm, later head of the SA and who had fought in the First World War, noted, "Soldierly comradeship, cemented with blood, can perhaps temporarily relax, but it can never be torn out of the heart, it cannot be exterminated." Röhm, who was homosexual, further recalled that the gender-specific experience of military companies forged a unique emotional linkage between men that at times consciously excluded women. "The wife of a soldier in my company," he wrote, "whose political convictions were far removed from mine, said to me on one occasion: 'In the heart of my husband, his captain takes the first place; there is nobody to outrank him. Only then come his mother and I.' "[27]

Insofar as a network of comradely relations, rather than external actions, appeared to create the structure of *Die endlose Straße*, the play illustrated a dynamic slice of National Socialist life. Though it is difficult to ascertain to what extent Graff's work was theoretically informed by National Socialism and conversely to what extent the National Socialist project was propelled by successful productions of the play, the play's detailed representation of front-line comradeship among German soldiers surrounded it at least briefly in the 1930s with a political aura few other war plays had procured. In the domain of Graff's identity as a veteran of the First World War, *Die endlose Straße* was also perhaps the product of more personal processes, a therapeutic excavation in which Graff attempted to recover the unresolved narratives of his First World War experiences—perhaps most intimately those associated with Verdun. Given the rigorously docudramatic, politically neutral voice of the text, however, it is ironic that shortly after completing the play, Graff himself wholeheartedly embraced the Nazi creed. In any case, both sound dramaturgical instincts and a receptive political environment appeared to have helped Graff the soldier reinvent himself as a playwright in the first years of the Third Reich. As the textual and performative forum in which this transformation was negotiated, *Die endlose Straße* therefore staged soldiers as actors, and actors as soldiers, in maintaining to interwar audiences that war was, for better or worse, Germany's national theatre.

III

At Aachen, *Die endlose Straße* ran for a limited engagement of five performances. For years afterward, Graff repeatedly noted that the premiere was one of his favorite productions of the play. Aachen audiences apparently concurred that it was one of theirs as well. "A quarter hour after the final curtain," Graff recalled of opening night at the 1,100–seat house, "the audience was still standing in the lobby as quietly as the walls."[28]

Under the direction of Hermann Albert Schroeder, the play was set in a highly naturalistic environment. Archive photos reveal a striking attention to detail. For the first act a dugout was literally reconstructed on stage.[29] Elements in the mise-en-scène included candles, lanterns, tin cups, pails, helmets, rifles, grenades, gas masks, canteens, playing cards, telephone wires, bunks, blankets, bottles, packs, walking sticks, wooden crates, sheets of corrugated steel, a clothesline, a wash basin, a broken mirror, and a small cast iron stove—most of which were likely surplus items obtained from the German army. Each of the actors wore an authentic German army-issue uniform from the First World War, what the soldiers affectionately referred to as the *Feldgrau* (field gray), appropriate to his character's military role and rank. With the exception of the paymaster, all of the soldiers were staged as filthy; mud-covered hats, coats, boots, and gloves testified to the existence of a subterranean race more akin to moles than human beings.

In the archive photos, none of the men are smiling; they have been posed to evoke solely the grim visage of war. In awkward tableaus they stand, sit on crates, or lay languidly on the floor. Many of them are touching other men, resting an arm on a shoulder, a foot on the leg of another. In the cramped space of the dugout neither privacy nor autonomy exists. Even the captain and lieutenant, who sit at a small table down right, are jammed intimately together, elbow to elbow, and surrounded completely by men.

The most striking aspect of the dugout photos is the ironically comfortable atmosphere they convey. The impression is that the soldiers have been existing for so long in close proximity to one another that they have long since given up on carving out even the semblance of a personal niche for themselves. As a result, a communal identity pervades the space. Even in the act 2 photos of the behind-the-lines hut to which the men retreat is this identity apparent. Like the dugout, the hut offers little room for privacy or autonomy. And while it is somewhat cleaner, it is no less inhospitable. Both spaces are represented on stage as fundamentally temporary; they have been quickly set up in order to be quickly torn down. Visually, they emphasize that the greater arena of the front was not created for men to live in—but to die in.

Constructed of similar materials, encompassing a similar size, and requiring a similar amount of time to build, the theatrical settings oddly mirror the actual front sites they represent. And yet they are not the actual sites, nor do the stagings of the front experience they engender operate according to stakes of the battlefield. Between the set for *Die endlose Straße* at Aachen and the muddy trenches of northern France it represented is a problematic gap in space and time. In naturalism or "documentary realism" of this style this gap must always be negotiated by the audience. As James E. Young observes, "the principal aims of such a style are to efface a work's constructedness, in order to foster the illusion of actuality, which rhetorically persuades the audience of a work's objectivity."[30] In this sense, did the documentary realism of *Die endlose Straße* in performance generally intend to present the facts of the front experience or an argument as to how those facts emerged in the first place? If the latter, then how were those facts used to support a particular explanation of events at the Western Front?

In the three politically volatile years between its premiere and the close of 1933, *Die endlose Straße* was performed in over 350 German cities, an astonishing number of which were middle-sized. In Hintze's home of Magdeburg, for example, a town roughly the size of a Berlin suburb, the play ran for 125 performances, suggesting that its voice resonated across a broad demographic spectrum. In 1933, Graff adapted the text for younger audiences in a widely distributed "school-use" edition, and in 1935 published it as a radio play.[31] As the critic Herbert Ihering noted, however, by the time the play arrived in Berlin in 1932, "for neutral plays such as this it was already too late." By "neutral" what Ihering meant was that the wheels of the Nazi propaganda machine had already been set into motion and would be supportive of only those works that manifestly supported the far-right (or far-left) theories and practices of the Third Reich.[32]

In Ihering's view, an 18 November 1933 production of *Die endlose Straße* at Berlin's Plaza, "the theatre of three thousand," may therefore have been the play's swan song, or one of the final productions of it in which its discourse on the front was publicly applauded rather than contested by the Reich. In an editorial in the *Neue Preußische Zeitung*, Graff indicated the significance of the Plaza production to his personal dramaturgical goals. Of the *Volk* who would fill the theatre the following evening he reflected, "This audience, which typically goes to the theatre for a single mark, although it barely has a mark remaining and for even less money could go to the movies, is the audience that I love, for which I write and to which I confess."[33] While on the one hand such a statement carefully aligned itself with the Reich's portrait of the artist as a populist hero, a public servant creatively employed by the vast German working classes, on the other it revealed Graff's perception of theatre as a popular art form that both entertained and instructed. In this respect, the large capacity of the Plaza appeared to represent for Graff an important opportunity to premiere his play before the German working class, a group he deeply identified with and hoped would find his memories of the front illuminating.

Given its subject matter, *Die endlose Straße* is not a humorous play. Within the dialogic intimacies exchanged by its cast of soldiers, however, humorous moments may have emerged for a large audience that perhaps collectively understood the context of the front all too well. Further, it is likely that a significant percentage of the Plaza audience was comprised of actual veterans of the First World War trenches represented on stage, men who saw in the Eleventh's staged soldiers brief yet incandescent reflections of themselves. For these members of the Volk—many of whom had enlisted or would be drafted to fight in the coming Second World War—the production occupied a unique time and space indeed, a hyper-reality in which past, present, and future converged in a timeless theatrical simulation. Graff himself desired that all members of the Volk would respond to the play in this manner, discovering in it the unique racial and historical characteristics that defined their national identity. The Plaza production of *Die endlose Straße* would therefore function as a true occasion of *Volkstheater*, he mused, "a theatre in which the *Volk* can laugh heartily, but not only laugh, in which the *Volk* can also now and then discover that gravity at which they alone are entitled to laugh."[34]

Directed by Peter Stachina of the Altes Theater in Leipzig, the Plaza production was, in sharp contrast to the play's premiere at Aachen and Schiller-Theater engagement the prior year, a spectacular exhibition of Nazi politics and culture. Here the shifting political climate was reflected in the explicit ideological marking of the theatre space. Like other sites at which high-ranking Nazi officials were scheduled to appear, the Plaza was lavishly adorned with the iconography of the Nazi Party. The critic F. Morgenroth, for example, began his review of the production's opening night with the following description: "Flowers, flowers everywhere; with black-white-and-red banners and flags bearing swastikas adorning the theatre's broad columns. To the right and left large iron crosses against a silver-gray background admonish [the audience] with their serious and stern demeanor."[35] As Morgenroth noted, Berlin audiences that had been acquainted with *Die endlose Straße* the previous year at the smaller Schiller-Theater were necessarily re-introduced to it in an entirely different light. The immense physical dimensions of the space itself, for example, may have directly assisted the play's representation of a vast windswept battlefield in France. In stark contrast to the house, the stage was left relatively barren in order to emphasize the desolate core of the front experience. Using primarily the actors' bodies and lighting, Stachina partitioned the playing area into the polarized and compressed physical spaces in which the identities of Graff's soldiers were staged: base camp versus the front.

The presence of a variety of Reich dignitaries and authorities in the Plaza audience likely further heightened the experience of the play for the *Volk* and engulfed the event in the heady atmosphere of Nazi ritual. Shortly after 8:00 P.M., for example, the first *Heil* cheer resounded throughout the house. Princes Eitel Friedrich and Oskar, accompanied by Princess Oskar of Prussia and a processional of distinguished Reich officials, thereby entered the space. As Morgenroth reported, the Plaza audience grew increasingly festive as curtain-time approached: "Jubilation, which awakes and ascends, fills the theatre as Bundesführer Franz Seldte follows the parade in. New *Heil* cheers are continually raised, each with continually more enthusiasm, each louder than the one before it, until *Reichsminister* Dr. Goebbels gestures to the tiers of seats that it's time to begin. It grows dark—and quiet. The production has begun."³⁶

The opening tableau of *Die endlose Straße*—in which a group of battle-dazed and badly wounded soldiers huddled by candlelight in a front-line trench—likely ruptured the Plaza audience's reverie with startling swiftness. Further, just after the curtain had risen, a particularly heavy explosion appeared to blow out all the candles, transforming the stage's artificial light into the preternatural darkness of a foxhole or shallow grave. While artificial light quickly returned when the soldiers relighted the candles, these first moments of the performance established a foreboding sense of danger that attempted to approximate the battlefield. Morgenroth's description of the final moment of the play—in which the sounds of the soldiers' marching feet were heard even after the curtain had fallen—reveals that Stachina may have been successful in conjuring this essence for the Plaza crowd:

> The final act—the soldiers' march upon the endless road to the front—is over. The curtain falls. For a moment the house remains quiet, then erupts with a thunderous applause. The curtain rises and there before us is a picture which will never be forgotten. Body to body, shoulder to shoulder, over the width of the stage the soldiers stand in their muddy, gray, noble uniforms, their bodies perfectly motionless as their strong, quiet eyes blink beneath their helmets. The picture issues a challenge: to remember the immense, mute sacrifice. Time and again the curtain must be raised over this picture, until finally its creator, Sigmund Graff, takes his place in the middle of the soldiers. His face—with lips trembling—mirrors that of every spectator: emotion and gratitude.³⁷

For Morgenroth, the primary function of *Die endlose Straße* was to remind audiences of the unfathomable number of German men that had been lost in the First World War. By merging the spaces of the battlefield and the stage, the play implied that soldiers were their nation's actors, men who played their roles—as paymaster, cadet, lance-corporal, and so on—and then, when the play was over, sacrificed their lives. Here Graff's soldiers functioned as theatrical apparitions of actual soldiers who had died in the line of duty. For an overwhelming number of Germans in the 1930s who had been related to or acquainted with a soldier who had been killed in the war, the play therefore provided a therapeutic forum in which the senseless loss of human life was not rationalized as an act of heroic nationalism (as some Nazis at the Plaza may have understood the play's intent), but questioned. To the extent that several thousand performances of the play in Germany between 1930 and 1936 facilitated this questioning on a mass scale, the play may have assisted the nation more in coming to terms with the carnage of its youth in the First World War than it exalted soldierly sacrifice as the highest form of national service in the Third Reich. Graff himself later observed that the irony of these diametrically opposed interpretations—the former evoking pacifism and the latter militarism—was reflected at the heart of the individual soldier's existence. "The soldier," he wrote at the height of the Second World War, "who represents the highest power of a land and people, rejects all violence."[38]

NOTES

1. Sigmund Graff, *Unvergesslicher Krieg: Ein Buch vom deutschen Schicksal* (Leipzig, 1936): 58.
2. For brief summaries of German front plays, see Hermann Wanderscheck, *Deutsche Dramatik der Gegenwart* (Berlin, 1938): 75–93.
3. Friedrich Bethge, *Reims* (Berlin, 1934): 57. Act 2, scene 3 of *Reims* appears in Wanderscheck, *Deutsche Dramatik*, 80–87; the play is briefly discussed in H. F. Garten, *Modern German Drama*, 2nd ed. (London, 1964): 233–34.
4. Wanderscheck, *Deutsche Dramatik*, 90–91.
5. Ibid., 91–92.
6. Sigmund Graff and Carl Ernst Hintze, *Die endlose Straße*, in *Von der Republik zur Diktatur: 1925–1933*, vol. 2 of *Zeit und Theater*, ed. Günther Rühle (Frankfurt, 1972): 757. Subsequent references will appear in the text.
7. Alfred Kerr's review in *Berliner Tageblatt*, 24 February 1932, in Günther Rühle, *Theater für die Republik, im Spiegel der Kritik: 1917–1933* (Frankfurt am Main, 1967): 1052.
8. Herbert Ihering's review in the *Berliner Börsen-Courier*, 24 February 1932, in Rühle, *Theater für die Republik*, 1049.
9. In Wanderscheck, *Deutsche Dramatik*, 78.
10. Rawson's soldiers employ somewhat more formal terms when addressing their superiors than do Graff's. See, for example, Sigmund Graff, *The Endless Road*, ed. and tr. Graham Rawson (London, 1930): 6.
11. For Graff's personal account of the play's history, see Sigmund Graff, "Der Weg zu 'endlose Straße,'" *Neue Preußische Zeitung* (Berlin), 17 Nov. 1933: 6.
12. Rühle, *Theater für die Republik*, 1047.
13. A production of Erwin Kolbenheyer's drama, *Heroische Leidenschaften*, was originally scheduled for 3 June 1934. It was withdrawn from the program at the last minute when the play's leading actor became ill. The production of *Endlose Straße* that had appeared earlier that year in Dresden was substituted in its place.
14. See Wanderscheck, *Deutsche Dramatik*, 305.
15. Rainer Schlösser, "Aufführung von Kriegstücken," *Die Deutsche Bühne: Amtliches Blatt des Deutschen Bühnenvereins* 26, no.5 (23 April 1934): 89.
16. Sigmund Graff, "Die endlose Straße im Berliner Osten," *Neue Preußische Zeitung* (Berlin), 15 Nov. 1933: 10.
17. For a postwar variation on this theme see, for example, Samuel Beckett's *Waiting for Godot*. The refrain, "Nothing to be done," appears at several junctures in the text at which Vladamir and Estragon rationalize their powerlessness in the face of violence.

18. Hitler's "Address on Art and Politics" at Nürnberg, 11 Sept. 1935, in Henry Grosshans, *Hitler and the Artists* (New York, 1983): 27.
19. Garten, *Modern German Drama*, 223.
20. In Rühle's commentary to the play, Graff and Hintze, *Die endlose Staße*, 833.
21. Graff, "Der Weg," 6.
22. Ibid.
23. Sigmund Graff, *Erinnerungen eines Bühnenautors: 1900–1945. Von SM zu NS* (Munich, 1963): 52.
24. For a year-by-year description of various theatrical openings of the era and their respective political backdrops, see Michael Patterson, *The Revolution in German Theatre: 1900–1933* (London, 1981).
25. In Wanderscheck, *Deutsche Dramatik*, 77.
26. Joseph Goebbels, *Michael: Ein deutsches Schicksal in Tagebuchblättern*, quoted. in George L. Mosse, ed. *Nazi Culture* (New York, 1966): 111.
27. Ernst Röhm, *Die Geschichte eines Hochverräters* [The history of a traitor], quoted in Mosse, *Nazi Culture*, 101–2. For a discussion of (homo)sexuality and comradeship among First World War German soldiers, see "A Soldier's Love," in Klaus Theweleit, *Male Fantasies*, vol. 1, tr. Stephen Conway (Minneapolis, 1987): 52–62.
28. Graff, *Erinnerungen eines Bühnenautors*, 85.
29. Production photos of *Die endlose Straße* are located at the Theatermuseum der Universität zu Köln in Porz-Wahn.
30. James E. Young, *Writing and the Holocaust: Narrative and the Consequences of Interpretation* (Bloomington, 1988): 65.
31. The *Schulgebrauch* edition of *Die endlose Straße* appeared in *Deutsche Lesebogen* 185, an educational publication intended for use in schools; a copy is at the Schiller-Nationalmuseum, Deutsches Literaturarchiv, Marbach am Neckar. The text of the radio play is located at the Theatermuseum der Universität zu Köln at Porz-Wahn. The editions are virtually identical, suggesting that Graff presumed the radio play would gather an audience comprising, at least in part, students who had read the text in school. The radio play includes notes for sound effects of rifles, shells, and so on.
32. Rühle, *Theater für die Republik*, 1048.
33. Graff, "Die endlose Straße im Berliner Osten," 10.
34. Ibid.
35. F. Morgenroth, "'Die endlose Straße.' Festaufführung in der 'Plaza,'" *Neue Preußische Zeitung* (Berlin), 19 Nov. 1933: 8.
36. Ibid.
37. Ibid.
38. Sigmund Graff, *Über das Soldatische* (Berlin, 1943): 95.

5

Eberhard Wolfgang Möller: Politically Correct Playwright of the Third Reich

Rufus J. Cadigan

Eberhard Wolfgang Möller (1906–1972) was one of the most celebrated of the Nazi playwrights. His career began in 1929 when he published two right-wing dramas, *Douaumont* and *Kalifornische Tragödie*. In 1931 the young playwright joined the Nazi Party; two years later with Hitler in power, Möller was appointed Chief Dramaturg at the prestigious Königsberg Theater. Goebbels personally tapped him to work in the Theater Division of the Propaganda Ministry in 1934. By the age of twenty-eight, Möller was an establishment figure who wrote his own politically correct dramas and censored those of others.

Douaumont and *Kalifornische Tragödie* thematically set the tone for Möller's plays written between 1933 and 1939. The former is a modern version of the Homeric myth. One of the few German survivors of the World War I battle at Fort Douaumont, the veteran Ulysses returns for a traumatic homecoming after a twelve-year absence. His wife Helen greets him with indifference; she has taken in lodgers, a businessman and a teacher, and has no more room for him. *Kalifornische Tragödie* is based on the life of the nineteenth-century American settler Johann Jakob Suter. His "tragedy" occurs when gold is discovered on his property and swarms of prospectors illegally descend on it. The government is sympathetic to Suter's predicament but lacks the military force needed to protect him from the lawless hordes. Suter dies brokenhearted and poor.

The allegorical nature of these two dramas would have been clear to German audiences. In *Douaumont* Ulysses represents Germany's angry young men, the veterans of the World War who suffered rejection from a society anxious to forget the war and the sacrifices of its soldiers. *Kalifornische Tragödie* is an indictment of the lawless Weimar Republic, which lacked the force to protect its people from foreign and domestic invasion.

After the overthrow of the Weimar Republic, Möller did not cease to write about it. Between 1933 and 1938 he published six more dramas that continued to condemn the Jewish, capitalistic, and foreign influences that had "contaminated" the German *Volk* in the 1920s and early 1930s. His first play under the Nazi regime was *Rothschild siegt bei Waterloo* ("Rothschild Wins at Waterloo," 1934). The anti-hero is Nathan Rothschild (1777–1836), a London banker of Jewish descent. Supposedly based on a historical incident, the drama reveals how Rothschild used advance knowledge of the outcome of the famous battle to stage a financial victory at the stock exchange. He is portrayed as a despicable parasite who becomes wealthy through war-profiteering. As a result of his treachery, the government is threatened and Englishmen go bankrupt.

In the opening scene, against the backdrop of the raging battlefield, Rothschild enters as a cowardly spectator, not a military participant. While the Aryans are defending their country's honor, Rothschild slinks at the corners, always at a safe distance from the major engagement. His mission is to discover the outcome of the battle before the general public so that he can play the stock market to his advantage. Rothschild's insensitivity to the carnage around him is compared with the compassionate attitude of his employee, O'Pinnel. The latter sees a wounded Frenchman crawling toward them.

> *Rothschild:* What are you saying? There's a corpse?
>
> *O'Pinnel:* He's still creeping.
>
> *Rothschild:* A corpse, I'm sure of it. Why are you getting so excited about a corpse?
>
> *The Frenchman (creeps nearer):* I . . . I
>
> *Rothschild:* Let's go on.
>
> *O'Pinnel:* Yes, we'll go on. But there are so many, so many, Herr Banker.[1]

Other soldiers approach with dying requests and pleas for water, but Rothschild remains callous. He rebukes O'Pinnel for his weakness and sympathy: "These men are only pieces of death, why dirty your hands for them?"[2]

Rothschild's cold-bloodedness is motivated by greed. He sees money as the only thing worth caring about: "My money is everywhere and money is friendly, the friendliest power on earth, fat, round, and happy."³ Through money, Rothschild can be a ruthless manipulator, buying power and bribing others into betraying their own best interests. When Rothschild discovers that Wellington is the victor, he attempts to rush back to London to put his plan into action. But a fierce storm arises and most sailors refuse to ferry him across the ocean. Eventually he finds a young man willing to risk his life and his family's future security in return for a considerable sum of money. The sailor's wife is afraid her husband will drown in the storm:

The young wife: You mean you'll hoist your sails?

The young sailor: He is rich.

The young wife: Yes, he is.

The young sailor: The richest man in London.

The young wife: But what does that matter to us?

The young sailor: How can a poor fellow like me argue with a man like that?

The young wife: Refuse to do it for me.

The young sailor: I can buy a house.

Rothschild (very confidently): You can become a ship owner.⁴

The implication would be obvious to the audience: Everyone has a price, and unless the Jews are separated from the rest of Germany, the *Volk* will become infected with their materialistic values, their "racial" characteristics. If we true Germans mingle with Jews long enough, Möller suggests, we will begin to worship money more than our families and country.

When Rothschild arrives at the British Exchange, he mournfully announces to the other brokers that the English have lost "in the heroic struggle for freedom."⁵ Single-handedly, he initiates a financial panic that sweeps the country. Publicly he sells hundreds of shares of government stock, thus encouraging others to sell as well. Rumors spread that Waterloo is lost and the government has no more security. While this gigantic hoax is being perpetrated, Rothschild has secretly hired brokers to buy everything they can at the new panic prices. When Wellington finally arrives to announce British victory, the stock market soars to a new high. "Jewish guile" has engineered a scheme to rake in millions of pounds while simultaneously destroying the hopes and savings of many British citizens. Rothschild, not Napoleon or Wellington, has won the war. Möller's characterization supports the notion that Jews are a sinister, destructive people who draw on the lifeblood of others. The play is a warning through historical fable: stop the Jew before he stops you. It is such propaganda as this that helped develop the popularity or at least the public acceptance of government policies that foreclosed Jewish business and allowed gangs of roaming soldiers to raze Jewish stores on *Kristallnacht* (the night of broken glass) in 1938.

Möller's next play, *Volk und König* ("The People and Their King," 1935), offered the protection plan needed for a society seeking to rid itself of corrupt characters such as Rothschild. In this one-act dramatic fable, an evil minister and his son plot to kill the king so that they can steal his lands. But the soldier Wilhelm catches wind of the scheme and assaults the two criminals with his fists before any real harm is done. When the king finally recognizes that the soldier and not the minister is his true subject, he rewards the former with a beautiful bride. At the wedding service the king pronounces the military message of *Volk und König:* "The King needs soldiers and the king needs soldiers who know how to help."[6]

Möller continued his law-and-order campaign the following year with his play *Panamaskandal* ("Panama Scandal"). The setting is Paris during the 1880s and 1890s when Ferdinand de Lesseps was forming the Universal Panama Interoceanic Canal Company. Patriotic citizens rejoice at the prospect of building a French Panama Canal and buy up millions of francs worth of stock to give de Lesseps the financial support needed. Unknown to de Lesseps and the people, however, a group of bankers and politicians are hard at work sabotaging the project.

Panamaskandal is a white-collar crime story. The financial guarantor for the company, Baron Reinach, encourages the board of directors to give kickbacks to politicians, journalists, and pressure groups. In return, the French Chamber of Deputies votes to establish a lottery system, the profits of which will return to the company. Rumors of illegal activity reach the public, and social pandemonium erupts. The Minister for Public Works, Monsieur Baihut, who is himself receiving personal checks from the company, tries to stall criminal investigation by announcing, "The government can take no course of action until there is the utmost certainty of fraud."[7] Even after scandal is uncovered and the government falls, nothing changes. A member of the new government asks the de Lesseps family, "How much money can we expect from you?"[8] Capitalistic vultures eventually devour the victimized company. Contractors raise the ceiling on their prices and bankers lend money at usurious rates. As a last resort de Lesseps tries to liquidate his assets, but when Baron Reinach demands his loan back he is forced to declare bankruptcy. As a result thousands of French citizens lose their life savings just like their English counterparts in *Rothschild*.

Möller dwells on themes of economic hardship for the common man with good reason. Having suffered through the massive inflation and the Depression of the Weimar Republic, audience members were to understand that survival was not possible in a capitalistic conspiracy that exploits the masses. Möller wrote *Panamaskandal* and *Rothschild* to show that there was only one true alternative, National Socialism. His two allegorical dramas dredged up atrocities of the Weimar Republic ad infinitum so that no one would escape the dictum that life before the Führer was fraught with chaos, evil, and danger.

Having vilified the Weimar Republic with its Jews and capitalists, Möller turned his venom next on foreign Catholic rulers with a visually spectacular play, *Das Frankenburger Würfelspiel* ("The Frankenburg Game of Dice," 1936). Opening on 2 August 1936 as part of a gala international celebration for the Olympic Games in Berlin, the play was produced in a huge outdoor theater environment, the Dietrich-Eckart-Bühne. This was the largest of a number of Nazi arenas for political pageantry called *Thingplätze*, a modern equivalent of the ancient *Thing* where Nordic tribes assembled to administer justice. Plays of *Volk* justice, or *Thingspiele*, were promoted by the Propaganda Ministry in the early 1930s to become the national drama of the Third Reich. Möller's play was the latest example of this form, which was stripped of its "significance to the Reich" in 1937.[9] On this impressive Berlin stage ground, a cast of twelve hundred gathered to show the world a drama of Teutonic victory over the oppressor.[10]

The historical setting for the drama is seventeenth-century Austria at the time of the Thirty Years War. A massive chorus played the peasants and soldiers who have suffered wanton death and destruction under the hated Emperor Ferdinand and his co-conspirators. The perpetrators of historic crime are brought to trial in the present age of *völkisch* justice:

> To God the highest and in the name of the people who say: you multitudes assembled here, hear this play which is both a play and a tribunal.
>
> Great is the master who offers grace to a people and his patience stretches far. But suffering will befall those brought before this tribunal of justice.[11]

Seven judges presiding over this court ask Ferdinand if he is indeed guilty of betraying the trust of the *Volk*. He admits that some have died but argues that those of the "right faith" have not been hurt. His counselor, Lamormaini, a foreign Catholic, reaffirms that the *Volk* had to be destroyed "so that a faith might live."[12] When another counselor, von Herbersdorf, accuses the *Volk* of disobedience, the chorus engages him in a shouting match, crying: "Liberate us from tyranny and oppression, dear God. . . . Give us your hero's courage. This must be."[13] It is a significant request soon to be answered. Because the charges and counter charges are confusing the central issues, the judges call for a re-enactment of the events from 1625, including the historic game of dice in Frankenburg, Upper Austria.

Reversing his promise of clemency, and as punishment for their rebellious ways, von Herbersdorf forces the peasants to play games of dice with each other; the losers will be executed. Eighteen peasants lose and are sentenced to mass execution. In 1625, the peasants were hanged; in 1936, at this climactic moment a deus ex machina figure dressed in black armor emerges from the group of judges. He is of course the courageous hero for whom the *Volk* has yearned. Confidently he challenges Ferdinand and his counselors to a second game. This time von Herbersdorf and the other defendants, who had oppressed their Austrian *Volk*, lose.[14] After a wait of centuries, the peasants' honor has been restored; they are understandably grateful. In unison they clamor loudly, "Oh, God, you are wonderful" a number of times.[15]

Although this play deals with the same theme of alien exploitation of the *Volk* as in Möller's earlier full-length dramas, it differs sharply from them with its happy ending. Other plays instruct audiences in the historically tragic consequences of foreign, Jewish, and capitalistic infiltration, but *Das Frankenburger Würfelspiel* moves a step beyond by creating a new legend that reveals how historical wrongs done to the *Volk* can be righted by a messianic figure sent from above. Wrapped in the center of this pomp and glory piece is the crucial notion that the past is being re-created through Hitler, Germany's spiritual warrior. Through him history is rewritten to make defeat become victory. To a generation still suffering the humiliating wounds of World War I and the subsequent Treaty of Versailles, the play was meant to be seen as a joyful announcement that Germany's enemies were God's enemies and His justice was forthcoming against them.

In 1937, Möller focused his theme on German leadership abroad with *Der Sturz des Ministers* ("The Fall of the Minister"). Whereas *Das Frankenburger Würfelspiel* taught audiences about the evils of foreign rulers in Germany, this drama preached the virtue of the reverse: German rulers had a necessary place in foreign government even if they were not wanted. In this pseudo-historical drama, the Danes are shown to need German leadership in order to survive and prosper. The German leader who proves Möller's point is a physician named Struensee who in the late eighteenth century seized the Danish government from its king. Struensee is able to transform the backward country into a progressive new society. However, there is a tragic turn of events: some of the Danes resent Struensee's leadership in Danish affairs and form a political faction that succeeds in sentencing the German to death.

Appearing at a time when Hitler was arguing for the German annexation of more European territory, *Der Sturz* was an ideal piece of propaganda. Möller showed his audiences a robust, energetic member of the "master race" who deserved to lead others. By contrast the Danish King Christian VII is sickly and syphilitic. Appointed to be the royal physician, Dr. Struensee gradually assumes full power over Denmark. Möller carefully points out that Struensee is not a power-crazed man scheming to wrest control from rightful leaders but someone who is forced into this position. Christian VII leads a life of drunken debauchery, totally unresponsive to the concerns of the state, so Struensee's motives for claiming control are shown to be purely humanitarian. When asked if he is ambitious for power, the "noble healer" replies, "Ambition? How can you say that when helpless patients cry for their doctor?"[16]

Möller's missionary of the Enlightenment has been called forward to expel the ghosts of Danish tradition. He establishes himself as an uncompromising dictator over the Danes, dismissing their parliament and stripping the court of its responsibilities. Keeping the country abreast of the latest social concepts, he boasts: "I have constructed highways, strengthened the army, created a new government. I have thrown corrupt officials out of their tenured positions. . . . I have given peasants their freedom."[17] Singlehandedly, he has lifted Denmark out of the Dark Ages. The key to his success, of course, is his national background, as he well knows: "I am a German. Who does not call on Germany when they can go no further? Who is not thankful when the Germans have come and unselfishly treated a foreign problem as if it were their own concern?"[18]

Not surprisingly, there are those Danes who do resent his presence. They seem not to recognize the benefits they are receiving from him and wish to depose him, crying out for revolution and a return to Danish rule. Struensee offers a simple response for dealing with these rebels: "I see that one must drown them in blood. . . . I have the power for this. Guards with weapons and guns cocked for firing. I shall have them shot down unmercifully like animals."[19] *Der Sturz* goes far beyond showing the positive nature of German intervention into foreign affairs. It openly advocates violence against foreigners who reject the concept of German domination. Mass murder is a commendable solution for those lacking in gratitude to the master race. Before Dr. Struensee is able to execute his threats of bloodshed, he is arrested for treason. He pleads for mercy on the basis that he was just being a good German trying to help out a neighbor, but the Danes are unmoved and kill him anyway. This unhappy ending suggested that sacrifice, even martyrdom, might be necessary if Germany were to bring its vision to the world.

Möller's final play during the Nazi peace years was *Der Untergang Karthagos* ("The Fall of Carthage"), published in 1938 and first produced on 23 October of that year at the Thalia Theater in Hamburg.[20] It was another large cast spectacle, this time designed to open the Hitler Youth Theater Festival.[21] Fitting to this theatrical occasion, the soldier hero of the drama is a young fiery nationalist named Hasdrubal who exhorts his countrymen with every breath to take up arms against the Romans who have conquered them. He urges them to prepare for a bloody struggle:

> Listen to me! The moment is fateful. It is certainly the last time that you have free choice to decide whether Carthage is a whore or a figure of purity, ready to defend her virgin honor at knife-point. . . . For thirty

years Carthage has been cowardly and weaponless while the worms have eaten her limb for limb.[22]

Such bellicosity, however, is opposed by industrial figures, one of whom, the business tycoon Baat Baal, has proclaimed that "the world lives for the fruit of peace, not the laurel wreath of war."[23] Baal thinks the city should forget its past battles and live to enjoy "the profits of the newly achieved peace."[24] He is one of "the rich Jewish horses"[25] in the play whose pacifism is motivated by money rather than patriotism.

The peacemongers also include government leaders greedy for power at any cost. The President of Carthage bows to the Roman decree that his city be kept an unarmed, defenseless nation. He assures the Roman Senate that Carthage has "neither the means nor the intention of building up our military."[26] Such cowardly rhetoric inflames Hasdrubal's followers, one of whom proclaims the government a national disgrace filled with "grovelers, spit-lickers, pettifogging officials bound by their red tape . . . chancellors of high treason, bigwigs of the party . . . who are nobodies filling their pockets."[27]

The rest of this overblown plot unwinds tragically as if it were some lost Wagnerian opera. The President poisons one of the national heroes, an old army general named Suffet, out of fear that the military will seize political power. When Hasdrubal tries to expose this treachery, he is thrown into prison. In the meantime the Romans decide to occupy Carthage to halt a mounting revolution. As the legions noisily approach, a Carthaginian traitor secretly agrees to open the city gates. Overwhelmed by despair, Hasdrubal refuses to witness the final outrage. He orders his mother to stab him to death, which she devotedly does. However, even in death he does not lose his noble stature. When the Roman soldiers discover his corpse, they carry it back to Rome so that he will receive a hero's military funeral.

Once again Möller used his historical substitution formula showing the Weimar Republic, this time represented by Carthage, to be a body of cowards and swindlers who accept defeat, shrinking borders, and disarmament without protest. The Hitler character Hasdrubal cannot save his country from invasion, internal and external, because the *Volk* has not vowed to follow him completely. *Der Untergang Karthagos* is an appeal to join Hitler's army, written one year before the war.

An overview of Möller's six peacetime plays presents a comprehensive picture of his political beliefs. Each featured a *Volk* searching for an end to injustices suffered. The *Volk* in his dramas is shown to be in desperate need of a strong military Führer to combat the evil alien who is a Jew, a greedy capitalist, a traitorous politician, or some combination of the three. Without a Führer the *Volk* is lost. The leaderless people in *Rothschild* and *Panamaskandal* fall easy prey to corrupt financiers. Nevertheless having a strong leader does not ipso facto guarantee success. The Danes are deprived of their

German Führer Dr. Struensee when he is executed by royal courtiers. The Carthaginians suffer when Hasdrubal is thrown into prison by his own government. The *Volk* must stand obediently behind the leader as the soldier in *Volk und König* and the peasants in *Das Frankenburger Würfelspiel* do before the community can be purged of alien forces.

Möller's six peacetime dramas were all pep rallies for war. Like the rhetoric of Hitler, their message was simple, passionate, uncompromising: conquer or be conquered. The challenge for Möller was how to say this endlessly and still draw in a crowd with each new production. His solution lay in the art of colorful packaging. By varying the setting and period of each of the six plays starting with the Battle of Waterloo and harkening back through the centuries to the fall of Carthage, Möller could stir audience imagination again and again and still just repeat himself. He could promise a taste of something new each time while reheating the same Nazi gruel.

But Möller had to do more than create exotic locales to sustain audience interest. His characters and plots had to be entertaining, too. To meet this challenge the playwright created people who spoke exclamatatory dialogue from the moment they entered the scene. As the *Volk* group together, individuals start to seethe in a cauldron of emotion, ranting radical politics. They have much to settle, for theirs are lives of perpetual persecution. Treachery, destruction, and murder lurk everywhere. The Evil One stalks his hapless prey without rest; the *Volk* pines for the Good One, the Warrior, to arrive in time. Reading Möller's plays today is not unlike watching violent children's cartoons on television. Both ride the tide of grand melodrama.

Party support and public interest kept Möller's melodrama with a message produced and published while Germany girded its loins. The frenzied political climate of the peace years allowed him and other hacks some measure of success in a country that had glittered with cultural sophistication in previous eras. Certainly one of the keys to Möller's effectiveness lay in his psychological ability to appeal to people's basest instincts. He enabled his audiences to repress their humanitarian consciences by indulging in an exercise of mass hatred instead. He taught them what they wanted to know: it was not only legitimate but a patriotic duty to hate.

Möller's opus of hatred continued to focus on the Weimar Republic five years after it had been clubbed to death by Hitler in 1933. This was not a bizarre technique of overkill. The playwright was making an important contribution to the Party cause. His plays sanctioned by implication the vicious housecleaning of leftover politicos and Jews that became an accepted part of national life. Moreover, their strident outcry helped to drown out any lingering voices that might question the virtues of a dictatorship over a democracy. Most importantly, Möller's dramas set up past villains as target practice for the future campaign of war.

The playwright was programming his audience to be a fighting force so dedicated to national revenge that it would sacrifice everything to the cause. Hatred was vital as a raw source of energy; without it a nation of warriors would be lethargic and incapable of conquest. It would keep the *Volk* in fighting trim until the Führer needed to harness its power. Möller created the dramatic villain as a symbolic figure, conveniently identifiable, to prepare the *Volk* for the real one ahead, that is, everyone beyond Germany's borders. Hate artists suchas Möller were literary matadors goading the bull with red so it would charge forward in blind fury.

NOTES

1. Eberhard Wolfgang Möller, *Rothschild siegt bei Waterloo* (Berlin, 1934): 16.
2. Ibid., 25.
3. Ibid., 43.
4. Ibid., 67.
5. Ibid., 78.
6. Eberhard Wolfgang Möller, *Volk und König* (Berlin, 1935): 24.
7. Eberhard Wolfgang Möller, *Panamaskandal* (Berlin, 1936): 42.
8. Ibid., 77.
9. See Henning Eichberg, "The Nazi *Thingspiel*: Theater for the Masses in Fascism and Proletarian Culture," *New German Critique* 11 (Spring 1977): 133–150.
10. Ferdinand Junghans, Afterword [*Nachwort*] to Eberhard Wolfgang Möller, *Das Frankenburger Würfelspiel* (Berlin, 1937): 60–61.
11. Möller, *Würfelspiel*, 6.
12. Ibid., 13.
13. Ibid., 21.
14. In the version used for the 1936 premiere, the Figure in Black Armor casts "infinity": "the measure which has never been measured, and the number which has never been counted." The defendants are defeated by supernatural force—*Ed.*
15. Möller, *Würfelspiel*, 53–56.
16. Eberhard Wolfgang Möller, *Der Sturz des Ministers* (Berlin, 1937): 29.
17. Ibid., 30.
18. Ibid., 132.
19. Ibid., 99.
20. Cf. the preface to Eberhard Wolfgang Möller, *Der Untergang Karthagos* (Berlin, 1938).
21. See Oscar G. Brockett and Robert F. Findlay, *Century of Innovation* (Englewood Cliffs, NJ, 1973): 432, for a picture of a later production of the play at the Hessisches Landestheater, Darmstadt.
22. Möller, *Untergang*, 27.
23. Ibid., 8.
24. Ibid., 7.
25. Ibid., 81.
26. Ibid., 33.
27. Ibid., 81.

6

Ordained Hands on the Altar of Art: Gründgens, Hilpert, and Fehling in Berlin

William Grange

Although the theatre "played a vital part in National Socialism and was one of Hitler's dominant passions,"[1] National Socialist ideology had no clearly defined portrait of the theatre director. When Nazi leaders referred to artistic leadership in the theatre, they made vague inferences to the *Führerprinzip* (leadership principle), a term usually placed within political or military contexts. They applauded the authoritarian leadership tradition in German theatre history, but recent leadership in the German theatre troubled the National Socialist outlook. Nazis regarded directors such as Otto Brahm, Max Reinhardt, Leopold Jessner, and Erwin Piscator as negative influences on the German theatre, and at their doorstep National Socialists laid blame for the theatre's "decline." These directors had unleashed modernist, decadent, and altogether "un-German" tendencies in acting, design, and playwriting. Nazi ideologues called for a new principle of artistic leadership to "cleanse" the German theatre of its deviant putresence.

Nazi Party pronouncements on culture in the late 1920s and early 1930s were jeremiads on the general state of decay in German cultural life. Nazi ideas about culture, like Nazi ideas about nearly everything, derived from various "racial, anti-Semitic, biological, and pan-German concepts, along with others of an emotional, pro-peasant, anti-civilization, militaristic, and pseudo-religious nature."[2] Hitler acknowledged that he and other Party leaders could not recall the origin of such ideas; nor did he know, for example, the origin of *Aryan,* a word commonly used in the study of linguistics. Yet he "needed a label to give his drive for power a scientific legitimacy"[3] and began to advocate Aryan culture, even an "Aryan" theatre, though neither had previously existed. Hitler was less concerned, however, with Aryanizing the German theatre than he was with ridding it of "diseases" infecting "almost all domains of art and general culture in Germany."[4] The metaphor of disease and decay appeared frequently in Nazi ideology, perhaps (as Martin Esslin has noted) because Nazi ideology was itself a product of decay. The breakdown of bourgeois culture in Germany after 1918 "dissolved the optimistic certainties of the 19th century," Esslin stated, "and Nazi ideology was a waste product of that dissolving social order."[5] Hitler naturally preferred to view himself and his movement as the savior of an entire cultural tradition. The crisis of the twentieth century, in the Nazi scheme of things, was a collusion between capitalism in the West and Marxism in the East. Both were working "to destroy the European spirit."[6] Its manifestations in art were "futuristic and cubistic representations," Hitler said, along with such abominations as "exhibitions of so called dadaistic 'experiences.'"[7] To Hitler it was all "spiritual lunacy," while "the theatre sank visibly deeper," exhibiting "symptoms of decay of a slowly rotting world."[8]

Hitler's statements set the tone for subsequent Nazi pronouncements, which were intended to provide the culturally bewildered with a comforting alternative. As cultural ideology the Nazi alternative was an "eclectic synthesis of all reactionary tendencies" and a syncretist amalgamation of "purpose bound trivia."[9] Yet it appealed to audiences convinced that German theatre had become too politicized, nihilistic, Jewish, or a combination of all three. The leading cultural polemicist among the Nazi leadership was Alfred Rosenberg, whose *Mythus des 20. Jahrhunderts* ("Myth of the 20th Century," 1930) not only echoed Hitler's ruminations in *Mein Kampf* but articulated anti-modernist, anti-Semitic attitudes toward the theatre specifically his own.[10] Rosenberg founded the *Kampfbund für deutsche Kultur* (Militant League for German Culture) in April 1929, intending to publish position papers on Nazi cultural perspectives; instead it generated a vituperative stream of philippics against prominent directors, identifying them as "agents of a threatening anti-Western invasion" originating in the Near East and Africa. The goal of such directors was the desecration of European culture; their legacies were not only Judaism but "nigger Americanism" and the "Mongolian sources of bolshevism."[11] The league targeted Jessner, director of the Schauspielhaus am Gendarmenmarkt in Berlin; Jessner was not only a Jew but an active, influential member of the Social Democratic Party (SPD) who had imposed his "hyper-modern, Bolshevistic, mollusk-like and neuraesthenic aesthetics" upon German classics such as Schiller's *Wilhelm Tell* and *Die Räuber*. He had staged Shakespeare's *Hamlet* in contemporary evening wear with a Jewish actor (Fritz Kortner) in the title role; Jessner had also cast Kortner in the leading role in *Macbeth* and as

Gloucester in *Richard III*. Such productions were "absolutely un-German," Rosenberg claimed, because directors such as Jessner had no comprehension of an audience's need for "German peoplehood." He called for an overhaul of casting practices and the ouster of such influential directors so that "German sensibilities would not be injured" by "foreign racial influences."[12] The best way to ensure "racially oriented criteria" among directors and to defend against "bastardized mestizoism in art"[13] was the establishment of a state bureaucracy enforcing those criteria. Only the state could convince errant directors, echoed Robert Ley, that "our culture in Germany is a product of blood and our race."[14]

I

When Hitler assumed the office of Reichskanzler on 30 January 1933, the new government began immediately to impose its cultural vision on the German theatre. The Nazis implemented that vision under the precept of *Gleichschaltung*, a word normally associated with electrical engineering. It meant transforming different wattages into one uniform line of service, and an analogous transformation of German theatre life began under the new government. The process continued throughout the peace years, so by the outbreak of war in 1939 the German theatre found itself completely *gleichgeschaltet*. It involved coordinating," or "bringing into line" the local organization of theatre throughout the Reich with a centrally planned policy originating from Goebbels's newly formed *Reichsministerium für Volksaufklärung und Propaganda* (Ministry for Popular Enlightenment and Propaganda). The ProMi, as it came to be called, was a cabinet-level agency chartered to oversee, regulate, and censor the flow of information within the Reich; its purview also included all aspects of the performing arts. Before Goebbels could imprint his personal stamp on the German theatre he had first to secure legal sanction to do so. The *Reichstheatergesetz*, or National Theatre law, made that possible; the Law had numerous provisions, but its major thrust was to make theatre a national concern, whereas it historically had been subject to local jurisdiction. The ProMi then had direct supervision of all but a half-dozen theatres in Germany, and in 1935 the President of the Reich Theatre Chamber, Otto Laubinger (a frustrated actor who had played walk-ons for Jessner) could report to Goebbels that "a secure inception of the theatre arts along national, *völkisch* lines" had taken place.[15] Prior to the promulgation of the Reich Theatre Law, Goebbels had assembled the directors of leading theatres around the country and described to them a "new age of the German theatre." In the new Germany, he said, "old values are sinking and new values are rising. At this moment the artist cannot say, 'This has nothing to do with me.' It has a lot to do with him. If he misses out on this re-ordering of artistic priorities under the new principles, he cannot wonder then if life passes him by."[16] He then described his idea of the direction art would take under his leadership: "German art of the next decade will be heroic, steely romantic, factual without sentimentality, and mindful of its communal duty, or it won't exist. That is the essence of what I am here to make clear to you today."[17]

The ProMi had numerous departments to facilitate *Gleichschaltung* within its jurisdiction; its Theatre Department was divided into three principal bureaus. The first dealt primarily with personnel matters (for example, hiring only Aryan performers); second was the dramaturgical bureau, headed by Reichsdramaturg Rainer Schlösser, which had oversight of production questions, especially those of repertoire selection and play content; the third oversaw budgets and all business procedures in German theatres. The Theatre Department's initial task in 1933 was to display in every German theatre lobby a large poster carrying Hitler's proclamation titled "The Renewal of the German Theatre." In it, Hitler declared that theatre's renewal must

> come from within. And people who think they can now just go along and perpetuate old things under new masks . . . must re-learn from the ground up. He who will not re-learn destroys himself, and we won't have to lift a finger. I will not be deterred. I will do everything to purge mendacity and mediocrity. The artist really prepared to do this does not need to cry "Heil!" The genuine artist will come to us of his own accord. [18]

All "genuine" artists were gathered under the umbrella organization of the *Reichstheaterkammer* (Reich Theatre Chamber), which subsumed constituent organizations under it, including official organizations for producers, directors, actors, singers, dancers, playwrights, composers, publicists, publishers, and musicians. Non-members of the offical organizations were unemployable: Jews, homosexuals, Jehovah's Witnesses, Social Democrats, Marxists, and anyone "who cannot vouch unconditional loyalty to the national state" were excluded under terms of the *Gesetz zur Wiederherstellung des Berufsbeamtentums* (Law for the Restoration of the Professional Civil Service).

The new government provided generous subsidies, and an increase in government spending meant more theatre performances and more jobs for actors. In its first year alone, the new Germany witnessed twelve new theatres in operation (for a total of 248) and a 14 percent increase in actors employed (from 25,663 to 29,263).[19] Artists benefited from the new policy, said Goebbels, because Hitler had an intense interest in and an indisputable knowledge of art. "You live today in a great and fortunate time," he told them. "You see above you a man as Führer of People and State who at the same time is your most powerful and understanding protector. He loves artists because he is himself an artist. Under his blessed hand a new

Renaissance age is today descendant upon Germany."[20] Other hands bestowed blessings on the theatre besides: the Labor organization Strength Through Joy organized thousands of theatregoers for group sales causing concomitant increases in box office revenues. Theatre of Youth organized groups of school pupils and provided them with tickets.[21] The *Reichsministerium für Kunst, Volksbildung, und Wissenschaft* (Ministry of Art, Education, and Research) apportioned funds for working-class audiences; the *Nationalsozialistische Kulturgemeinde* (National Socialist Cultural Community) touted theatre attendance among Party members as part of their national duty. Support from so many official and quasi-official sources meant unaccustomed augmentation of cash inflow, for rarely had the German theatre enjoyed such widespread assistance and promotion. In 1936 alone, theatres received twelve million marks merely to cover the costs of refurbishments.[22]

II

Refurbishments and renovations were the most extensive, and subsidies most lavish, in that erstwhile cesspool of theatrical degradation, Berlin. The regime paradoxically saw Berlin as the jewel in its crown, a crown it wanted to wear proudly before the eyes of the theatrical world. Money lavished on Berlin theatres had less to do with Nazi cultural aims and ideals, however, than it did with the fierce competition between Goebbels and Göring for the unofficial title of Reich Theatre Impresario. Among the many titles Hermann Göring already had (Economic Overlord of the Reich, Air Minister, Speaker of the Reichstag, Marshall of the Air Force, and National Master of the Hunt) was Minister President of Prussia; in that capacity he controlled all Prussian State Theatres. As Speaker of the Reichstag, however, he managed to get an exemption from the Reich Theatre Law for his theatres, permitting him to operate them independently of the ProMi. That exemption enabled Göring to take on Goebbels head to head in Berlin, where the regime wished to display itself most ostentatiously. Göring's duel with Goebbels continued throughout the period; the first parries came only four weeks after the new regime took office, when on 26 February Göring hired Gustaf Gründgens to run the Schauspielhaus am Gendarmenmarkt. Gründgens's most pressing and immediate task, Göring told him, was to sign as many big-name actors and actresses for the Schauspielhaus before Goebbels got them for his theatre, the nearby Deutsches Theater in Schumann Straße.

The competition between Goebbels and Göring hastened the abandonment of many polemical planks in the Nazi Party's cultural platform. They kept anti-Semitism, of course, and continued to pay lip service to anti-Marxism. They also banned the performance of plays by writers they did not like or simply could not understand. The imposition of the Naxi lexicon on the entirety of German theatre became secondary, however, to an old-fashioned reverence for theatre they had learned as schoolboys. They wanted a theatre whose "brilliance reflected flatteringly on its keepers," as it had done in decades previous. "Official" Nazi culture, John Rouse has noted, "proposed itself as the legitimate heir of the national culture," and the objective of Goebbels and Göring in particular was "to preserve the grand style of the grand culture."[23] German directors had created that culture; in order to continue it, Goebbels and Göring realized they needed men in the mold of Brahm and Reinhardt. Thus the directors they chose to run their theatres and to "embalm German culture," in Grunberger's colorful metaphor,[24] were not Party members nor even sympathizers with the Nazi cause; they did agree, however, with the Nazi leadership in one specific sense, namely that "German culture" must at all costs be preserved. Convincing outstanding directors to remain and continue working was not difficult; many believed they could accommodate themselves to the new conditions while remaining somehow unpolitical. There were of course political consequences in remaining unpolitical, as Fritz Stern has shown; using culture to remain unpolitical is a long tradition in Germany, Stern noted, and directors in the Third Reich, like many Germans, "used their greatest achievement, their culture, to augment and excuse their greatest failure, their politics."[25] They thus accepted the government's denial of rights and liberties to certain of its citizens in exchange for advantages bestowed on German culture at large. They saw the government's willingness to overlook one's previous affiliations as a sign of good faith. Erich Engel had premiered many of Brecht's plays and was one of Brecht's most trusted colleagues; he signed on with Heinz Hilpert at the Deutsches Theater. Jürgen Fehling worked with Jessner in the 1920s and staged some of the most "neurasthenic" exercises imaginable, yet he was hired by Gründgens to work at the Schauspielhaus. Karl-Heinz Martin worked extensively with Piscator and premiered several Expressionist works; he directed numerous films during the peace years and later worked for Goebbels at the Theater am Horst Wessel Platz (the former Volksbühne). Goebbels and Göring were fully prepared to make compromises needed to retain a director whose services would reflect positively on their respective domains. "Besides," as Göring noted, "it is always easier to make an artist into a National Socialist than the other way around."[26] After Göring hired Gründgens, Goebbels was most concerned in finding a man who could compete successfully with Gründgens and give the ProMi an edge over Göring.

Heinz Hilpert (1890–1967) was the man Goebbels sought. His long association with Reinhardt included the direction of numerous outstanding premieres, most of which Nazi ideologues had considered decadent and/or perverse. Hilpert was a good administrator and Goebbels knew of his outstanding reputation among theatre artists. He was director of the Volksbühne in 1932–33, and Goebbels planned to liquidate that "Marxist" theatre in 1934. In December 1933 he wrote in his diary, "Tonight

Volksbühne *Die Kaiserin* by Fall. Incomparable Käthe Dorsch, piquant Lucie Mannheim, brilliant direction by Hilpert. I will get him when I have the theatre."[27] Though Goebbels had in effect expropriated the Deutsches Theater from Reinhardt, Hilpert took over its direction in September 1934, intending to preserve Reinhardt's tradition of excellence, and in the process he even secured Reinhardt's written blessing to do so. Goebbels meanwhile permitted Hilpert to hire two "questionable" designers, Caspar Neher and Ernst Schütte. Neher's professional association with Brecht was more extensive even than Engel's, and furthermore Neher was Brecht's closest personal friend. Schütte had designed extensively for Hilpert and Reinhardt, and he was separated from his Jewish wife but refused to divorce her. Hilpert himself was romantically involved with Annelies "Nuschka" Heuser, a Jew whom the director had known for many years. Hilpert later concealed her in the Deutsches Theater, had her hair dyed blond in the theatre's make-up department, and smuggled her across the Swiss border. Yet Goebbels permitted Hilpert to visit her in Zurich on a regular basis, just as he permitted the hiring of Neher and Schütte, along with many other questionable persons. Goebbels referred to Hilpert's personnel as "a concentration camp on leave,"[28] yet he exercised a relatively tolerant policy with Hilpert because he fancied himself and Hitler as "artistically sensitive." "We feel ourselves as more than politicians," he said, "but also as artistic individuals. I am even of the opinion that politics is the highest form of art, because sculptors shape stone . . . and poets shape words. The statesman, however, shapes the masses so that the masses emerge as a people."[29] Goebbels the frustrated novelist and Hitler the frustrated painter saw art as a "sublime realm," where "only ordained hands have a right to serve at the altar of art."[30] The most concrete motivation for Goebbels's tolerance with Hilpert, however, was Göring's similar policy at the Schauspielhaus with Gründgens.

Gustaf Gründgens (1899–1963) had little experience as a director and no administrative experience whatsoever, but he was one of the most glamorous and appealing actors anywhere on the German stage. He had established himself as a star in Hilpert's 1928 production of Ferdinand Bruckner's *Die Verbrecher*. Prior to that he had worked extensively in provincial theatres and with his wife Erika Mann, her brother Klaus (children of the novelist Thomas Mann), and Pamela Wedekind (daughter of the playwright Frank Wedekind) in their cabaret act, "Review of Four." Gründgens was extremely versatile, with extraordinary vocal and dance skills to complement his appeal as an actor. He played a wide variety of roles, but the one with which he remained most closely identified was Mephisto in Goethe's *Faust*. He debuted as Mephisto in Berlin in Lothar Müthel's production at the Schauspielhaus am Gendarmenmarkt in 1932, the centennial year of Goethe's death. His performance left strong impressions on everyone who saw it, including Göring, who at the time was courting Gründgens's colleague at the Schauspielhaus, Emmy Sonnemann. When he hired Gründgens, Göring assured the new Intendant that his homosexuality would not be problematic and that he had nothing to fear from the new regime.[31] Göring later appointed Gründgens Prussian State Councilor, giving him the Minister President's personal protection and immunity from arrest.[32] Göring asked in return that Gründgens hire the biggest names in German theatre; Gründgens obliged, and by 1934 the Schauspielhaus was able to boast an ensemble far more glamorous and star-studded than its competitor on Schumann Straße.

Gründgens not only had Werner Krauß, Emil Jannings, Käthe Dorsch, Käthe Gold, Maria Koppenhöfer, and other famous performers under contract, but he also had the services of the most talented, unpredictable, and temperamental of any German director: Jürgen Fehling (1885–1968). Fehling was among the most accomplished of German directors in the Weimar Republic, with a wide variety of productions to his credit. He had premiered plays by Kaiser, Toller, and Barlach—all of whom the Nazis banned; he had also premiered Hermann Essig and Richard Billinger, whom the Nazi press had celebrated and whom the new regime wanted to promote. Fehling's distinctive Shakespeare productions had not generated controversy like Jessner's, but Nazi critics condemned them as examples of "cultural Bolshevism"; his productions of Grabbe, Raimund, and Nestroy were, according to the same critics, appropriately *völkisch*. Fehling had an ability to "take weak plays and turn them into 'events,' " said Bernhard Minetti, an actor who worked with Fehling on numerous productions.[33] That had been the case with Toller's *Masse Mensch* as well as with Billinger's *Rauhnacht*. Even with weak plays he made demands on the audience, according to critic Herbert Ihering, "never going for the cheap effect but always for the audacious."[34]

Fehling's audacity made him a difficult colleague. He paid no attention to rehearsal schedules, pushed actors to the limits of their endurance, never worked with a *Regiebuch* (production book) because he constantly improvised and re-improvised staging as rehearsals progressed, and he never permitted the playwright to see the play performed until opening night. That worked well with Barlach and Else Lasker-Schüler, but it infuriated Brecht; when Fehling staged the Berlin premiere of Brecht's *Edward II*, Brecht accused the director of putting the actors into some kind of trance. When Fehling tried similar techniques in *Mann ist Mann*, Brecht insisted that Fehling be dismissed (Fehling was in fact fired numerous times). Fehling accused Brecht of "purging magic from the theatre"—an accusation with which Brecht no doubt agreed.[35] Siegfried Melchinger characterized Fehling's artistic ethos as "North German mysticism" and Ihering called it "Protestantism in the true sense of the word, not spiritual or puritanical but pro-active and volatile."[36] Alfred Mühr, Gründgens's Dramaturg at the Schauspielhaus, described Fehling as "a rebellious outsider . . . with absolutely no talent for organization or structure [who] in rehearsal paid no attention to time or costs."[37] Most who were acquainted with Fehling agreed that he was unpredictable, impulsive, inconsistent, and dangerous to have around; those same individuals also agreed that he was a director whose productions were unmatched during the Third Reich for their imaginative sweep and histrionic intensity. For all the reasons cited above, his work would seem "wholly alien to the Nazi aesthetic," as John Willett has argued; yet the Nazi "aesthetic" was a mercurial thing, dependent upon the personal whims of leading Nazi mandarins. In the final analysis, one may conclude, as does Willett, that Fehling's productions under the Nazis "were unlike anything prior to 1933."[38] One Fehling production, *Richard III*, was unlike any director's until 1945, for it dared to ponder political questions. With that production, Fehling alone preserved a tiny sliver of the German theatre's ravaged integrity.

III

Hilpert and Gründgens were less independent than was Fehling, for they were not only directors but also administrators. Theirs was the daily battle with zealous bureaucrats hoping to place a Nazi intaglio on their work; Hilpert particularly felt the officiousness of Goebbels's ProMi, especially its dramaturgical bureau headed by Rainer Schlösser. Schlösser, like Rosenberg, remained an unreconstructed true believer in earlier Nazi pronouncements on German culture; he consistently pestered Hilpert to present dramas by Billinger, Rehberg, Burte, and Möller, playwrights whose work enjoyed widespread production in provincial theatres. Hilpert relented twice in 1935, staging Möller's *Panamaskandal* and Billinger's *Die Hexe von Passau*; once in 1936 with Rehberg's *Friedrich I*; and in 1937 with Burte's *Herzog und Henker*. Of his 44 productions prior to World War II, however, Hilpert concentrated mostly on Goethe, Schiller, Shakespeare, and Shaw, successfully resisting Schlösser's demands for a more *völkisch* repertoire. Hilpert pleased Goebbels with *As You Like It*, his inaugural production at the Deutsches Theater; it sold out for weeks after the opening. Rosenberg and his colleagues at the *Völkischer Beobachter* greeted the production unenthusiastically, although reviewer Heinrich Gruber discovered new "racial truths" in the character of Orlando: he represented "noble races" such as the Germans, who "through genetic predisposition can overcome oppression."[39] "How do we like it?" Gruber asked. "We don't!" Goebbels ignored opposition from Party functionaries and the Nazi press (in 1936 he banned all critiques in favor of "cultural reporting" and descriptions); subsequent entries in his diary attest to his general approval of Hilpert. After seeing *The Winter's Tale* in 1935 he wrote, "A magnificent performance with [Theodor] Loos and [Lil] Dagover. A masterpiece of Hilpertian direction. I am deeply moved. That beautiful Dagover!"[40] After *Don Carlos* in 1937, Goebbels exulted, "Perfect in casting, design, staging. A masterpiece by Hilpert. . . . I am happy. I have experienced Schiller in his greatness anew. Wonderful, stimulating. What a genius. A storm of applause."[41]

Goebbels recorded some problems with Hilpert, but during this period he paid little heed to complaints of Schlösser, Rosenberg, Walter Stang, or other purists. Goebbels was enjoying himself too much to crack down on Hilpert: "It is so beautiful to be a patron," he wrote, "and to be able to assist art."[42] Goebbels's assistance included support for Hilpert's numerous Shaw productions. Of the director's 1938 production of *The Apple Cart*, Goebbels wrote, "Magnificent direction by Hilpert. The play is almost antiquated, but it is funny and well done. A real fun show. I had a lot of fun."[43] The Nazi embrace of Shaw was a result of Shaw's support for Hitler and the playwright's critique of parliamentary democracy; Shaw even sent Hitler a congratulatory telegram after the 1938 Anschluß with Austria. Goebbels had personal reasons for supporting Shaw plays staged by Hilpert, however: Gründgens's portrayal of Henry Higgins in the 1935 film of *Pygmalion* had been enormously popular. Although Goebbels's ProMi had in part financed the film, its success reflected mostly on Gründgens, and Gründgens's success reflected on Göring.

Gründgens enjoyed adulation not only in film roles while he was Göring's Intendant; he acted in eighteen productions at the Schauspielhaus, six of which he directed himself, up to World War II. All of them attracted large audiences. A great personal triumph was the title role in his 1936 production of *Hamlet*; his "signature," however, remained Mephisto in *Faust* I and *Faust* II.[44] His first important production as Intendant was Lessing's comedy *Minna von Barnhelm*, in which he cast Emmy Sonnemann as the eponymous heroine; Sonnemann played Minna with unaccustomed ladylike qualities. Berlin audiences were used to girlish interpretations such as those of Agnes Sorma. Sonnemann played the role with a "quiet, cultivated soberness" befitting her imminent retirement from the stage.[45] She later married Göring amid great pomp at the Berlin cathedral. Her presence in this production, combined with Gründgens's virtuoso performance in a flashy but minor role (that of the adventurous Frenchman Riccault de la Marliniere), generated more curiosity than authentic artistry.

Gründgens's first Shakespeare production boasted more stars than Hilpert's, but the results were less than stellar. *King Lear* opened 23 December 1934 with a cast featuring three actors who had already played the title role in Berlin productions (Werner Krauß, Friedrich Kayßler, and Eugen Klöpfer), yet the performance never gelled as an ensemble piece; the result was strangely passionless and detached. The evening's loudest applause came at the entrance of Göring into his private box.[46] Subsequent Gründgens productions suffered a similar mismatch between the allure of stars and their incongruence as cast members. The plays he directed were not the well-integrated, finely wrought ensemble pieces of Hilpert, but they were not mere vehicles for popular performers either. Ihering described Gründgens as a director capable of instilling in actors specific attributes of timing, effective entrances and exits, clear recitation of dialogue, use of pauses, precise handling of props, and maintaining focus within the stage space.[47] In comparison to Hilpert's "dry, sarcastic, and bitter" production of *Twelfth Night*, Gründgens's was "sweet and cloying."[48] Nazi critics acknowledged the enormous popularity of Gründgens's productions but complained that they were too detailed; Wolf Braumüller, for example, warned that Gründgens might be fostering a "Meininger Renaissance" in a 1935 production of *Egmont*. Goethe's words had "drowned in splendor and in the expansiveness of the scenery" as actors used props to fill out the drama, and the drama had to struggle to make any impact at all.[49] Göring, like Goebbels, paid little attention to what Braumüller or other orthodox Nazis had to say; Gründgens likewise knew he had to please only Göring, the most conspicuous member of his growing audience.

Though Gründgens and Hilpert enjoyed the favor of their masters, neither director was at liberty to make artistic choices wholly independent of political pressures. Both directors pushed at the boundaries set for them, but rarely did they succeed in anything more than stretching the leash attached to the muzzle. Hilpert once proposed doing Georg Kaiser's *Das Los des Ossian Balvesen* after the playwright had signed an oath of allegiance to the government; Hilpert also tried to produce Ödön von Horváth's *Glaube Liebe Hoffnung* when that playwright "sought to assure the new authorities that he was by no means to be identified with people like Piscator and Brecht" and had in fact been "a communist refugee."[50] Neither proposal found approval within the ProMi, and Hilpert did not press the issue. Though Goebbels later gave him greater responsibilities (the directorships of the Salzburg Festival and of the Theater in der Josefstadt in Vienna, after the 1938 Anschluß), Hilpert concentrated on resisting increasing pressure from Schlösser and Party officials to turn his theatres into platforms for Nazi ideology. Gründgens claimed that as a German director he was like most German actors: "politically uninterested. There have been very few politically engaged actors," he said (conveniently forgetting the examples of Alexander Granach, Helene Weigel, Kurt Gerron, and scores of others in exile or in concentration camps). "Before 1933 there were few communist actors, and after 1933 there were few fascist actors. For actors, good roles are a higher priority than politics. This lack of political education the German actor shares with the German population in general."[51] Gründgens was probably correct, as Fritz Stern has noted above. Yet he departed from those sentiments in one crucial instance, and that instance resulted in the most important production any time during the Third Reich.

When Gründgens permitted Fehling to stage *Richard III* at the Schauspielhaus in 1937, the new Germany experienced a major theatrical scandal. Fehling conceived the production in terms diametrically opposite to those set forth by Goebbels in his speech to directors in 1933 and to those of Hitler in his 1933 proclamation. The production was not "steely" or "romantic" or "factual" or "mindful of its communal duty." It was instead an abstract meditation on what Clare Trask of the *New York Times* called "diseased ambition [and] a relentless will to wickedness."[52] With designer Traugott Müller the director set the play in a "disrobed landscape," a landscape stretching 144 feet from the apron to the back wall across a bare stage. Müller augmented the sense of depth (and a resulting sense of insignificance for the individual characters) by fashioning a series of eight false proscenium arches progressing toward the back. For interior scenes, scrim walls flew in to define the space momentarily, but the walls were transparent so the sense of depth and character isolation remained acute. Fehling conveyed the inner torment of characters by having actors deliver lines "with tense muscles, blank staring eyes, and invisible foam on their lips," said Siegfried Melchinger, as "emotions boiling up inside them collided with a tightened musculature and tense skin. Invisible radiations proceeded from them. Fever, electricity, explosiveness. You could smell the hatred. You could sense the demands placed on them. You breathed in, and you could breathe the horror."[53] Werner Krauß as Gloucester hobbled around with a clubfoot, "an apparent Goebbels take-off," according to Boleslaw Barlog[54]; more indicative of Fehling's conception of Gloucester was the six-foot-long broadsword Krauß carried with him everywhere. The actor stood only five feet, seven inches tall, so the sword was obviously more than a mere prop. With it, Krauß laughed and frolicked his way through his machinations, a "dangerous comedian" with weapons he hardly knew how to use. And in fact he never did use the sword, because Fehling cut the final battle scene; when King Richard saw Richmond, he exclaimed the famous "My kingdom for a horse!" line and collapsed, dead, onto the sword. The villain's accomplices had more literal contemporary analogies; the murderers of Clarence came on in brown shirts and jackboots, bearing a distinct similarity to Nazi Storm Troopers. When Gloucester became king, a phalanx of eight men in black uniforms accented with silver bijouterie accompanied him; their resemblance to Hitler's SS was both immediate and frightening, as many audience members looked upon such obvious parallels with fears of guilt by association.[55] Fehling's emphasis on stylization gave the five-hour-long performance "its agonizing supernatural strength," said Trask; the audience, said another critic, sat "spellbound, as if they knew theatre history was being made."[56]

Göring was one audience member uncaptivated by the production. He demanded that Fehling be dismissed and the production removed from the repertoire of the Schauspielhaus; if this was not a case of cultural Bolshevism, he must have reasoned, nothing was. Gründgens refused to fire Fehling. In Curt Riess's biography of Gründgens, Göring reacted to his Intendant's insubordination by grabbing him by the necktie and shoving him against a nearby wall. "If you don't get rid of Fehling," Riess quoted Göring, "I'll kill him!" Gründgens reportedly responded with "Herr Minister President, if you dismiss Fehling I am no longer your Intendant." After a lengthy pause, stalking back and forth across the room and pondering his options (which included loss of face to Goebbels), Göring relented: "You've won again," he said. "You can keep your goddamned Fehling."[57] Not only did Gründgens get to keep Fehling, he kept *Richard III* in the repertoire for the rest of the season. Fehling, meanwhile, proceeded on his unpredictable way to direct the world premiere of *Am hohen Meer* by Nazi favorite Richard Billinger, the German premiere of Shaw's *Mrs. Warren's Profession*, and his last production of the peace years, *Richard II*, with Gründgens in the title role.

When German troops initiated World War II on 1 September 1939, observers noted the absence of enthusiasm with which most Germans greeted the news. There were no popular expressions of support for the Führer, no outbursts of patriotic fervor, no spontaneous affirmations of faith in the government. There was instead a sense of powerlessness and isolation, according to Bernt Engelmann, as "here and there people gathered around newsstands, talking quietly, depressed and anxious."[58] Years later, critic Paul Fechter recalled parallel images from Fehling's *Richard III*, "as if viewed through the opposite end of a stereoscope . . . [where] actors stand, walk, shout—and what they do has a tiny significance."[59] The significance of Fehling's work, however, takes on a much larger, metaphorical dimension within the context of petty rivalries, venality, corruption, and boorishness swirling about the theatre of the Third Reich. When Werner Krauß as Richard III cried out at the performance's conclusion and fell to his death, it was as if the German theatre itself was crying out for its lost identity as a moral institution. Its cry, like Richard's, remained isolated and unheeded.

NOTES

1. George Mosse, *Masses and Man: Nationalist and Fascist Perceptions of Reality* (New York, 1980): 214.
2. Joachim C. Fest, *The Face of the Third Reich*, tr. Michael Bullock (New York, 1970): 164.
3. Eberhard Ahleff, ed., *Das dritte Reich* (Hannover, 1970): 11.
4. Adolf Hitler, *Mein Kampf* (Munich, 1927): 355.
5. Martin Esslin, Introduction to *The Enthusiasts*, by Robert Musil (New York, 1983): 9.
6. Henry Grosshans, *Hitler and the Artists* (New York, 1983): 23.
7. Hitler, *Mein Kampf*, 353–54.
8. Ibid., 355.
9. Respectively, Georg Lukács, *Die Zerstörung der Vernunft* (Berlin, 1954): 622 and Ronald Taylor, *Literature and Society in Germany, 1918–1945* (Totowa, NJ, 1980): 251.

10. Among the more provocative were his opinions of Gerhart Hauptmann, who, despite winning the Nobel Prize for Literature in 1912, had not really created art but had "merely gnawed at the rotten roots of the 19th century middle classes and constructed theatre pieces from newspaper reports." Alfred Rosenberg, *The Myth of the Twentieth Century*, tr. Vivian Bird (Torrance, CA, 1982): 272.

11. Rosenberg, *Myth*, 272.

12. Ibid., 274.

13. Quoted in Hildegard Brenner, *Die Kunstpolitik des Nationalsozialismus* (Hamburg, 1963): 16.

14. Robert Ley, *Wir alle helfen dem Führer* (Munich, 1937): 150.

15. Otto Laubinger, "Ein Jahr Aufbauarbeit," *Deutsches Bühnen-Jahrbuch* 46 (1935): 6.

16. Joseph Goebbels, "Rede des Propagandaministers vor den Theaterleitern, 8. Mai 1933," *Das deutsche Drama in Geschichte und Gegenwart* 5 (1933): 31.

17. Ibid., 36.

18. Ruth Freydank, *Theater in Berlin, von den Anfängen bis 1945* (Berlin, 1988): 432.

19. Joseph Wulf, *Theater und Film im Dritten Reich; Eine Dokumentation* (Gütersloh, 1964): 43.

20. Ibid., 49.

21. Ibid., 72.

22. Günther Rühle, *Zeit und Theater*, vol. 3, *Diktatur und Exil, 1933–1945* (Berlin, 1974): 27.

23. John Rouse, *Brecht and the West German Theatre: The Practice and Politics of Interpretation* (Ann Arbor, 1989): 20.

24. Richard Grunberger, *A Social History of the Third Reich* (London, 1971): 345.

25. Fritz Stern, "The Political Consequences of the Unpolitical German," *History* 3 (1960): 107.

26. Quoted in Freydank, *Theater*, 444.

27. Michael Dillmann, *Heinz Hilpert: Leben und Werk* (Berlin, 1990): 98. *Die Kaiserin* was the last Berlin production in which Lucie Mannheim (1899–1976) appeared until after 1945; she was Jewish (Goebbels's interest in her notwithstanding) and emigrated to Great Britain in 1934, where she frequently performed on stage and in such films Alfred Hitchcock's *The 39 Steps*.

28. Wolfgang Drews, *Festgabe für Heinz Hilpert* (Göttingen, 1965): 21.

29. Quoted in Wolf-Eberhard August, "Die Stellung der Schauspieler im Dritten Reich" (Ph.D. diss., University of Cologne, 1973): 94–95.

30. Ibid., 89.

31. Heinrich Goertz, *Gustav Gründgens* (Reinbek, 1965): 21.

32. Ibid., 81.

33. Quoted in Gerhard Ahrens, ed., *Das Theater des deutschen Regisseurs Jürgen Fehling* (Berlin, 1987): 144.

34. Herbert Ihering, *Regie* (Berlin, 1943): 23.

35. Jürgen Fehling, *Die Magie des Theaters* (Hannover, 1965): 21.

36. Respectively, Melchinger in Fehling, *Magie*, 23; Ihering, *Regie*, 47.

37. Alfred Mühr, *Mephisto ohne Maske: Gustav Gründgens, Legende und Wahrheit* (Munich, 1981): 36.

38. John Willett, *The Theatre of the Weimar Republic* (New York, 1988): 188.

39. Quoted in Dillmann, *Hilpert*, 330.
40. Ibid., 137.
41. Ibid., 137.
42. Ibid., 126.
43. Ibid., 139.
44. The role of Mephisto became a metaphor for Gründgens's entire career in Klaus Mann's "novel of a career," *Mephisto*. Mann drew a distinctly unflattering portrait of his former brother-in-law and lover; Gründgens's *Doppelgänger* in the novel is Hendrik Höfgen, a neurotic sycophant with abundant talent and unscrupulous ambition. The novel was the basis for Ariane Mnouchkine's 1979 production in Paris and for the 1984 motion picture starring Klaus-Maria Brandauer.
45. Edda Kühlken, *Die Klassiker-Inszenierungen von Gustaf Gründgens* (Meisenheim, 1972): 81.
46. Ibid., 32.
47. Ibid., 58.
48. Goertz, *Gründgens*, 75.
49. Kühlken, *Klassiker*, 108.
50. Quoted in Willett, *Theatre*, 188.
51. Goertz, *Gründgens*, 109.
52. Clare Trask, "Richard III Adorns a Berlin Stage," *New York Times*, 7 May 1937: n.p.
53. Ahrens, *Theater*, 171.
54. Ibid., 174.
55. Ibid., 173.
56. Otto Ernst Hesse in *BZ am Mittag* (Berlin), 3 March 1937, quoted in *Jürgen Fehling der Regisseur* (Berlin, 1978): 151.
57. Curt Riess, *Gustaf Gründgens: die klassische Biographie des grossen Künstlers* (Hamburg, 1965): 214.
58. Bernt Engelmann, *In Hitler's Germany: Daily Life in the Third Reich*, tr. Krishna Winston (New York, 1986): 169.
59. Quoted in *Jürgen Fehling*, 50.

7

Werner Krauß and the Third Reich

William R. Elwood

Until recently, research on any aspect of the Third Reich seemed to have a specific bias. It was centered around the effects of the evil system and how individuals and institutions resisted, survived, or sold out to the regime. It showed how the Nazi reign of terror meant a gradual and incremental absorption of the ordinary lives of the citizens, including the intelligentsia and artists. It showed how the arts were dominated, with countless individual responses ranging on a continuum from heroic to darkly self-serving. Yet life under the Nazis was considerably more difficult and intricate, as each individual tried to make a living and survive, if not flourish. For specific minorities—Jews, communists, homosexuals, Jehovah's Witnesses, and so on—there were fewer options and greater risks. There were no easy choices, or at least the difficulties surrounding them clouded the options.

Scholarship is now considerably less monolithic in its approach, perhaps because of increased globalization of political institutions and structures. Research in the theatre of the Third Reich should no longer delineate sides; it should—without apologizing—explore the complexities of adapting to the regime.[1] It should examine the community of artists that actively engaged in the practice of the art and that attempted to function in a society that had bought into Hitler's madness.

To bring some perspective about the theatre in the Third Reich, it is essential that we examine attitudes of the practitioners during that difficult time. Werner Krauß (1884–1959) provides a particularly significant example. He was a major theatre artist, prominent before and after 1933, whose artistic and political record was scrutinized closely after 1945. His career under the Nazis is of present interest: I will attempt an assessment of his attitudes toward the Nazi hierarchy, with a brief chronology, a statement of his place in the history of German-speaking theatre, a description of his acting style, and finally my view of his attitudes vis à vis National Socialism.

Krauß began his career around 1903 in the provincial theatres of Breslau, Aachen, and Nürnberg. By 1914 he was recommended by the agent Eugen Frankfurter to Max Reinhardt at the Deutsches Theater in Berlin, and under Reinhardt's direction Krauß had the opportunity to play many important roles. He performed in approximately 160 productions for the Reinhardt theatres. He acted in five plays of the celebrated Wedekind Cycle, which starred Frank and Tilly Wedekind: *Franziska* (as Laurus Bein), *Erdgeist* (as Escerny and Schigloh), *Stein der Weisen* (as Pater Porphyrion), *Kammersänger* (as Professor Dühring), and *Marquis von Keith* (as Konsul Kasimir).[2] Krauß played Schiller's Wallenstein, Kaiser's Cashier (in *Von Morgens bis Mitternachts*), and Shakespeare's Shylock. In 1924 he moved to Leopold Jessner's Staatstheater, but in the same year toured with Reinhardt when the Austrian director brought *Das Mirakel* to New York.[3] He appeared at Reinhardt's Salzburg Theatre Festival and regularly at the Burgtheater in Vienna. His list of major stage roles extended beyond 1933. In addition to his stage work, there were a number of film roles in his career. Two of his films are most prominent in film history: *Das Kabinett von Dr. Kaligari* (1920) and *Jud Süß* (1940). *Dr. Kaligari* is significant as the prototype of German Expressionist cinema and *Jud Süß* as a notorious anti-Semitic Nazi film.

Krauß achieved his fame and fortune with a compelling acting style that seduced his audience into believing the character and the story portrayed. There was an ingenuousness about his acting style that audiences found compelling. There are three basic interrelated constituents of his style: personal shyness, the "magic circle," and the demonic nature and transformative power of the human mask.[4] His shyness, according to some, was a result of his feelings of low self-esteem.[5] He always felt intimidated by being on stage. "My greatest successes came from overcoming a sense of shame. I was no Reinhardt actor; I was always terrified to step on stage, and because of that I invented the mask."[6] Shyness per se is not a constituent of acting style, unless one plays shyness in some unique way. Krauß used it as a kind of flight behavior into levels of aesthetic reality that were more comfortable for him.[7] He translated shyness by projecting himself into his roles, by escaping self. He acted "in order not to be myself."[8] He felt the need for a projection of self from self.[9] And he was convincing in this flight, luring spectators into his "magic circle."

The magic circle is the power of illusion on stage, directed primarily by the actor as he manipulates the elements of production. Krauß biographer Alfred Mühr explains it this way:

All powers belong to the magic circle on stage, to the destined space of illusion, of costume, make-up, color and the true emotions from the heights and depths of the uniquely changeable human soul. . . . The magic circle is for Krauß the continued world of thought, the empire of fantasy.[10]

Krauß saw the creative act as a departure from self and an immersion into the essence of the story to be portrayed. He saw himself entering the magic circle armed with costume, make-up, and so on, articulating for the audience the core of being of the character portrayed.

It is clear from what we know of his work that he had a power and a talent resembling that of the shaman. He was possessed of a demonic nature that the audience found appealing. He is quoted as saying that his only goal was "to enchant, to enchant."[11] Krauß believed that stage make-up existed to make the human mask.[12] To escape shyness, Krauß sought refuge in characters on stage, tapping into the magic circle and utilizing the most subtle of all masks, the persona, on stage. His acting possessed a kind of demonic and powerful charm.

Essentially his theatre was the theatre of idea manifested in physical form. German belles lettres and theatre have long thought of the mind as the primary channel of communication, from artist to art form, from theatre to spectator. Krauß seemed to possess an extraordinary talent for binding his audience to him. In his book on Krauß, Wolfgang Goetz tells us that Krauß reached out from his artistic core and drew the spectator into the soul of the actor or into the soul of the character.[13] Reinhardt said it well: Krauß was the "legitimate heir" of the famed Burgtheater actors Bogumil Dawison (1818–1872) and Friedrich Mitterwurzer (1844–1897). Krauß had the ability to project "his life intensively into each role, so that he transformed himself physically by an unusual process of autosuggestion. However the change did not occur with a fake belly, but through experiencing the life of the role. Herein lies the art of acting in its most profound aspect."[14]

Krauß's style lay in enchantment. He lured the spectator into the illusion of the character and of the mise-en-scène. Those who saw his work were not always able to distinguish between illusion and reality; they lost their own reality for his. His prominence and his ability to bind his audience made him particularly attractive to the Third Reich. It can be said that the Nazis recognized his brilliance as an effective weapon for their drive to manipulate the populace. Germany had for centuries revered its theatre. What better weapon than an actor with such hypnotic force?

Krauß was clearly active during the Third Reich—in Berlin he was a principal actor at the Staatstheater (the Preußische Schauspielhaus am Gendarmenmarkt) and occasionally starred at the Burgtheater in Nazi Vienna. He made eight films between 1935 and 1943. He was also honored by the new government: in September 1933, Propaganda Minister Goebbels named him Deputy President of the Theatre Chamber, under President Otto Laubinger, a more politically acceptable but less famous actor. In 1934, the Minister-President of Prussia, Hermann Göring, honored him as State Actor (*Staatsschauspieler*) among fifteen significant theatre artists including Gustav Gründgens.[15] He was awarded the Goethe Medallion in 1938.

Did he use his magnetic appeal in the service of his overlords? How conscious was Krauß's choice to work for the National Socialists? Motivations are always difficult to establish and prove, especially during so horrendous a time as that of the Third Reich. There is no question about his prominence in the German theatre world. Indeed, were he not so prominent, the Nazis would have not courted him for his usefulness to the propaganda effort, nor would the postwar authorities have seen fit to ban him from the stage for a period of time. In an interesting work entitled *Theaterpolitik in faschistischem Deutschland*, Jutta Wardetzky wrote that the Propaganda Minister "wasted no time in calling the most prominent artists into positions in the Reichskulturkammer, such as Richard Strauß, Wilhelm Furtwängler, Heinz Hilpert, Werner Krauß, to name only a few. These names were particularly useful in the early years."[16] Although she goes on to say that Goebbels replaced them as soon as they were no longer useful, the fact remains that these famous artists were co-opted. Apparently Krauß did not especially like it, but he did not mind.

In 1945 Krauß was brought before Allied authorities on charges that he was a Nazi *Mitläufer* (fellow traveler).[17] In that year the authorities levied an *Arbeitsverbot* (work ban) on him. He was required to leave Austria in 1946. Three times he was brought before the courts to clarify his relationship with the Nazis. Such leading theatre figures as Carl Zuckmayer, Käthe Dorsch, and George Bernard Shaw spoke on his behalf. In 1948 he was fined heavily and allowed to work, but at first no German Intendant would hire him.[18] His career would begin anew in Vienna.

The primary evidence against Krauß included his continued prominence in Nazi performance and in the cultural hierarchy. There are lesser indications regarding his culpability or at least his ability to be compromised. In 1934 he was "required" to play Napoleon at the Staatstheater, in the Benito Mussolini–Giavaccino Forzano epic drama *Hundert Tage* ("Hundred Days"); thereafter he quoted the Italian dictator's comment to him: "You are the only lion who allows himself the strength to run free in this civilized time."[19] That Krauß would cite this as an honor in his memoir does not reflect well on his attitudes, especially when he protests his association with the Nazis.

If Mussolini attracted Krauß' respect, Hitler earned special consideration, as mandated by the times. Krauß sent Hitler autographed pictures of himself and in 1939 a telegram from Vienna wishing the Führer well.[20] Moreover, he was not above invoking Hitler's name when it suited his purposes or his ego. In 1933, Goebbels requested a meeting with Krauß, which would be attended by Göring, Heß, Lammers, and Hitler. Since Krauß was scheduled to go to London after the meeting,[21] the Propaganda Minister arranged a special flight for him. He was then taken to the Salzburg airport and when asked by a member of Reinhardt's staff what he was doing there, he replied *"proudly,"* or so it seemed to one auditor, that he had just come from Hitler.[22]

There are several other episodes that call Krauß' discretion into question: the "Baumeister affair" is an example. Apparently a young woman in circles close to Hitler had connections to the German Ambassador to Belgium. Indiscreetly, she kept a diary which could prove embarrassing to the Nazis. Krauß heard of the diary and promptly reported the information to Göring, complete with names and addresses. When told to do so, he broke off relations with the people involved.[23]

The centerpiece of the case against Krauß, without question, is his performance in *Jud Süß*. The film was made in 1940 at the behest of Goebbels, and is notable as one of the most vicious anti-Semitic films ever made.[24] It is a perversion of Lion Feuchtwanger's *Jud Süß*, written in 1925 (itself derived from German history and a novella of the same title by Wilhelm Hauff, 1827). Feuchtwanger's novel is not anti-Semitic, nor was the English film version, entitled *Power* (1932), directed by the Jewish director Lothar Mendes.[25] But as the "Final Solution" was being planned, Goebbels wanted a propaganda interpretation with a strong anti-Semitic bias, and consequently the film portrays Jews in the most despicable light possible. There is a clear indication of menace in the Jewish characters Krauß portrayed.[26] Krauß played no fewer than thirteen Jewish caricatures, from "the cunning secretary Levy" to "the grasping Rabbi Loew." He was thought so true to (stereo)type in these roles "that he asked Goebbels to announce publicly that he was not Jewish, but a loyal Aryan merely playing a part as an actor in the service of the state."[27] Although Krauß does not bear sole responsibility for the effects of the film on the Jews, *Jud Süß* has been linked to the Nazi terror: there is documented evidence that the film inspired violence against the Jews.[28]

If Gottfried Reinhardt is to be believed, Krauß was a willing participant in this kind of anti-Semitic propaganda. When Max Reinhardt bowed to pressure to recast the part of Mephistopheles given to Max Pallenberg for the Salzburg Festival because Pallenberg was "racially inadequate," Gottfried refers to Krauß as the "unashamed anti-Semite" who took over the part.[29] Krauß's prejudices, Gottfried concluded, "would draw him to the Nazis, whose luminary he would become.[30]

Although he presumably played sympathetic Shylocks for Reinhardt in 1914 at the Deutsches Theater, in 1915 at the Volksbühne (replacing Rudolf Schildkraut) and again in 1921 at the Großes Schauspielhaus, Krauß later adopted an anti-Semitic interpretation. In 1943, when he recreated the role in Hitler's Vienna, he earned elaborate praise from the Nazi Party organ, the *Völkischer Beobachter*:

> Words are inadequate to describe the linguistic and mimic variety of Werner Krauß's Shylock.... Every fiber of his body seems impregnated with Jewish blood; he mumbles, slavers, gurgles, grunts and squawks with alarming authenticity, scurries back and forth like a rat, though he does so the hard way—knock-kneed; one literally smells his bad breath, feels the itching under his caftan and senses the nausea that overcomes him at the end of the court scene. Everything demonic is submerged in the impotent rage of the little ghetto usurer; in the wobbling of his body, in the frantic blinking of his eye lids and the arching of his arms, he becomes a caricature, especially together with the no less realistic Tubal of Ferdinand Maierhofer. An infernal puppet show.[31]

It is somewhat damning to be so praised for a performance as Shylock by the Nazi Party organ.

The argument Krauß and others have used is that they were coerced into playing such propagandist roles. To resist meant heavy penalties. Yet Gottfried Reinhardt accused Krauß of being more than willing to serve the Nazi state: "Krauß volunteered, among other breaches of taste, to caricature no less than thirteen Jews in Goebbels's infamous film *Jud Süß*."[32] To justify his actions, Krauß would readily shift responsibility to Goebbels or others, giving the impression that he did what he did out of fear and coercion. Walter Huder compared the more accurate English film version of *Jud Süß* with the Goebbels version and in so doing rendered an opinion of Krauß's behavior: the English version "is the true opposite of the Goebbels hate film of the same title. A dark stain also for the Fascistic collaboration of a Werner Krauß."[33]

What is the other side of the story? We do not have incontrovertible evidence that Krauß consciously launched his own attacks or used his position of prominence to aid and abet the Nazis. He continued to appear at the pre-*Anschluß* Burgtheater and to act with racial emigré Reinhardt. Krauß claimed that Goebbels made him Deputy President of the Theaterkammer without his knowledge or permission.[34] There is a membership list of individuals in the Reichstheaterkammer and the Reichskultursenate indicating membership in the Nazi Party with date of entry and membership number. Krauß is listed in the official organization but was clearly not a member of the Party.[35]

Krauß's contract with the Staatstheater was to expire 31 January 1933, and he knew he was being considered for the position of Intendant. He was invited to a tea party at Goebbels's home. Krauß declined, fearing that he would be named to the post. He did not renew his contract and went to

Switzerland on 1 February.[36] In 1935, in Montevideo, he was invited to a National Socialist Party social event. He refused, saying, "Deliver me from your stupid party [*Scheißpartei*]."[37] Apparently Hitler vetoed Krauß for a film about Frederick the Great because he did not like the actor.[38] Finally, Göring is quoted having said to his wife that Krauß was not a good National Socialist.[39] Even in light of such evidence, the "case" against Krauß still remains rather strong.

The Nazi Party wanted only true followers of the Reich in positions of importance. In a letter to Goebbels, Otto Laubinger in nominating Alfred Nöller for a position as Intendant speaks of the importance of the Party line in such appointments: "he should embrace the idea of the truly National" Socialist work ethic."[40] In the end, we have no irrefutable insight into Krauß's state of mind. We must be fair and understand a little of what it was like to have suffered the takeover by, or gradual subscription to, the darkness of National Socialism. People had to earn a living. One does not quickly and easily believe that the menace will come so close to home.

Historians appeared to take a harsher view. Julian Petley took fellow film historian David Hull to task for whitewashing artists who continued or expanded their careers under the Nazis; the following quotation could also include Krauß:

> Hull's particular combination of special pleading, wishful thinking and political innocence can be explained partly by his naive reliance on interviews with and statements by the likes of Veit Harlan, Leni Riefenstahl and Luis Trenker, who have clearly taken this as a welcome opportunity to remove black (or brown) spots from their pasts. But Hull also clearly has not the slightest notion about the workings and nature of ideology in general, and of fascism in particular; anecdotes about and statements by directors, actors and actresses who claim to have been hostile or indifferent to the regime are quite irrelevant to a film's ideological significance, which is a matter not of "personality" or intention but of that film's meaning, place and function *within the historical conjuncture*.[41]

Werner Krauß was at the height of his career when Hitler came to power. He was forty-nine years old in 1933. To have been courted by Goebbels or Göring and not to have known what the Third Reich stood for would mean that he had lived in a complete cultural vacuum. Actors may choose not to participate in politics, but they have to know what is going on in order to perform in works that are relevant to current events. Certainly Krauß's fear that he be mistaken for a Jew because of *Jud Süß* demonstrates his keen awareness of anti-Semitism. He needed to prove his Aryan heritage in order to belong to the Theater Chamber and consequently to hold acting positions in theatre or film. It is perhaps too harsh to condemn him as an active fascist or Nazi. His complicity, however, cannot be excused in the same way in which a lesser figure might have failed to see the larger issues. Krauß was one of the most famous actors in the German-speaking theatre at a time that the German theatre was a particularly favored art form of the state. He was flattered that Mussolini called him a bold lion and he was proud to invoke Hitler's name when it suited his needs. When he called the NSDAP a *Scheißpartei,* or when Göring deemed him to be less than satisfactory as a Nazi, his culpability is ameliorated somewhat, but his case remains full of complexity.

I would imagine that Krauß tried to play both ends against the middle, even detesting the party hierarchy and wishing that it would fail. He did not become an exile as Georg Kaiser and others did, however; he did not turn his back on an evil institution that had taken over his country; he did not become an "inner emigré." He remained active in his craft; conditions sometimes mandated that he participate in virulently anti-Semitic artistic work. The best case one can make for Krauß is that he was a true professional and put his art above all else, and as such, he allowed himself to be drawn into the web of the Third Reich. At best, by focusing solely on his profession—to interpolate for him—he committed the sin of omission. Others found he had committed many sins of commission.

We cannot be smug about the evils perpetrated in Germany during that time. We can, however, continue to conduct such research so that we might accomplish two things: (1) to bring events into more human and complex perspective and (2) to provide some direction about ethics and the arts, about choice and implication. Werner Krauß had ample opportunity to exercise choice. He chose to play along with the new cultural bureaucracies in the hopes that they would go away. History confirms that there are always choices. The artist can take an important lesson about fame, prestige, money, and the temptations to power, for the theatre in Third Reich Germany had its impact on the culture outside the stage door. Krauß had choice and he opted for the Nazis.

POSTSCRIPT

After World War II and the collapse of the Third Reich, Krauß reemerged at the Vienna Burgtheater, where he had performed during the 1928–29 season and frequently from 1933 to the Anschluß (13 March 1938). After the union with Germany, Krauß continued to perform only occasionally at the Burgtheater. In Nazi Vienna he played the title role in *Wilhelm Tell,* which had a gala premiere 20 April 1938 to celebrate Hitler's birthday and the Anschluß, Rudolf II in Grillparzer's *Bruderzwist in Hapsburg* ("Fraternal Strife in the House of Hapsburg," opened 6 December 1941), and the notorious Shylock of 1943. After postwar censure and a temporary work ban, Krauß was brought out of his forced retirement by Austrian Cultural

Minister Egon Hilbert and Burgtheater artistic director Josef Gielen. Krauß's postwar premiere was as Charles Josse in Jacques Deval's *Die Frau deiner Jugend* (*La femme de la jeunesse*, 18 November 1948, with Käthe Dorsch as Fernande Josse). His subsequent roles included Philip of Spain in Bruckner's *Elisabeth von England* (1949, with Maria Eis as Elisabeth), Ibsen's John Gabriel Borkmann (1950), the title role in Carl Zuckmayer's *Hauptmann von Köpenick* (1950), Iago (1951, with Ewald Balser as Othello), and Rudolf II in Grillparzer's Hapsburg tragedy (1957). When the Burgtheater toured to Berlin, Krauß was booed and the performance had to be cut short. The Berlin engagement was subsequently cancelled.[42]

Interestingly enough, Krauß toured Munich, Stuttgart, Frankfurt, and other German cities without incident. Berlin was the only city that opposed his performance, although by 1953 when he appeared there in Shaw's *Don Juan in Hell* he was greeted with 29 minutes of applause.[43] Berlin's attitude had apparently shifted. In 1954 Krauß was selected by a committee of German, Austrian, and Swiss theatre professionals to receive the coveted Iffland Ring as the greatest German actor.[44] At his death, the ring and honors, at Krauß's direction, passed to Josef Meinrad. Meinrad began his impressive acting career at the Burgtheater in 1947; there was no question about his political status.

As Petley indicated, an actor has a responsibility to be aware of the impact on society of his or her status and of the roles chosen to play. While there is no absolute proof that Krauß agreed with the Nazis, he chose enough roles such as those in *Jud Süß* and he clearly did not oppose the regime in sufficiently overt ways to justify his claim of innocence. He tried to walk a fine line, but it is arguable that he often stepped over to the side of evil.

NOTES

1. For inquiries regarding the theatre and its role in the Third Reich, see William R. Elwood, "The War Conscience on the Berlin Stage," *Quarterly Journal of Speech* 53, no. 4 (Dec. 1967): 378–79, and Eckart von Naso, "Events at the Prussian State Theater," in George Mosse, ed., *Nazi Culture* (New York, 1968): 185–88.

2. Heinrich Huesmann, *Welttheater Reinhardt* (Munich, 1983): production numbers 745, 747, 863, 750, 751, respectively.

3. According to Alfred Mühr, Krauß had a falling out with Jessner, and Reinhardt took him back with star billing in October 1926 as the title character in Wolfgang Goetz's *Neidhardt von Gneisenau*. Alfred Mühr, *Werner Krauß, Das Schicksal auf der Bühne* (Berlin, 1933): 46–47.

4. Krauß was primarily an actor who built upon German stage tradition, realizing the aesthetic needs of the German-speaking theatre audience. He is given credit for some innovation: he was the first, apparently, to play Mephisto as a blonde character—with interesting ethnic dimensions. Werner Krauß, *Das Schauspiel meines Lebens*, ed. Hans Weigel (Stuttgart, 1958): 112. Some of the best sources

regarding his acting style were written before his involvement in the world of National Socialist politics. See Hugo Fetting, ed., *Max Reinhardt, Schriften* (Berlin, 1974); Henning Rischbieter, ed., *Gründgens* (Hannover, 1963); Wolfgang Goetz, *Werner Krauß* (Hamburg, 1954); and Alfred Mühr, *Großes Theater. Begegnungen mit Gustaf Gründgens* (Berlin, 1950) and *Die Welt des Schauspielers Werner Krauß* (Berlin, 1928).

5. See Goetz, *Krauß*.
6. Krauß, *Schauspiel*, 111.
7. Off stage he was thought to be aloof, although one source describes him as shy and sober. He apparently did not have many friends, was subject to depressions, and periodically felt repressed in daily life. Goetz, *Krauß*, 189–90.
8. Goetz, *Krauß*, 181.
9. His style included the unique ability to blend his private life with that of the character. Mühr, *Werner Krauß*, 50.
10. Mühr, *Werner Krauß*, 59, 61.
11. Ibid., 9.
12. Ibid., 10.
13. Goetz, *Krauß*, 188.
14. Reinhardt, *Schriften*, 345.
15. Boguslaw Drewniak, *Das Theater im NS-Staat* (Düsseldorf, 1983): 155, and Bundesarchiv, Abteilung Potsdam, Deutsche Reichsbank, Akte 3566: 111.
16. Jutta Wardetzky, *Theaterpolitik in faschistischen Deutschland* (Berlin, 1983): 35.
17. Christa Haan has detailed the ban on Krauß after World War II and his eventual rehabilitation. Christa Hann, "Werner Krauß und das Burgtheater," diss. University of Vienna, 1970.
18. Krauß, *Schauspiel*, 225.
19. Krauß, *Schauspiel*, 158. The play was later filmed under Franz Wenzler's direction, with screenplay by Karl Vollmöller. It premiered 22 March 1935. Krauß recreated the Napoleon role in the film.
20. Drewniak, *Theater*, 147; telegram dated 17 June 1939, Berlin Document Center.
21. He went to London to play in Hauptmann's *Vor Sonnenuntergang*, where he was booed: "We don't want Nazi actors."
22. Goetz, *Krauß*, 174.
23. Krauß, *Schauspiel*, 212. This story surfaced in 1952, although Frau Göring denied that it was true. Her justification was that her husband would have mentioned it to her, but this is a weak defence.
24. See Julian Petley, *Capital and Culture: German Cinema 1933–1945* (London, 1979).
25. David Stewart Hull, *Film in the Third Reich* (New York, 1969): 161.
26. Interestingly enough, the portrayal of the German attitude is equally disturbing to the modern conscience. When Süß appears in the home of Sturm, the young man Faber is quite vicious in his anti-Semitism as well. It is a subject for another article.
27. David Welch, *Propaganda and the German Cinema 1933–1945* (Oxford, 1983): 291. Since this statement is rather significant, I cite Welch's source: W. A. Boelcke,

Kriegspropaganda 1939–41. Geheime Ministerkonferenzen im Reichspropagandaministerium (Stuttgart, 1966).

28. Joseph Wulf, *Theater und Film in Dritten Reich* (Gütersloh, 1964): 447.

29. Gottfried Reinhardt, *The Genius* (New York, 1971): 242. He elaborates further: "As early as 1921, during rehearsals for *The Wolves* by Romain Rolland, Krauss had let himself go in a venomous tirade against the 'brothers Goldman's [the original Reinhardt surname] slatternly way of doing business' on the stage of the Deutsches Theater, because he was irritated by some contractual controversy."

30. Reinhardt, *Genius*, 42.

31. Otto Horny review in Richard Geehr, *Karl Lueger, Mayor of Fin de Siècle Vienna* (Detroit, 1990): 361, n. 122.

32. Reinhardt, *Genius*, 42.

33. Walter Huder, "Zur Ausstellung, Filmretrospective und Konferenz," in Lothar Schirmer, ed., *Theater im Exil 1933–1945* (Berlin, 1979): 18.

34. Krauß, *Schauspiel*: 174.

35. Bundesarchiv, Abteilung Potsdam, Reichsministerium für Volksaufklärung und Propaganda, Microfilm no. 6436, photograph no. 3589207.

36. Goetz, *Krauß*, 171–72.

37. Ibid., 178.

38. Ibid., 216.

39. Ibid., 179.

40. Bundesarchiv, Abteilung Potsdam, Reichsministerium für Volksaufklärung und Propaganda, Akte #296: 134.

41. Petley, *Capital and Culture*, 4.

42. Krauß, *Schauspiel*, 239.

43. Ibid., 240.

44. Ibid., 250. Although its age and early history are subject to speculation, tradition holds that the ring, with diamonds and portrait of actor August Wilhelm Iffland (1759–1814), was passed to Ludwig Devrient upon Iffland's death. It was then passed on to Emil Devrient, Theodor Döring, and Friedrich Haase. Haase is the first known to have possessed the ring. On his death in 1911 it passed to his choice, Albert Bassermann. Because Bassermann's three designated choices (Alexander Girardi, Max Pallenberg and Alexander Moissi) predeceased him, he put the ring into Austrian trust in 1935 before he left Europe. Bassermann died in 1952; in 1954, a committee selected Krauß. According to statute, Krauß named his successor in a document opened on his death. See Minna von Alth, ed., *Burgtheater 1776–1976. Aufführungen und Besetzungen von zweihundert Jahren*, vol. 1 (Vienna, 1979): 682, 718.

8

Nazi Berlin and the Großes Schauspielhaus

Yvonne Shafer

The Großes Schauspielhaus in Berlin was a theatrical showcase in several incarnations. The building itself was initially a great market situated near the Spree River in the center of Berlin. In the later part of the nineteenth century it was converted to an enormous circus, which drew crowds to see outstanding exhibitions of horsemanship and other circus acts. It also served as a great meeting hall for such events as Robert Koch's international congress dealing with tuberculosis in 1890.[1] The large amphitheatre in the building was a symbol for the growing population of Berlin and its increasing prosperity. The history of the various uses to which the theatre was put in the twentieth century is an important reflection of the changes in German society in the period. During the time of the Third Reich, it was an important element in culture and propaganda under the direction of Dr. Joseph Goebbels. This chapter analyzes the unusual architecture of the theatre and the productions of several plays that were important during the Third Reich.

Before looking at the theatre as it was used by the Nazis, it is necessary to make a brief examination of its theatrical history up to that period. The first use of the building as a theatre occurred in November 1919. The creative genius Max Reinhardt conceived a "great theatre without loges and balconies, the stage sticking out into the auditorium. No court theatre, no peep-hole theatre, rather a theatre for the masses."[2] In this theatre he presented plays for a united audience, calling up the idealism and grandeur of the ancient Greek theatre. This concept was symbolic of the idealism of the early days of the Weimar Republic. Reinhardt hired the architect Hans Poelzig to convert the circus arena to an unconventional theatre without any of the traditional class-oriented separation into orchestra seats, loges, and lower-priced balcony seats. The audience of three thousand was to be massed together in a democratic whole. Reinhardt anticipated many of the effects of modern staging. He told Poelzig,

> We must move out of the proscenium and eliminate the division between the actor and the public! But it is not enough to bring the stage into the auditorium; no, the whole tired tradition that the stage and the auditorium are two realms separate from one another must be destroyed. The viewer must feel that he is a participant in the development of the proceedings. But the curtain must disappear, the actor should, whenever it is possible, move through the auditorium, and it should be decorated in harmony with the scenery.[3]

In order to create spectacular effects, the theatre was equipped with a *Kuppelhorizont* (skydome), a main stage with a revolving floor in it, and a large forestage to bring the actors in closer contact with the audience. Poelzig was faced with a number of difficulties. The first was the fact that there were iron supports throughout the building that could not be removed. An obvious problem with a theatre for three thousand was the acoustics. This was particularly important in relation to the huge dome over the stage. To replace the contoured ceiling with a flat surface would have been acoustical suicide. Poelzig's innovative solution to these problems gave the theatre its unique quality. He decorated the eight-sided dome and the supports with hanging stalactite-like configurations, which created an excellent room for acoustics.[4] The stalactite-covered supporting columns were also the sources of indirect lighting. The nickname of the theatre was the *Tropfensteinhöhle* (stalactite cave).

The first production was Aeschylus' *Oresteia* in an adaptation by Karl Vollmöller. It has been described as the most important German theatrical event of the period. In *The Theatre of the Weimar Republic*, John Willett briefly noted the symbolic significance of Reinhardt's production in this theatre:

> Here, watching some of Germany's finest actors—Moissi as Orestes, Agnes Straub as Clytemnestra, Werner Krauss as Agamemnon, and others of Reinhardt's prewar ensemble—was the new republican society, from the chancellor down, melting into an anonymous mass unbroken by the old theatre's traditional distinctions of level.[5]

Reinhardt was successful in creating a new theatre for the people, but his work in many other theatres in Germany and abroad often took him away from this theatre. Financial difficulties caused him to sell the theatre. His last work there was a 1931 production of *Tales of Hoffmann*. The darkness of the opera, with its images of death and the grotesque, no doubt reflected his feelings about the changing Germany. He had dreamed of creating a German National Theatre in the Großes Schauspielhaus, but his work in theatre would no longer be in Germany. In 1933, he surrendered ownership of his remaining Berlin theatres to the German nation, writing in an open letter that not only did he lose his theatres, but his home as well.[6] Reinhardt was unacceptable to the Nazis because he was Jewish, of course, but also because the whole aura of his theatre, his outlook on art, his work with designer Ernst Stern on such plays as *Lysistrata* (opened at the Großes Schauspielhaus 11 June 1920, for 55 performances), and his work with Hans Poelzig were regarded as examples of *Kulturbolshewismus* (cultural Bolshevism).[7]

Before Reinhardt left Germany, the theatre had been put to other uses that were unacceptable to the rising Nazi Party. First, on 24 January 1924, as the reports of Lenin's death arrived, thousands of workers gathered in the Großes Schauspielhaus. "On the stage was a chorus of male workers and an agit-prop group of the Communist party."[8] Such a mass meeting was naturally repugnant to Hitler and his supporters because the power of the Communists, particularly in connection with the labor unions, was of great concern. In June 1925, *Trotz alledem!* ("Despite Everything!"), an agit-prop revue that took its title from the martyred socialist Karl Liebknecht, ran for ten days at the theatre. It presented in music and dance "the struggle of the German working class from the beginning of the World War to the murder of Rosa Luxemburg and Karl Liebknecht. The text was by Erich Weinert and Ernst Toller, with direction by Erwin Piscator."[9]

Given the history of the Großes Schauspielhaus, the Nazis were very eager to take over control of the building. The theatre was immediately attractive to the Party, and especially to Goebbels, because, ironically, the idealistic dream Reinhardt had of creating a unified mass audience and the success of the agit-prop revue prefigured Goebbels' use of the theatre. A description of the effect of *Trotz alledem!* might be a description of the mass Nazi meetings that took place in the 1930s:

> The masses began to participate. The theatre was reality for them, and soon it no longer was stage against auditorium, rather a *single* great auditorium, a *single* battleground, a *single* great demonstration. This unification on this definitive evening was the evidence of the power of agitation of political theatre.[10]

On 13 March 1933, six weeks after Hitler took control of the government, the central organization for the control of art was established with Dr. Joseph Goebbels as the Head of the *Reichsministerium für Volksaufklärung und Propaganda*. The control of the theatres was a very important element.[11] Theatre artists were divided into two categories: those who were supporters of the government and were "properly" using their God-given gifts, and those who were politically suspect. Goebbels made a yearly list with notations about every theatre artist, which he gave to Hitler.[12] Naturally, one of the first acts regarding artists was to "cleanse" the theatres by getting rid of non-Aryans. Such actors as Elisabeth Bergner and Fritz Kortner were considered "not the real artists and figures after the hearts of the German people, but merely typical charming creatures of the night."[13] Both Göring and Goebbels were profoundly impressed by the power actors exerted in society and were very interested in getting them under their control. Göring (who would marry an actress, Emmy Sonnemann) remarked that "he could make a very good National Socialist out of an actor, but that he could not make an actor out of a National Socialist."[14] Goebbels set up a mass meeting with theatre professionals early in 1933 and made his intentions quite clear, saying, "We will stand by you, if you will stand by us."[15]

Goebbels and Göring, rivals in many ways, were also rivals in the area of theatre. Göring controlled the Staatstheater with Gustaf Gründgens, and Goebbels directly controlled the former Großes Schauspielhaus. Given the power he enjoyed, it is not surprising that Goebbels assembled a first-class acting ensemble in the Großes Schauspielhaus, although he misused his power to cast a few actresses who were not equal to the rest of the company. When the theatre opened in January 1934, Goebbels had a direct hand in all aspects of its changes and in the first production. The new name of the theatre was the *Theater des Volkes* (Theatre of the People). Of course, the term *Volk* was very important in the Third Reich. It referred to the Nazi belief in a racially homogeneous German people, and it was used to indicate the importance the Nazis placed on integration of the ordinary people within society. An obvious element of this was the extension to the *Volk* of consumer products formerly unavailable to workers, such as the *Volkswagen* and the *Volkskühlschrank*, a refrigerator. This effort was called the *völkisch* cause.[16] Goebbels wanted to increase theatre going and said, "We want to lead art [back] to the people [*Volk*], in order to be able to bring the people to art."[17] The company in the newly named theatre was to be the *Theater der Nation*—a national theatre.

The size of the "giant house," as it was so often called, was a particularly desirable element to the Nazis, as the intention was to fill it with workers and control their leisure time. The man to do that was Robert Ley, who headed the *Kraft durch Freude Gemeinschaft* (KdF). This organization to bring "Strength Through Joy" to the German workers was in intimate connection with the Theater des Volkes. Membership in the organization was allegedly voluntary, but benefits were offered and pressures of various kinds were applied. The KdF was part of the *Deutsches Arbeitsfront* (DAF, German Labor Front), which Ley headed. It was "an educational-propaganda structure to turn Germans into believing National Socialists."[18] In 1933, the organization had 4.7 million members, and by 1939 there were 22 million members out of 25.3 million workers.[19] This organization not only took over the funds of former unions, but even hobby organizations of workers. Ultimately, the DAF had enormous funds at its disposal, and (not surprisingly) there were charges of corruption. Initially the plan was to exercise control over the workplace, but ultimately Ley said, "We must organize leisure anew. This means not only the hours after work, but the total man from morning to night.... The care [read "control"] of the German people at the workplace, after hours, in their free time, at home, and in the family is the highest goal of the DAF."[20] Millions of Germans took part in the "Strength Through Joy" activities, which included concerts, extensive travel, theatre "and other amenities which in the past had been reserved for the middle and upper classes in Germany."[21] Despite the "regimented leisure" inherent in the organization, many historians have expressed the view that the "KdF was one of the few really benevolent aspects of the Nazi regime."[22] One estimate is that the KdF brought workers to 8.1 million theatre performances and concerts.[23] One of these occasions was the opening night of the Theater des Volkes, for which thousands of workers received free admission, free programs, and free coat checks.

In his book *Zwischen Zucht und Ekstase* ("Between Discipline and Ecstasy"), Dieter Bartetzky points out the close relationship between the architecture of the Großes Schauspielhaus and the later architecture by Albert Speer and other Nazi architects. The Großes Schauspielhaus relates to Egyptian and Greek buildings as well as other antique buildings. The yearning for the past, the sense of tradition, and the concept of great societies and great architecture that existed in the past and would exist again when the Third Reich triumphed were expressed in this architecture. In buildings early in the century, such as the Großes Schauspielhaus, "the foundations for neo-classic, old-oriental, and sometimes, Expressionistic tendencies, as a synthesis of historical style and form" were developed and subsequently became the elements of fascist architecture, both for buildings and for outdoor showplaces. Audiences, whether for plays or political speeches, were capable of being controlled and influenced by the architecture, the lighting, the sound, and all the visual elements. Bartetzky refers to the "magical atmosphere somewhere between cosmic symbolism and cult theatre" in the Großes Schauspielhaus.[24] He describes the parallels between the theatre and fascist building practice and theory. There was "a yearning for greatness, the eternal, enchantment, etc., in the face of an anguished society and environment."[25] In the presentations in Poelzig's Großes Schauspielhaus, massive architecture and mass control complemented each other. In his "theatre for all," the people were drawn in and moved to states of excitement or ecstasy by the costumes, the lighting, and the theatre design. The architect transformed the gigantic circus into a building with "mystical reality, stereometric rows and strange symmetry, an overpowering impression which was increased through the perfect installation of spotlights."[26] The fact that the audience was on three sides of the forestage meant that the communication, or synthesis of audience and actors, was another means of creating a mutuality of purpose and feeling in the theatre. Bartetzky concludes his discussion of the effects produced in the theatre by saying, "The sense of massiveness which was engendered in the Großes Schauspielhaus was a forestudy for the architecture of the Third Reich."[27]

In this theatre the audience could be excited yet controlled, and individuals lost their sense of loneliness and alienation by becoming part of a unified mass with shared goals and beliefs. This was, of course, the technique used by Goebbels when he staged the mass rallies in which Hitler dynamically roused the crowds to support him. The same techniques were used in the *Thingspiele*, the great historical pageants performed in the 1930s. Goebbels contemptuously spoke of the mass of people as something to be cynically manipulated for the ends of the Nazi Party: "The mob is a weak, lazy, cowardly group of people. . . . [One must] bring the largest part of them into a unity, so that ultimately they will take their place in [our] triumphant advance."[28]

A typical example of the success of the combination of theatricality and politics was the production of Goethe's *Götz von Berlichingen*. A brief description of this production, which opened on 21 November 1935, will indicate the essence of the audience response in this period. The production starred Heinrich George, who was closely associated with the Nazi Party throughout the 1930s and the war. As one critic wrote, in this production "the pulse beat of the people [*Volk*] is felt." He continued, "Here is the storm of revolution, here wave the flags of the awakened peoples, and here a Germany is dreamed of, which will be great and free. The breath of youth that this work exudes informs all the scenes, blood from a fiery heart springs in the spoken words and gives them weight and strength." He concluded that the audience had experienced an evening in which great things were attempted and achieved and that the public responded appropriately to a jubilant theatrical success.[29] Director Richard Weichert, using a larger-than-life, heroic acting style and all the technical capabilities of the theatre, with the designs of Ludwig Hornsteiner, presented Goethe's monumental Sturm und Drang play with color and excitement, moving through twenty-seven scenes (reduced from fifty-four) with technical facility. This was to be the effect of many of the plays presented in the Großes Schauspielhaus under the control of the Minister of Education and Propaganda, Dr. Goebbels.

The productions in the Theater des Volkes fall into two segments. In the early and mid-1930s, there was an acting ensemble headed by Heinrich George, with the important directors Dr. Hanns Riebedene Gebbard, Walther Brügmann, and Richard Weichert. Later in the thirties, the theatre was turned over to operetta, with a large and outstanding collection of actors, singers, and dancers. The opening production in the Theater des Volkes was carefully chosen and rehearsed. Goebbels was involved in the decisions about the production and attended rehearsals, often giving advice to the director.[30] *Die Räuber* ("The Robbers") by Schiller opened 18 January 1934. Despite the emphasis on opening-night free admission for the workers and the democratic seating, an important architectural change was made by Goebbels: loges were built in the theatre for himself, Hitler, and other notables to use.

The critics raved about the setting by Benno von Arent, especially the scene in the Bohemian Forest (described as "a fantastic view," with trees in the foreground and peaks of trees in the background) and the scene by the Danube, which was enhanced by shafts of brown, yellow, and green lighting.[31] There were excellent mass scenes with a large number of actors. In the leading role of Karl Moor, Heinrich George was praised by all the critics, and the ensemble received great praise as well.[32]

The play, the staging, the direction, and the acting all achieved what Goebbels desired: the audience fell directly under the spell of the presentation and individuals united to become a connected mass. An anonymous critic said that the workers became a community with the same ideas and goals. He believed this was brought about because the actors were capable of drawing the audience in to feel it had experienced all that the characters had experienced in the play.[33] Erich Krafft noted that the actors often used the side stages for monologues and to make direct contact with the audience.[34] Heinz von Lichberg, the critic for the Party's newspaper, *Der völkische Beobachter*, concluded his review by noting the "colossal effect" that moved from the stage to the audience, enchanting the viewers continuously.[35] The opening was an immense success for the company and a personal success for Dr. Goebbels, as several critics noted. Other important figures in the Nazi regime, including Hitler's Deputy, Rudolph Hess, and Head of the DAF, Robert Ley, were in attendance. At the conclusion of the play, "the size of the audience response [shouts and applause] paralleled the size of the enormous theatre."[36]

Another major success opened in September 1934. This was an enchanting production of *A Midsummer Night's Dream*, directed by Walther Brügmann. Critics agreed that Brügmann's direction was highly successful and that he "played with the whole room." The magical, exotic quality of the architecture was mirrored in the scenery of the play and the style of the production. A path on the left went out along the auditorium and was used by the aristocratic characters in Athens, while the mechanicals danced along a similar path on the right. The action was enhanced by enchanting elves and fairies who danced several times.[37]

Again, Benno von Arent made full use of the technical facilities of the theatre, the dramatic lighting, and particularly the revolving stage.[38] "When Hermia made her flight, the stage turned 360 degrees, whereby continuously new surprising prospects appeared: bats, frogs, and strange trees gave a sense of a refined fairy-tale type of decoration." Actors costumed as mushrooms and other plants moved about, and all was a "many-colored, intoxicating" presentation—"Shakespeare as revue."[39] At the end of the production there was massive cheering for all the actors, of whom Paul Wagner was most impressive as Theseus. One reviewer suggested that the director and designer had succeeded in enchanting the audience so that their eyes were as dazzled and mystified as those of the characters in the play.[40] Another concluded that the Theater des Volkes was at the beginning of a long run of lively, beautiful evenings.[41]

Although all the critics expressed admiration for the production, several expressed concern that perhaps the director was in danger of pandering to the taste of the audience. All agreed it was beautifully designed and performed but that in appealing to a mass audience, it appealed to the lower type of taste for *Variété*. One critic began by noting two important needs of the Theater des Volkes: artistic success and "winning over the common people [*Volksgenossen*—the ideologically faithful] who previously had little connection with the institution of theatre."[42] Another noted that the program carried the phrase *Volksgenossen, Dein Theater* (Comrades, your theatre), emphasizing the point that it was the theatre of the ordinary man (who was committed to the new government).[43] The implication in the reviews was that in attempting to appeal to common, unsophisticated theatregoers, Brügmann had moved in the direction of kitsch.

Although the Theater der Nation was an ensemble company with many excellent actors, several of the plays were selected as vehicles for the powerful, large-scale actor Heinrich George (1893–1946). His acting style was appropriate for such a large theatre space. He was an early champion of Expressionism, acting in Kokoschka's plays and later working with Fehling and Piscator. He appeared in many theatres and was particularly notable as Falstaff in all three of Shakespeare's plays with that character.[44] His successful performances at the Theater des Volkes led to one of its major theatrical events, in the celebration of Schiller's 175th birthday, 10 November 1934. Schiller's *Wallenstein* trilogy was performed in two parts, beginning at 3:00 in the afternoon, with a one-hour dinner pause, and concluding at 10:30 at night. The director of this monumental theatrical performance was Dr. Richard Weichert, whose production of Hasenclever's *Der Sohn* (1916) at the Mannheim National Theatre in 1918 "set the style for Expressionistic productions: stylized set, emphasis on lighting, and use of follow lights."[45] *Wallenstein* called up an emotional response to the German poet much praised by Dr. Goebbels and to the subject matter.

As was usual in the productions in this theatre, a full orchestra performed music composed for the production. As part of the mass event, Weichert included a number of folk dances. He was praised for carrying out the production on a large scale and going to the limit with the staging.

Designer Eduard Sturm created a simple but powerful setting with Jessner-like broad steps, giant columns, and a sky filled with stars, which were appropriate for the "great spirit of the poet."[46] One of the many settings featured a dimly lit room with a view of the landscape on the right and a giant tent-like covering on the left. The stage was filled with soldiers, aristocrats, and peasants in seventeenth-century costumes. Reviewer Herbert Pfeiffer remarked that in order to take in all the action, the spectator had to turn his head 70 degrees. In one scene, George, as Wallenstein, stood watching on a side stage as the revolving stage turned, changing the scene from a hall to a landscape of ruins with broken columns and a "wonderful, mysterious, darkened sky."[47] The play began on a quiet note with a prologue delivered directly to the audience by the excellent actor Karl Zander. It ended with Wallenstein contemplating his death, walking alone "between giant columns into a grey background, from power to nothingness"; the dramatic death scene took place at the top of the flight of stairs.[48]

The role of Wallenstein is one of the greatest characters of dramatic literature, and both the characterization and the long performance were a great challenge to an actor. George was apparently staggering in his power, his vitality, his changes in mood, and the great use of his voice and gestures. His voice could fill the giant theatre with a roar or, when it sank, to a whisper, as he pointed to the stars. His was a larger-than-life portrayal and was complemented by similar outstanding performances by Paul Wagner and others in the ensemble. Pfeiffer noted at two points in his long review that nuances were missing.[49] Given the heroic style of the acting and the size of the house, that lack of nuance was not only inevitable, but purposeful. In *The Merry Wives of Windsor* George would be described as "grotesquely comic." The style of the plays in this period and space, then, was not naturalistic but borrowed some of the highly theatrical qualities of Expressionistic acting and staging.

The critics gave praise to the Propaganda Ministry and the DAF, under whose auspices "the Theater des Volkes has undertaken the most difficult task of this Schiller-Year, and has scored a great success."[50] Anton Dietzenschmidt called the production "a truly worthwhile, serious Schiller celebration with the full use of all the arts and all the [technical] means."[51] The evening ended in a spirit true to the Theater des Volkes. Not only were the actors on stage, but so were the director, the conductor, the designers, the technicians, and even the ticket-takers to receive the cheers and "jubilant thanks of the full house for the monumental presentation of the work of a powerful playwright."[52] Subsequent performances, into 1935, alternated *Wallensteins Lager/Piccolimini* with *Wallensteins Tod*.

In February 1935, Walter Brügmann directed another successful production, *The Merry Wives of Windsor*, with George in his immensely popular role of Falstaff. Many of the productions at the Theater des Volkes were very long, prompting some critics to remark that if the theatre was designed to help the workers, perhaps it should not keep them up so late. This production was four hours long and filled with spectacle. Twice two big crowds of men roared and stomped across the wide stage in search of Falstaff. Ludwig Hornsteiner's settings and designs pleased everyone. His Windsor was a *bürgerlich* English town with houses, narrow streets, a park with trees merrily suspended from a gridiron, a beautiful moon that rose behind them, cocks crowing, a dog barking, and a marvelous mummery with characters in fantastic, grotesque costumes.[53] Herbert Ihering began his review by noting the inherently interesting quality of the theatre and the possibilities for staging such a comedy in it. He went on to say that the production of a comedy here in this large theatre must be very clear and lightly handled.[54] Other critics commented on the style as broad and revue-like, as was Brügmann's *Midsummer Night's Dream*. Again, there seems to have been an effort to play simply and rather broadly for the mass in this great theatre. Another critic suggested that the size of the theatre had encouraged the director to summary characterizations.[55]

Ihering and others noted that the 1929 translation by Hans Rothe (made for Reinhardt's Deutsches Theater) was too modern, and that he altered the play too much. Almost everything else was highly praised, including the music, based on old airs. Paragraphs were devoted to describing how funny Heinrich George was as the fat knight: he was funny just walking on stage. In fact, his entrances were enhanced by Hornsteiner's setting, which featured narrow doors, difficult for Falstaff to maneuver. Despite his weight, "he played with bright humor and drollery and dancingly, as on a seesaw, moved from one adventure to another."[56] George's great voice blared like a trumpet to the last rows of the "stalactite cave," and he was at his comic best when emerging from the laundry basket and escaping disguised as a woman. He was a positive danger to the audience: people might fall into fits from laughing so much.[57] Ihering said it was so wonderful to see him in this role that he would like to see him in the two Henry plays as well. George clearly dominated the play, but Paul Wagner and others were also praised for fine acting.

The merry wives, it was noted, were not merry enough. This was not the first time that a few actresses had been criticized (and it is interesting that the critics dared to do it!) as being weaker than the men. Goebbels was a noted womanizer, and Poche and Ludwig wrote that he had taken some women from the demimonde and turned them into starlets.[58] Despite the relative weakness of some of the actresses, the play was a hit. It was "a full beaker of humor foaming with mirth and spirits."[59] Goebbels was observed enjoying the production in his loge with a great Falstaff of earlier times, Werner Krauß, who had appeared in Reinhardt's 1929 production of *The Merry Wives* (at the Deutsches Theater).

The production of Ibsen's *Peer Gynt* (in the 1912 nationalist adaptation by Dietrich Eckart) in March 1936 was connected directly to the overall plans of the KdF. Part of its program was enriching the lives of the workers so they would feel a part of the society and support the government, as opposed to agitating against it. To do this, the KdF arranged elaborate, affordable travel tours. Many workers had traveled little, even within Germany, and now the KdF made trips to Italy and other countries possible. One of the larger efforts of the KdF was to order the construction of a cruise ship (named the *Kraft durch Freude*) that would take workers to see the Nordic beauty of Scandinavia. So when *Peer Gynt* opened, the critic Dietzenschmidt began his review by noting that the beautiful scenery of the play would remind the hundreds of spectators of the fairy-tale beauty of Norway that they had seen on their KdF vacations, and that hundreds more would now want to take such a cruise. He concluded by saying that the presentation brought many thousands of spectators closer to the fantasy-laden play.[60]

Hornsteiner and Brügmann had worked together to create a production that seemed a perfect complement to the architecture of the Theater des Volkes and that utilized its facilities in an imaginative way. Accompanied by Grieg's music, the ten Ibsen-Eckart scenes were presented to the audience with dances to bridge the changes. The lighting, as usual, was very important. The critic Gerhard Weise wrote that it created a mood, both during and between the scenes, of darkness, mystery, and fantasy, which emphasized an allegorical quality. He also spoke of an "oriental richness of the scenery, and the exotic quality of the costumes in some scenes in contrast to the beautifully colored traditional folk costumes in the Norwegian scenes."[61] These folk costumes, naturally, called up the feeling of national pride exhibited in ordinary life by the wearing of the *Tracht* (folk costume).

The scenes that particularly impressed the critics were the "brain-destroying picture of the madhouse," with swirling and flashing lights; a ship that moved across the wide stage through a storm and overwhelming waves and finally exploded; Solveig's mountain hut with its light shining through a scene covered with snow; and the play of light and color as Peer returned to his homeland. The Troll King's realm was a fantastic nightmare calling up memories of E. T. A. Hoffmann's tales.[62] "The appearance of the Dover palace in the fairy-tale grotto created a fantastic-romantic ghostliness which the supernatural Troll world swirled about in raving fury; an intoxicated ecstasy of color, bodies, masks—an insane bacchanal."[63] Many other effects captured the fancy of critics and audiences: the end of the bacchanal was enhanced by the voice of the Troll King being broadcast throughout the audience by loudspeakers. (This was an unfamiliar technique at the time, and credit on the program was given to the Siemens Company.) The Boyg (the *Krumme* in Germany) always presents a challenge to designers. Hornsteiner solved it by showing only "two giant goggle-eyes which glowed forth through the mountain forest like a dazzling picture in a children's book."64

The cast was enormous. When the farm girls danced around the bride, they encircled the whole stage. The acting, dancing, and singing were praised without exception. Unlike many present-day productions featuring several actors in the role of Peer, a single actor, Herbert Hübner, played the role. Gerhart Weise called him a Peer Gynt "of flesh and blood—laughing, crying, shouting, loving, hating, dancing, raving—in a Life Dance and a Death Dance, alternately robust and pale, and dazzling and gloomy."65 Another critic said he enchanted the giant audience and never lost a syllable. He played the young Peer with a charming naiveté and then, with an outstanding actor's craft, was convincing as the aged wanderer returning home.66

Ibsen had long enjoyed popularity in Germany, and this play, known as the *Nordisches "Faust,"* was dear to German hearts. The 1912 free translation by the anti-Semitic poet Dietrich Eckart altered Ibsen's play considerably and thereby appealed to the nationalism fostered by the Nazis.67 The play itself successfully drew the audience into that unified state that Goebbels desired. This was particularly noted in the scene in which Aase dies: "When the curtain closed noislessly, not only had Peer Gynt's mother died, there was no one in the audience who did not have the memory of a final farewell of a loved one."68 When the play ended, "the spectators, having traveled through this colorful world, felt themselves elevated through each act to a kind of pious harmony. The solemn consecration of the poet pulled them upwards and the theatre became a temple—the highest achievement of dramatic art."69

It was mentioned by several critics that not only was this the perfect theatre for this production, but it was also the best use made of the theatre by this ensemble. Brügmann and his helpers "played with the giant apparatus of this giant theatre as has seldom been done before and created a wondrous fantasy."70 Weichardt spoke of the dream of theatre, the colorful magic, the journey into the soul of man that was realized because of the architecture and equipment of this theatre; of all theatres, the Theater des Volkes was the one capable of this success.71

Ironically, this was one of the last plays in the Theater des Volkes by the Theater der Nation. The acting ensemble was broken up and the actors moved to other theatres. Heinrich George went on to act in propaganda films for the Nazis and to play classical roles at the Volksbühne and the Schiller Theater. In 1937, dressed as Götz von Berlichingen, he was awarded a sword and given congratulations by the Führer and Dr. Goebbels in a celebration of his twenty-fifth year as an actor.72

Before the theatre was turned exclusively to the performance of operettas, there was a major cultural propaganda effort. This was in connection with the Berlin Olympics of 1936. *Freut Euch des Lebens* ("Enjoy Your Life") opened several months before the Olympics, on 30 April, and was performed while the city was filled with visitors for the athletic competitions. The revue was a *"KdF-Monsterschau"* (monster show) with staging by Benno von Arent, intended as a mirroring of happy German life, "a frolic of peace and a contented society."[73] This large-scale show was designed to unite the German public and to create a positive impact on the visitors from around the world. The music and dancing and the beautifully costumed, attractive performers impressed the visitors. This was an important propaganda effort by the Nazi Party.

From 1936 into the 1940s, the Theater des Volkes became the home of operetta, chiefly under the direction of Rudolf Zindler. There was a belief in this period that the operetta was a valid art form. Furthermore, it was noted that operetta could lead the uninitiated to an appreciation of opera.[74] The *Deutsches Bühnen-Jahrbuch* of 1943 pointed out that, after their hard day's work, hundreds of thousands of ordinary folk found pleasure sitting in the theatre waiting for the curtain to rise on "a colorful, light-spirited world of merriment and melody" and went on to point out that bringing happiness to the workers was a task of military importance.[75] Earlier the goal at the theatre was to move the individuals in the audience to a sense of greatness and unity through the presentation of classics and performances reminding them of the traditions of German literature. Now the idea was to keep the audiences supporting the government, but to do it by presenting light, sentimental, traditional operettas that pictured life as it was in the good old days in Germany and would be again in the future. Here were blonde, blue-eyed Aryans (often in traditional folk costumes, the maidens with long braids) falling in love and finding happiness. The romantic and exotic settings and subject matter were selected to take the people's minds off problems in German society. Audiences were treated to the likes of *Eine Nacht in Venedig* ("A Night in Venice" by Zell and Genée, 1936), *Hofball im Schönbrunn* ("Court Ball in Schönbrunn Palace" by Peplächs, 1937), and *Hochzeit in Samarkand* ("Wedding in Samarkand" by Künneke and Kessler, 1938).

Architecturally, the theatre was also changed. What had been useful in creating the magical, mythic quality of the classics was not particularly appropriate to the operettas. It was finally decided that Poelzig's stalactite columns and dome were degenerate art and should be destroyed, so in 1938 Poelzig's monumental decoration was torn out in fifty-eight days.[76] In the war, as Berlin was bombed, the Theater des Volkes was partially destroyed. Like all the other theatres, it was closed in September 1944. After the war, it was restored almost immediately and put into use as the Friedrichstadt Palast until it was torn down in 1984.

The long history of the Großes Schauspielhaus is not easy to trace, because many of the documents relating to it were destroyed in the war and people in Germany are not eager to bring forth material about a period that brought shame to the country. The documents that still exist reveal the highly successful effort to make the theatre a part of a gigantic propaganda effort that utilized and controlled all of the arts. Because of its size, technical facilities, and architectural design, the Großes Schauspielhaus was particularly useful to Goebbels. The audience was encouraged to identify with the production, the traditions of German literature, and the motifs of glory, heroism, sacrifice, and love. The interaction between the audience and the stage was enhanced by the proximity of the audience to the actors, the use of direct address, and, on at least one occasion, the use of loudspeakers. In several of the plays there was an additional element of interaction of audience and actors: members of Hitler Youth groups acted as extras in the productions.

No doubt the reviewers were inclined to accentuate the positive in their critiques of plays closely allied to the Nazi Party. But even allowing for fulsome praise, the reviews indicate that the productions were successful in achieving the aims of the Minister of Enlightenment and Propaganda in elevating and uniting the audience in a mystical union. Adjectives such as *enchanting, intoxicating, monumental, massive, fantastic*, and *ecstatic* occur and re-occur in reviews as well as phrases such as "the great traditions of Germany's past" and "the soul of the German people." The presentation of plays by Schiller and Goethe made another appeal to German patriotism. The Theater des Volkes was an important factor in the culture of Nazi Berlin. In her *Theaterpolitik in faschistischen Deutschland*, Jutta Wardetzky commented, "Hitler, like Goebbels, spoke of the 'Art of Propaganda.' In it they saw a creative instrument for achieving power and later as a means of stabilizing and enlarging it. They always spoke of their resolution to use every means [including theatre] 'to bring the masses to their political viewpoint.' "77 Goebbels had the power, the cunning, and the imagination to use the Theater des Volkes as one of these means.

NOTES

1. Wolfgang Carlé and Heinrich Martens, "Berlin am Zirkus 1; Eine Geschichte des Friedrichstadt-Palastes," *BZ am Abend*, no. 24 (Jan.–Feb. 1976): n.p.; clipping file, Berlin Akademie der Künste.

2. Klaus Poche and Hans Ludwig, "Von der Markthalle zum Weltstadtvarieté," no. 7 (n. d.): 38; clipping file, Berlin Akademie der Künste.

3. Poche and Ludwig, "Markthalle," 38.

4. Carlé and Martens, "Berlin," no. 19: n. p.

5. John Willett, *Theatre of the Weimar Republic* (New York, 1988): 64. (The *Oresteia* opened 29 November 1919 for 73 performances. The cast configuration Willett describes was available only for a few of the performances. Reinhardt typically stacked his Berlin premieres with stars from his multi-theatre company. Replacements in central roles, drawn from less-seasoned members of the company—some subsequently famous—would come as early as the second perform-

ance. Reviews of the *Oresteia* premiere lauded a configuration never seen there again: the actors playing Agamemnon, Cassandra, and Aegisthus were replaced the second evening, Moissi was replaced 5 December (by Ernst Deutsch), Straub on 10 December (by Auguste Pünkösdy). Gustav Czimeg was the original Agamemnon, replaced by Krauß the second night (he was subsequently replaced in January by Walter Redlich). At a Reinhardt theatre, audiences seldom saw the brilliant actor configuration touted in the reviews.—Ed.

6. Reinhardt was forced by financial difficulties to sell the Großes Schauspielhaus to Alfred and Fritz Rotter in 1931.

7. Jutta Wardetzky, *Theaterpolitik im faschistischen Deutschland* (Berlin, 1983): 21.

8. Carlé and Martans, "Berlin," n. p.

9. Ibid.

10. Wolfgang Carlé, *Kinder wie die Zeit vergeht* (Berlin, 1987): 61.

11. Wardetzky, *Theaterpolitik*, 25.

12. Viktor Reimann, *Dr. Joseph Goebbels* (Munich, 1971): 216.

13. Wardetzky, *Theaterpolitik*, 19.

14. Ibid., 90.

15. Ibid., 24.

16. Ronald Smelser, *Robert Ley, Hitler's Labor Front Leader* (New York, 1988): 163.

17. Reimann, *Goebbels*, 210.

18. Smelser, *Ley*, 163.

19. Ibid., 161.

20. Ley in Ibid., 164.

21. Ibid., 210.

22. Laurence Van Zandt Moyer, "The *Kraft durch Freude* Movement in Nazi Germany: 1933–1939," Ph.D. diss. Northwestern, 1967: 3.

23. Smelser, *Ley*, 216.

24. Dieter Bartetzky, *Zwischen Zucht und Ekstase; zur Theatralik von NS-Architectur* (Berlin, 1985): 80.

25. Ibid., 82.

26. Ibid., 139.

27. Ibid., 139.

28. Wardetzky, *Theaterpolitik*, 16.

29. Erwin H. Rainalter, "Im Theater des Volkes 'Götz von Berlichingen,'" *Der völkische Beobachter* (Berlin), 21 Nov. 1935: 6.

30. Rolf Brandt, "'Die Räuber' im Theater der Nation," *Berliner Lokal-Anzeiger*, 19 Jan. 1934: n. p.

31. H. P., "'Die Räuber' im Großen Schauspielhaus," n. p., n. d.; clipping file, Berlin Akademie der Künste.

32. Heinz von Lichberg, "Eröffnung des Theaters der Nation in Berlin: 'Die Räuber' im Großen Schauspielhaus," *Der völkische Beobachter* (Berlin), 20 Jan. 1934: 9.

33. H. P., "Räuber," n. p.

34. Erich Krafft, "Das neue Theater des Volkes," n. p., 19 Jan. 1934; clipping file, Berlin Akademie der Künste.

35. Lichberg, "Eröffnung," 9.

36. Krafft, "Theater," n. p.
37. (Not surprisingly, the Theater des Volkes dropped the incidental music that had been traditional for German productions of the play since the mid-nineteenth century, that of Jewish composer Felix Mendelsohn-Bartholdy. New music by Edmund Nick was used for the 1934 premiere, but it was not received with the same enthusiasm as the staging. Music reviewer Fritz Stege complained Nick had been unable to capture the "magic of the forest." He also added—interestingly enough, considering the review was published in the *Völkischer Beobachter*—that Nick could have learned from Mendelsohn how to avoid "musical cuteness [*Geistreichelei*] or trivial salon style." Cf. Stege, "Die Bühnenmusik," *Der völkische Beobachter* (Berlin), 18 Sept. 1934: 5.—*Ed.*)
38. Anton Dietzenschmidt, "Eröffnung mit 'Ein Sommernachtstraum,' " n. p., 17 Sept. 1934; clipping file, Berlin Akademie der Künste.
39. Herbert Pfeiffer, "Eine Sommernachtstraum-Revue," *12-Uhr-Blatt* (Berlin), 17 Sept. 1934: n. p.
40. Ibid.
41. " 'Sommernachtstraum' im Theater des Volkes," n. p., 17 Sept. 1934; clipping file, Berlin Akademie der Künste.
42. Ibid.
43. Dietzenschmidt, "Eröffnung," n. p.
44. Henning Rischbieter, ed., *The Encyclopedia of World Theater* (New York, 1977): 114.
45. Ibid., 283.
46. C. W., " 'Wallenstein' im Theater des Volkes," n. p., 13 Nov. 1934; clipping file, Berlin Akademie der Künste.
47. Herbert Pfeiffer, "Wallenstein," *12-Uhr-Blatt* (Berlin), 12 Nov. 1934: n. p. The sky and the stars were important in the play because Wallenstein's actions are guided by the stars.
48. Ibid.
49. Ibid.
50. C. W., "Wallenstein," n. p.
51. Anton Dietzenschmidt, "'Wallenstein' im Theater des Volkes," n. p., 12 Nov. 1934; clipping file, Berlin Akademie der Künste.
52. C. W., "Wallenstein," n. p.
53. P. K., "Falstaff in Nöten," n. p., 4 Feb. 1935; clipping file, Berlin Akademie der Künste.
54. Herbert Ihering, "'Die lustigen Weiber von Windsor.' Theater des Volkes," n. p., 4 Feb. 1935; clipping file, Berlin Akademie der Künste.
55. J-r., "Die lustigen Weiber von Windsor," n. p., 5 Feb. 1935; clipping file, Berlin Akademie der Künste.
56. P. K., "Falstaff," n. p.
57. C. W., "Falstaff: Heinrich George," n. p., 5 Feb. 1935; clipping file, Berlin Akademie der Künste.
58. Poche and Ludwig, "Markthalle," 38.
59. C. W., "Falstaff," n. p.
60. Anton Dietzenschmidt, "'Peer Gynt' im Theater des Volkes," n. p., 6 March 1936; clipping file, Berlin Akademie der Künste.

61. Gerhart Weise, "Dietrich Eckarts 'Peer Gynt,'" *12–Uhr-Blatt* (Berlin), 6 March 1936: n. p.

62. Weichardt, "Peer Gynt," n. p., n.d.; clipping file, Berlin Akademie der Künste.

63. Ludwig Sternaux, "Irregang und Läuterung 'Peer Gynt' im Theater des Volkes," n. p., 6 March 1936; clipping file, Berlin Akademie der Künste.

64. Ibid.

65. Weise, "Dietrich," n. p.

66. Otto Ernst Hesse, "Großes Zaubertheater," *Berliner Zeitung am Mittag*, 6 March 1936: n. p.

67. (Eckart [1868–1923] had been an ideologic mentor to Adolf Hitler, who fondly remembered seeing *Peer Gynt* in Berlin with Eckart in 1921. The play adaptation was Eckart's greatest stage success, even before the Third Reich; See Chapter 9 of this book.—*Ed*).

68. Hesse, "Zaubertheater," n. p. It was not surprising that Goebbels wanted *Peer Gynt* performed. In addition to its propaganda value in the Eckart translation, the play had moved Goebbels immensely in 1925. He wrote in his diary, "Aase's death out of this world. I thought of my mother and could have wept." Joseph Goebbels, *The Early Goebbels Diaries, 1925–26*, ed. Helmut Heiber, tr. Oliver Watson (New York, 1963): 54.

69. Weichardt, "Peer Gynt," n. p.

70. Hesse, "Zaubertheater," n. p.

71. Weichardt, "Peer Gynt," n. p.

72. Möhrke, "Götz von Berlichingen," n. p., n.d.; clipping file, Berlin Akademie der Künste.

73. Carlé and Martans, "Berlin," no. 40 (1976): n. p.

74. Wardetzky, *Theaterpolitik*, 18.

75. "Verpflichtung und Aufgabe der deutschen Theater," *Deutsches Bühnen-Jahrbuch* (Berlin, 1943): 1.

76. Carlé, *Kinder*, 92.

77. Wardetzky, *Theaterpolitik*, 16–17.

9

The First National Socialist Theatre Festival—Dresden 1934

Glen W. Gadberry

The Dresden Theatre Festival, 27 May–3 June 1934, was the first national stage assembly of the Third Reich. The annual showcase was created and promoted by the Ministry of Popular Enlightenment and Propaganda through its subordinate theatre offices. It was to celebrate sixteen months of cultural rule and the first full season under the swastika. Its meetings and speeches helped shape the theatre for years to come, as did its performances: nine plays and eight operas graced the stages of the Saxon capital. The festival repertoire informed but did not oblige German producers as they prepared their 1934–35 season. It glorified the new National Socialist theatre spirit but offered a rather conventional dramatic configuration.

The Dresden Festival highlighted performance, but producers had not come to be entertained by the best Saxony could offer (all performances but one were by Dresden companies—see the festival schedule, below). They were much more interested in the official pronouncements of Reichsminister Dr. Joseph Goebbels (1897–1945). In the weeks and months before the festival, the Minister had reasserted his vision of theatre and its place in society. Dresden was the first opportunity to endorse his cultural agenda, with little room for compromise.

Within the context of 1934, the Dresden Festival may be viewed as a celebration of the importance and power of the stage and of the Propaganda Ministry. The arts were particularly dear to the Third Reich. Hitler felt he had been denied an artistic career by German destiny and thereafter let his aesthetics shape German art and politics.¹ His artistic prejudices were implemented by Goebbels and in a different manner by Alfred Rosenberg (1893–1946). In these first years of Nazi Germany, Goebbels and Rosenberg were the principal cultural rivals, with no love lost between them. They maneuvered against each other for dominance while trying to stretch Hitler's aesthetic range.² All three agreed that the arts were vital to the health of the nation and that under the Weimar Republic the arts—and particularly the theatre—had abused and lost the support of Germany's racially unified people (*das Volk*). Now in power, the Party would restore the intimate *völkisch* bond. "Non-Aryans," Communists, and decadent modernists would be removed from German stages. Objectionable forms of the late nineteenth and early twentieth centuries would be suppressed or reshaped. German classics and carefully selected international plays would still be performed: Schiller and Shakespeare (a "true Germanic playwright") remained in the repertoire while the government encouraged wholesome and heroic German themes in a new drama of *Volk* community. The new Nazi art would be hard, "manly," non-sentimental: it would be "steel-hard romantic" (Goebbels), or "heroically objective" (Rosenberg's aide, Thilo von Trotha).³ There would be a cultural renaissance consistent with Hitler's National Socialism, controlled from above.

The national arts agenda required central bureaucracy, and by the end of 1933 regulatory agencies were in place: Goebbels headed the Propaganda Ministry (March) and Culture Chambers (September) and had created the office of National Dramaturg (August). Rosenberg formed the arts advocacy Militant League for German Culture (1928) and a spectator organization, the National German Stage Alliance (April 1933); both were given special status by Hitler.⁴ Rosenberg was also editor of the Party newspaper, *Der völkische Beobachter*. Goebbels and Rosenberg had considerable opportunity to shape and influence the German stage, although lines of cultural authority were complicated. There was also the problem of other organizations (e.g., German labor's entertainment division, Strength Through Joy, formed 27 November 1933) and individuals (e.g., Prussian President Hermann Göring, who insisted on personally developing his own state theatres). But at the end of 1933, it seemed Goebbels had taken the lead in national cultural dominance.

In 1934, Rosenberg was given special authority over National Socialist ideology, over "content," which challenged Goebbels's authority over personnel. In New Year's telegrams to his top officials, published in the *Völkischer Beobachter*, Hitler congratulated Rosenberg for his long and successful fight for the ideas of the Party while he praised Goebbels for "ingenious propaganda" that won Berlin for the Third Reich.⁵ On 24 January, Rosenberg was given a new title: acting upon the motion of Robert Ley, Director of Party Organization and Head of the Labor Front, Hitler named Rosenberg "Führer's Designate for the Supervision of the Total

Intellectual and Ideological Education of the Nazi Party." Historians have observed that the title had little power and that it is inappropriate to regard Rosenberg as Third Reich Ideologue. But in 1934, the principals were unaware of those more carefully considered conclusions informed by hindsight.[6] Rosenberg found it appropriate to use the full title to authorize his activities and viewpoint. He could explore and expand pure National Socialist philosophy, while Goebbels, who was "merely" Minister of Propaganda, could publicize those ideas. Goebbels could look after arts memberships, paperwork, and the mundane operation of theatres, presses, and studios. Rosenberg thought himself the man with ideas and Goebbels the bureaucratic publicist.[7]

Goebbels responded aggressively; in the realm of theatre, he brought substantial changes to strengthen his position. The first Dresden Theatre Festival was planned at this critical time, and it was shaped by the subsequent actions of the Minister. One week after Rosenberg's appointment, Goebbels claimed he determined "Reich theatre politics" and hence his national censorship should replace local regulation. Ostensibly he wanted to eliminate inconsistency: it was illogical to have a play forbidden in one city and produced in another. In the future, state and local officials were to notify him in advance of their intention to censor (or allow) a play's production, so he could coordinate national policy.[8] The intrusion was paternal, but he was venturing into content and ideology, the recognized domain of Rosenberg.

On 12 February, Goebbels announced an agreement between his Culture Chambers and Robert Ley's Labor Front. Ley had nominated Rosenberg for Ideologue; Goebbels now pulled his arts workers out of Ley's national union and bound them to his own bureaucracy. There would be no split allegiance.[9] In April, he invited German producers to Berlin to discuss measures to bring theatre solely under the "hand of the Ministry." He designated three Berlin theatres to be the flagships of national policy and introduced their newly appointed directors: Count Bernhard Solms for the Volksbühne (previously associated with Piscator), Heinz Hilpert for the Deutsches Theater (Reinhardt) and Walter Brügmann for the Theater des Volkes (the former Großes Schauspielhaus of Reinhardt, now operated by Strength Through Joy). Goebbels promised to provide more specific guidelines for management, staff, and repertoire; they would be binding for Ministry theatres.[10]

At the start of May, Goebbels's Culture Chambers awarded prizes in film and literature; the arts audience was joined by Hitler, Göring, Hess, Funk, Frick, von Papen—everyone but Rosenberg and his fellow radicals—SS-Führer Heinrich Himmler, National Farm Führer R. Walter Darré, and Labor Chief Robert Ley. As featured speaker, Chamber President Goebbels reinforced the government's commitment to art as *"the most noble, spiritual expression of an era."* The state would continue *"to clear the way for the truly creative products of genius* and to keep that way unobstructed." But this did not mean "dictatorship over the arts. The Führer and all his co-workers think and feel too much like artists to believe that artistic process can be commanded with coercive measures." He then admitted current products had not fully achieved the political or aesthetic demands of the *Volk:* "everything great must have time to ripen; there is need for patience, so we can *truly* partake in greatness."[11] Goebbels would make this kind of apology several times during the next months and years, even at such an inopportune occasion as an awards ceremony.

While he critiqued artistic progress, he did not authorize others to do the same. After mundane governance had replaced the first rush of Nazi victory, there had been complaints: the revolution had not brought utopia or a better life fast enough (Rosenberg's radicalism contributed to this atmosphere). To protect the revolution and to smooth the way for more repressive measures, Goebbels launched a two-month campaign, rallies throughout Germany would discredit "defeatists and fault-finders, rumor mongers and do-nothings, saboteurs and agitators."[12] The technique is familiar: apparent problems are the products of critics, not of flaws in the system. One need only silence "fault-finders" and problems disappear. The Dresden Theatre Festival came mid-way in this campaign; producers were to endorse Goebbels's art policies as patriotic duty. Anything else would be interpreted as defeatism.

Ten days before the festival, Goebbels released the sweeping provisions he promised in April, published as the Unified Theatre Law.[13] Its interlocking measures seriously affected the structure and functioning of most German theatre. After coming to power, the government inherited subsidized state and city theatres; privately held companies (20% of the total, 41 of 205 in 1933–34) remained independent. Hereafter there would be no difference: all public performance spaces were German and hence subject to national racial and artistic aims. The Minister then added the usual reassurances: "Artistic freedom of theatre productions will not be altered in any way." Producers had only one obligation, to provide quality theatre, "conscious of national responsibility." Personnel would be bound to the producer in "faithful adherence" to achieve that political and artistic imperative. To ensure unity, Goebbels would appoint managers, producers, directors, choir masters, and head stage managers. Existing placements would remain in effect, but there was much to fear, especially in the previously private theatres.

As "chief Führer of the German theatre" (a considerable inflation of his title), Goebbels would also license theatres. Patents would be granted or withdrawn for "trust, artistic aptitude and economic capability"—allegiance to the Minister was more important than art or fiscal responsibility. The law also allowed him to move further into content. In January 1934 he had assumed avuncular intervention; now he could forbid or discontinue production of plays or operas which did not serve (his) artistic or national aims. Endorsed by Hitler, this "theatre law" allowed Goebbels to supervise text, space, and staff.

The only remaining subject of his sweep of German stage performance was the audience itself, and an additional proviso addressed Rosenberg and Ley's successes organizing audiences. The ideologic right found approved performances through Rosenberg's National German Stage Alliance, and German labor found regular amusement in Ley's Strength Through Joy. Because of the national importance of theatre and its inherent power over the *Volk*, the Ministry could intercede in such audience organizations (or in the performances of closed societies) if it "becomes important for the Reich"—an ominous phrase. In addition to cementing his own role in the theatres of the nation and challenging Rosenberg's authority over content, Goebbels could access the spectator and thereby weaken Rosenberg's power base.

As German producers examined the new theatre law, and just three days before Dresden, Goebbels calmed the theatre community.[14] *"In a National Socialist state too, art is the result of free vision."* But because theatre has such a "sweeping and powerful effect upon the *Volk*"—equal to the press, film and radio—it must serve the needs of the nation. Theatre would no longer turn its back on the *Volk*, as it had during the Weimar years. The government would continue to "safeguard the theatre"—presumably against the vagaries of the ticket office—"once a few inessential rights are cleared away." In a few months of political action endorsed by the Führer, Goebbels had centralized control, outmaneuvered Rosenberg, silenced critics, and tried to make everyone think it was all for the good of the theatre and the nation. Such was, of course, the genius of propaganda. The Dresden Theatre Festival, in part the annual assembly of German stage producers, attracted several thousand representatives of Germany's theatre scene. Goebbels had insured their interest and, from a distance, Rosenberg's as well.

Events on the Elbe—exhibits, concerts, speeches, public assemblies, and performances of opera and theatre—were coordinated by Goebbels's President of the Theatre Chamber, Otto Laubinger (1892–1935). The greatest and most frustrating question was whether Hitler would attend. At the last moment Hitler decided to come and, the day of the opening, to arrive by motorcade. There was a scramble to decorate the highway route through Saxony. Swastika banners were intermixed with ranks of freshly scrubbed Hitler Youth and Maids (HJ and BDM), "their faces lit by enthusiasm, full of faith," who stood along the last kilometers to the city limits. Some 58,000 SA and SS troops lined the route into the center of the city.[15] Hitler provided national glamour and authority to theatre, to Dresden, and especially to Goebbels's regulations.

Hitler remained for three days. He attended the opening ceremonies, which featured Goebbels's first major address and a performance of Wagner's *Tristan und Isolde*.[16] The next day he met with Richard Strauß, President of the Music Chamber, who had come to Dresden to attend *Rosenkavalier* and conduct *Arabella*. The last evening he went to a gala performance of *Peer Gynt*, in the 1912 adaptation by his mentor, Dietrich Eckart. Each day there were public appearances and tours of the city's sights—including the exhibit of decadent art at the Rathaus.[17] It was Hitler's first visit to Dresden since the Machtergreifung, and he basked in Saxon adoration and German art. But the visit was not a mere vacation from the cares of the capital: some historians believe Hitler came to Dresden to brief the Saxon military for the upcoming purge of the SA leadership, including Ernst Röhm and his personally selected officers. Hundreds of "old comrades" and Storm Troopers would die during the "Night of Long Knives" (30 June 1934) or in subsequent show trials. The Theatre Festival allowed Hitler to mix business with pleasure.

Goebbels opened the event with his speech *Triumph Richard Wagners*; it was broadcast to the nation, along with the first act of *Tristan*.[18] It was a superb opportunity to publicize his directions for the German stage. After Hitler's entry into the Semper Opera House, in white tie and tails, the curtain opened to reveal Goebbels, similarly garbed, standing before a huge silver Nazi eagle. In this way the Minister was spared the embarrassment of limping to the podium; a pause after the speech covered his exit. Because of the imminent performance and Hitler's preferences, Goebbels would close with praise for Wagner, whose "eternal art" had towered above the "grumbling know-it-all-better attitudes" of his contemporaries. That is, Wagner had triumphed over the same kind of "rumor mongers and agitators" who were being discredited in the Minister's two-month propaganda campaign. His music "surpassed all the pretentious, untalented, near gut-wrenching banalities of modern atonality!" Wagner was the Hitler-Goebbels ideal German genius to open and close the festival opera schedule, with *Tristan* and *Meistersinger*.

Praise for Hitler's favorite composer was hardly unexpected; the assembly was more interested in Goebbels's other remarks. He stressed he was a man of action, rather than abstraction; he preferred "facts" to "ideology." By rejecting mere theory, he was sniping at Rosenberg, a notable absentee. But Goebbels had a nominal theoretical foundation: revolution was a "spiritual act" which "forces everything into its circuit." Art and theatre were not exempt—the revolutionary "rhythm also resounds audibly in the holy temple of the Muses." The lofty phrasing and ideas were not new, but now justified the repressive, two-week-old theatre law. Once again he placated the professional: he was not going "to place art and artists under party-directed prior restraint"; the government would not "stifle creative genius" or interfere with "the organic growth of artistic endeavor." But it "had the political right and *also the spiritual duty* to bring art and artists into the correct relationship to each other and to the *Volk*." Once properly aligned, artists would "have full possibilities for active roles and for development." The message was clear and clever: there would be absolute and full artistic freedom, if the artist was fully and absolutely committed to Goebbels's National Socialism.

The Reichsminister then turned to familiar charges against "the liberal era of excessive individualism." The products of Weimar were merely "divertisements" or "at their best, interesting experiment." That was a liberal and bold remark, considering Hitler's blanket rejection of 1920s abstraction: Weimar "experiment" was never interesting and there was nothing that might be called the "best." But Goebbels recovered. The Nazis had "cleared away" that disorder, "so distant from true artistry." He would be more explicit four days later.

Goebbels then addressed another aspect of order and unity when he insisted "National Socialism *recognized only one German art, which is no longer bound to city and state borders.* Its concern is German theatre, not the special interest of Prussia, Bavaria or Württemberg; its concern is exclusively the *German character in its totality.*" It was an important restriction, particularly for German history plays—which had been given special favor by the Reichsdramaturg—because so much of German history recorded intra-German strife.[19] In the context of 1934, Goebbels might have been challenging Göring's assumption of cultural preeminence in Prussia, but more likely he was referring to Rosenberg. Goebbels must have known Rosenberg consecrated the premiere of one such play that day, August Hinrichs's *Die Stedinge; Spiel vom Untergang eines Volkes* ("The Stedingers; Play of the Destruction of a People"). The festival play recounted a brutal thirteenth-century massacre of German peasant Volk by an invading German army.[20] It was just the sort of work that fueled district strife, disrupting the Nazi ideals of Volksgemeinschaft and "One Volk, One Reich, and One Führer."

Goebbels closed with his obligatory laudatory on Wagner, and the Dresden opera company then performed *Tristan*. That was Sunday evening, 27 May; on the afternoon of the thirty-first, after four days of meetings and performances, the theatre audience reassembled for Goebbels's second speech, *Das deutsche Theater im neuen Reich.*[21] It was not broadcast, but the text was carried in the press. Hitler had already returned to Berlin. The session opened with the heroic romanticism of Beethoven's Overture to *Egmont* and closed with Wagner's Prelude to *Die Meistersinger*.

The Reichsminister restated much of what he had said on Sunday. Once again he dismissed the "reactionary" (meaning Rosenberg) in favor of artists who "rush in advance of the times." Yet he was not endorsing Weimar-era freedom, when "theatre had only been of concern to the police or fire department." On the twenty-seventh he said the "best" Weimar experiments were "interesting," but now *"theater will no longer be a laboratory."*[22] He left such works to displays of "decadent art." But what of the first Nazi dramatic experiments, written since the 1920s and now flooding

Nazi Central Publishing? Standing before these "fellow artists," as he had in May, he critiqued current playwriting. He commiserated with producers, because "there were no modern plays [of quality] available." In fact, he said, what had been written up to that point was the "most tedious kitsch [*ödester Kitsch*]. The ideas which stand behind the revolution have not as yet found their artistic form." It was a generally understood but not overtly uttered truth: Third Reich drama, was, at best, only on the threshhold of art. At his first National Theatre Festival, mid-way in his national campaign deriding negativism, Goebbels dismissed Nazi stage art.

It was easy to ridicule failure, but he was less clear about solutions: "We now await the new form. . . . The government can't be expected to lead the way for this new style. *That is the duty of genius.*" Faith in future genius would not help working playwrights, but he did offer prototype. On the twenty-seventh he praised Wagner, performed immediately thereafter, as an implied model for contemporary opera; on the thirtieth, he hailed the German classics and particularly Schiller, performed that evening. "Schiller stands closer to us today than the majority of modernist big-mouths" because he achieved a satisfying union of revolutionary sentiment and controlled form. "With thanks and reverence we bow to the classical authors as the great masters, the vanguard."

Waves of applause capped the Reichsminister's final remarks. "We unite our deeds and creations in solemn promise: all our efforts will be dedicated to the greatest object German spirit can create on earth: noble German art." The theatre was now officially recharged by this Heidelberg Ph.D. with artistic pretension.[23] He admitted the first works of the Third Reich were not artistically significant, despite the promotional efforts of his own propagandists. Without Hitler in the house, he could even use *Kitsch* to describe them.[24] The effect was striking, as some of those new national playwrights, creators of the "most tedious kitsch," were in the Dresden Opera House. The Minister was not always sensitive to artistic ego.

The government had instructed producers to search for Nazi genius and promised unequivocal support if they looked in the right places. Goebbels wanted playwrights to immerse themselves in the Volk, combine Third Reich revolutionary sentiment with a Sturm und Drang and/or Weimar-classic form, as Nazi Schillers.[25] The directives were confusing. New combinations had been tried without apparent success. Goebbels would await artistic miracle and do all he could to silence critics, suppress radical experiment, attack reactionaries, honor half-efforts with national prizes, and revere the classics. "There can be no better advice for the producers and actors gathered here, who come along with us," he told his audience, "than to talk of noble striving for the future, but also to maintain honor and attention to the great past."

Goebbels returned to Berlin immediately after the speech, and that evening Schiller's *Wilhelm Tell* was produced on the Dresden Festival stage.

REICHSTHEATERFESTWOCHE
Dresden 27 May–3 June 1934

Date	Play	Opera
27 May	*Prinz von Homburg* Heinrich von Kleist	*Tristan und Isolde* Richard Wagner
28	*Kabale und Liebe* Friedrich von Schiller (Weimar Naional Theatre)	*Alkestis* Christoph Gluck
29	*Peer Gynt* Henrik Ibsen/Dietrich Eckart	*Der Rosenkavalier* Richard Strauß
30	*Die Freier* Joseph von Eichendorff/Georg Kiesau	*Julius Cäsar* Georg Friedrich Händel
31	*Wilhelm Tell* Friedrich von Schiller	*Arabella* Richard Strauß
1 June	*Coriolanus* William Shakespeare	*Oberon* Karl Maria von Weber
2	*Iphigenie auf Tauris* Johann von Goethe (matinee)	—
	Zar Peter Otto Erler	*Fidelio* Ludwig van Beethoven
3	*Die Endlose Straße** Sigmund Graff and Carl Hintze	*Die Meistersinger von Nürnberg* Richard Wagner
Performaces at the State Theatre or Hellerau Baroque stage (Goethe)		Performances at the State Opera or Hellerau (Gluck, Händel)

*Substitute for Erwin Guido Kolbenheyer's *Heroische Leidenschaften, die Tragödie des Giordano Bruno*.

Perhaps more clearly than ministerial rhetoric, the festival repertoire suggested Goebbels's preferred dramaturgic configuration. He certainly approved the performance schedule; ten days after the festival was announced (20 January 1934), he was in Dresden and met with the head of the Saxon theatres who coordinated the performances.[26] The festival plays, as planned and performed, infer the Goebbels Propaganda Ministry ideal stage aesthetic; they are worth looking at in greater detail.

What is most striking is the absence of Nazi drama. Eleven plays received special consideration: eight had been planned, a matinee was added, one play was replaced in March, and one was substituted during the festival. Eight of the eleven had been written prior to 1870: Shakespeare's *Coriolanus*

(1607–08), Goethe's *Götz von Berlichingen* (1773, replaced by Erler), Schiller's *Kabale und Liebe* (1784), Goethe's *Iphigenie auf Taurus* (1787, added as a matinee), Schiller's *Wilhelm Tell* (1804), Kleist's *Prinz von Homburg* (1821), Eichendorff's *Die Freier* (1833), and Ibsen's *Peer Gynt* (1867). The bulk of Third Reich festival plays had been written before the formation of the Second Reich.

The remaining three plays were written in the twentieth century, none during the Third Reich. Otto Erler's *Zar Peter* replaced *Götz von Berlichingen*. Erler was a Dresden Gymnasium professor and Dramaturg. His historic tragedy premiered in Dresden in 1905; it examines father-son conflict and the issue of succession in the house of Peter the Great. The only twentieth-century play in the original schedule was Erwin Guido Kolbenheyer's *Heroische Leidenschaften, die Tragödie des Giordano Bruno* ("Heroic Passions, the Tragedy of Giordano Bruno," premiere Düsseldorf 1928). It was a revision of the playwright's first play, *Giordano Bruno, Tragödie der Renaissance* of 1902–3. At the last moment Friedrich Lindner (Bruno) took ill and the performance was cancelled; *Die endlose Straße* ("The Endless Highway," 1926) by Sigmund Graff and Carl Hintze, was transferred from the Dresden repertoire, where it had opened in March. The most modern play performed at the festival was there by accident, and in many ways *Endlose Straße* was atypical. It was more of a Weimar experiment than National Socialist drama (see Chapter 4).

Where was contemporary Nazi drama for this first theatre festival of the Third Reich? Although the government was only sixteen months old, there was a quantity of new scripts—four hundred premiered since the Machtergreifung and hundreds were being written and published.[27] But no new plays were produced, presumably because Goebbels thought them all the "most tedious kitsch." For the moment, the Goebbels stage would stay with a traditional, practically nineteenth-century repertoire: Kleist, Schiller, Goethe, with Shakespeare and early Ibsen thrown in as Anglo-Saxon-Nordic brothers. Twentieth-century plays were represented, but they were only remotely National Socialist.

With the possible exception of *Endlose Straße*, the most radical offering of the festival was the 1912 "free adaptation" of Ibsen's *Peer Gynt* by Dietrich Eckart (1868–1923). Augmenting his career as poet and playwright, Eckart had edited the anti-Semitic *Weekly for Order and Justice* (*Auf gut deutsch!* 1919–21), which was rolled over into the Nazi Party organ, *Der völkische Beobachter*. Just months before his death, Eckart was replaced as editor by his friend and protégé, Alfred Rosenberg.[28] Eckart "exercised the greatest influence on Adolf Hitler in the immediate postwar years."[29] Hitler lauded Eckart as ideologic mentor and dedicated the second book of *Mein Kampf*, as well as a number of buildings and monuments, to his memory. In 1942, Hitler fondly remembered seeing the *Peer Gynt* adaptation in Berlin with Eckart in 1921.[30] *Peer Gynt* was the only play Hitler saw at the festival, in the company of Goebbels.

While Eckart's other plays only found their audiences after 1933, the Ibsen adaptation had been an immediate success. It premiered at Berlin's Königliches Schauspielhaus in February 1914 and received one hundred performances in the next two years; most German theatres produced *Peer Gynt* in the Eckart version. In an essay on the adaptation, Rosenberg complained that Jewish directors took advantage of the work's success with "real" Germans.³¹ *Peer Gynt* was an expression of the reactionary, Nordic-Teutonic, Eckart-Hitler-Rosenberg aesthetic, which vied for dominance in the Third Reich with the vision of Joseph Goebbels.

Ibsen's visionary play, with its thirty-nine scenes and more than thirty-five sets, was not actually intended for the stage. It was to be read as "a long dramatic poem."³² Eckart wanted a stageable version suitable for twentieth-century German audiences; he retained fifty-six roles (plus extras) but reduced the play to ten scenes and eight sets. According to Eckart commentator David E. R. George, the adaptation stressed "Eckart's own racist feelings. . . . This was achieved by presenting the Jews as the epitome of materialism."³³ But text and production history do not seem to support that darker interpretation, which relies upon Eckart's later anti-Semitism.³⁴ George Mosse put the play into better focus: Peer "became, in Eckart's hands, a simple, just, and genuine man struggling for salvation and giving himself to the cosmic spirit. . . . What emerged was the model for a Volk hero who alone, according to Volkish ideology, could shatter the complex of contemporary society."³⁵ As a "Nordic" play, Ibsen's *Peer* appealed to the Third Reich; as a patriotic Volk play, Eckart's adaptation appealed to Nazi ideology and especially to Nordic supremacist Alfred Rosenberg.

According to the *Frankfurter Zeitung* the Ibsen-Eckart *Peer* was quite unlike the festival's more mundane slate of classics.³⁶ A "Germanic current" flowed through the gala that was altogether alien to Goebbels's theatre aesthetic. Reviews in the Munich and Berlin editions of the Eckart-Rosenberg *Völkischer Beobachter* were filled with *völkisch* slogans. The Munich critic wrote that the Ibsen-Eckart "Nordic stance" allowed Peer to transcend the "demonic powers in life." Peer replaced the torments of liberal individualism with a comforting *Volksgemeinschaft*. Instead of being "enough unto himself alone," Peer achieved *völkisch* redemption.³⁷ The Berlin reviewer, conjuring the authority of Rosenberg and his "master work," the *Myth of the Twentieth Century,* concluded that *Peer* showed "how decisive Nordic blood was, especially for the form of German life and German writing." This kind of "Nordic thinking and Nordic racial purity" were Eckart-Rosenberg solutions to contemporary problems.³⁸ Ibsen had been brought into radical Nazi Germany by Eckart's nationalism and by Hitler-Rosenberg's "Nordic" perceptions.

Why was it included at all in Goebbels's festival? Certainly it was a play Hitler admired in the adaptation of an early and respected mentor. It bore some of the mythic power of Wagner's music dramas when staged with

Edvard Grieg's musical score (all German versions used the *Peer Gynt Suite*). It spoke to that side of Hitler which worshipped Teutonism at Wagner's "mystic chasm" at Bayreuth and empowered Rosenberg as Ideologue. The production also happened to be the premiere of the adaptation in the city that had been Ibsen's home between 1869 and 1875. And Peer had been one of Otto Laubinger's early acting triumphs. The combination of overdue local premiere, honor to Eckart, deference to Laubinger, and reverence for Hitler certainly offset any objection by Goebbels. Because there was a separate opera performance schedule, the Minister probably planned on *Der Rosenkavalier* with Richard Strauß. But when Hitler decided to stay a third day, Goebbels joined the Führer for an evening of Ibsen-Eckart, Rosenberg-Nordic-Aryan *Mythos* in the (physical) absence and (ideological) presence of the Führer's Designate. "The performance, which began with thundering jubilation for the Führer, ended with respectful silence for Dietrich Eckart, the dead comrade of Adolf Hitler, who will live forever as the first poet of National Socialist Germany." "When the rapt audience finally responded, a triumphant feeling of newly-won *Volk* community burst forth over Führer and *Volk*, as a single flame of proud German consciousness."39 Hitler swept on stage to congratulate the actors and the director, the "old National Socialist," Rudolf Schröder. It could only have been an uncomfortable evening for Goebbels, who, after all, preferred the music to the text.40 Two days later, he attacked Third Reich kitsch and lauded Schiller as ideal playwright for the new Germany.

The festival closed with *Die endlose Straße*. The assembly returned to Germany's theatres to open summer productions and to prepare for the 1934–35 season under the watchful eyes of the Propaganda Ministry. While producers pondered the week's events and wondered how to recognize emergent Nazi genius, critics tried to give significance to the week-long cultural event. At the national level, Hans Knudsen praised the festival for clearly demonstrating the centrality of theatre to the cultural life of the Third Reich. Like Goebbels, he thought theatre could not be furthered by theory alone, but by "practical acts." Although all nine Dresden plays were the kind of " 'weekly schedule' which probably could not be maintained in the running repertoire" of a normal theatre, production of a select few would be "a marvelously encouraging example of what the German theatre can and must be." The classics were a solid foundation, but the government should continue to search for new playwrights. The classics should not become "the form for contemporary experience."41 There was also predictable praise from Goebbels's Reichsdramaturg Rainer Schlösser. The Minister's "directives laid the massive foundations of a new German spiritual life, in a surprisingly short amount of time. From its huge scale you can see and comprehend the future structure."42

A more vital response came from a Dresden reviewer. While he predictably hailed the festival as an event of international importance and the performances as a "mirror image of the German soul, a catechism of the German people, a text book of German duty," he thought the future of German theatre would be shaped by the broad theatre audience, as Hitler had urged. "Only when German theatre feels itself borne by new masses of spectators from all social levels, only then will it find the new style which speaks to the experience of our changing times"; only then could Goebbels's envisioned geniuses appear.[43] The future of Third Reich theatre depended upon the *Volk* as active spectators. This was also Rosenberg's view; as creator of a Party-sanctioned spectator organization, Rosenberg understood the centrality of a properly educated audience to theatre development. His recent efforts had been to bring the spectator to National Socialist ideas through affective performance. But try as he might to realize his policies, he was blocked by Goebbels's bureaucracies. The Dresden Theatre Festival and Goebbels's taunting speeches prompted Rosenberg's renewed efforts to shape German culture.

The day Schlösser's encomium was published and while the Reichsminister was fresh from his speeches in Dresden, Rosenberg complained in his diary that the opportunistic Goebbels had thrown together his organizations without regard to ideologic purity. Rosenberg objected to Goebbels naming

> old buddies of Jews as presidents, lawyers of the old red wing in influential positions, incapable "national socialists" [i.e., people who held important positions for political affiliation rather than talent or ability]. And here and there a few competent people who are dissatisfied with it all. And then Goebbels's speeches without content, in slippery style, evading all problems. It's hopeless. People put their hopes in *me*, but *in fact*, since a *National Socialist* is president of the Reich Culture Chamber, it's difficult to create other *party-level* organizations, *without* the Chamber, and especially if it's against it.[44]

The very next day, Rosenberg formalized a new organization to focus on the spectator, as the Dresden critic suggested. Rosenberg's Militant League for German Culture and million-member National German Stage Alliance merged with Robert Ley's Strength Through Joy to become the *NS-Kulturgemeinde* (National Socialist Cultural Community).[45] It was a national spectator organization for German workers that extended into every community and would be headed by a Rosenberg deputy, Walter Stang (1895–1945). Here was an opportunity to continue supervising the "total intellectual and ideological education of the Nazi Party," with access to thirty million worker/spectators. Through block sales and/or closed performances at reduced rates, Rosenberg hoped to influence the success (or failure) of any stage production, educate the workers, and serve his own ideology.[46] With great optimism, Rosenberg opened the first National Congress of the NS–Cultural Community in Eisenach a month later, having appropriated arrangements for the second assembly of the now-defunct National German Stage Alliance, 4–7 July 1934. The annual congresses became Rosenberg's counterpoints to Goebbels's National Theatre Festivals.

This organizational merger, solidifying Rosenberg's cultural authority, was the most significant cultural-political response to Goebbels's Dresden Festival. If the Reichsminister could control personnel and censorship, the Führer's Designate could influence spectators and, through them, the spread of ideas he endorsed. Goebbels would await dramatic genius to shape the legitimate stage and revive the classics in the interim. The Hitler-Goebbels art stage preferred heritage to ideology. By contrast, Rosenberg supported playwrights who argued "pure" National Socialist concepts, regardless of aesthetics. The Hitler-Rosenberg ideologic stage demanded the most recent in playwriting as a better expression of National Socialism than any play of the past, regardless of its national or international importance or interpretation put upon it in performance. Rosenberg advocated August Hinrichs and Hans Wilhelm over Schiller and Shakespeare; text and ideology were superior to theatre history and art.[47] His organization would educate the *Volk* to values the *Volk* ought to hold.

Hitler would ultimately reject both positions and endorse a theatre that served neither art nor ideology. His ideal theatre was more closely matched to broad spectator preference for entertainment, not Goebbels's classics or Rosenberg's ideologists. Privately, in 1938, Hitler remarked, "Performances must be 'illusion' for the masses. The little man knows only too well how serious life is. Because life is serious, his joys must be beautiful."[48] As Germany descended further into the Third Reich, a newly innocuous theatre resolved the Byzantine cultural strife in the house of Hitler. Newly empowered folk comedies and farces trivialized the German stage, despite the art productions at Goebbels's National Theatre Festivals or the ideologic productions at Rosenberg's Congresses of the National Socialist Cultural Community. Goebbels, the more flexible politician, embraced his Führer's preferences; Rosenberg was left to theorize greater glories to come.

NOTES

1. See Henry Grosshans *Hitler and the Artists* (New York, 1983). Hitler's art prejudices were well developed by the time he dictated *Mein Kampf* in 1924 and remained essentially the same over the next decades; cf. Adolf Hitler, *Mein Kampf*, ed. and tr. John Chamberlain, et al. (New York, 1939): 352–62, and Hitler's cultural address at Nürnberg, "Adolf Hitlers Rede auf der Kulturtagung der NSDAP. am 1. September [1933]," in *Die nationalsozialistische Revolution 1933*, ed. Axel Friedrichs (Berlin, 1935): 281–90.

2. Goebbels had sympathy for Expressionism, which Rosenberg (and Hitler) dismissed as an expression of spiritual madness. Rosenberg favored a more

"primitive," pre-Christian Teutonism. Both positions would be ridiculed by Hitler, notably at the 1934 and 1938 Nürnberg Party Congresses and at the opening of the House of German Art in 1937. See Robert A. Pois, "German Expressionism in the Plastic Arts and Naziism: A Confrontation of Idealists," *German Life and Letters*, 21, no. (April 1968): 204–14.

3. Joseph Goebbels, "Rede des Reichspropagandaministers Dr. Goebbels vor den deutschen Theaterleitern," in *Die nationalsozialistische Revolution 1933*, ed. Axel Friedrichs (Berlin 1938): 296. Thilo von Trotha, "Heroische Sachlichkeit: Gedanken über einen neuen Stil," *Der völkische Beobachter* (Berlin), 14 March 1934: 5. Trotha edited Rosenberg's speeches and essays and was a novelist (*Frauen*) and playwright in own right (*Engelbrecht* premiered 1937; *Gudrun*, 1938; and *Prinzessin Plumpudding*, 1938). He died in an auto accident in 1938 at age 29.

4. Hitler's deputy Rudolf Hess announced in the official *Völkischer Beobachter* that the Deutsche Bühne "was herewith recognized as the sole spectator organization for the Nazi Party" ("Der Kampfbund für Deutsche Kultur schafft die 'Deutsche Bühne,' " *Der völkische Beobachter* [Berlin], 16/17/18 April 1933: 1). The next month he made a similar announcement designating the Kampfbund "the sponsoring cultural organization for the Nazi Party" ("Anordnung," *Der völkische Beobachter* [Berlin], 28/29 May 1933: 2).

5. "Der Führer dankt seinen hervorragendsten Mitkämpfern," *Der völkische Beobachter* (Berlin), 2 Jan. 1934: 2.

6. The Nürnberg judges cited the title as evidence of Rosenberg's contributions to Nazi war crimes: Rosenberg's title became a hanging matter. See "Texts of Verdicts of the International Military Tribunal in Trial of German War Leaders," *New York Times*, 2 Oct. 1946: 22.

7. The right to determine ideology was not conferred at the time of appointment to Reichsminister, 13 March 1933, nor as a part of the "Duties of the Ministry," 30 June 1933: the office was to spread "enlightenment and propaganda within the population concerning the policy of the Reich government and the national reconstruction of the German Fatherland." It was not mandated to create policy. "Verordnung über die Aufgaben des Propagandaministeriums," in Axel Friedrichs, ed., *Die nationalsozialistische Revolution 1933* (Berlin, 1935): 280–81.

8. "Künftig einheitliche Regelung bei Verboten von Theateraufführungen," *Der völkische Beobachter* (Berlin), 31 Jan. 1934: 6.

9. "Eingliederung der RKK in die Deutsche Arbeitsfront," *Der völkische Beobachter* (Berlin), 13 Feb. 1934: 1.

10. "Theaterbesprechung bei Reichsminister Dr. Goebbels," *Der völkische Beobachter* (Berlin), 12 April 1934: 5.

11. "Die Festsitzung der Reichskulturkammer in der Staatsoper," *Der völkische Beobachter* (Berlin), 3 May 1934: 9.

12. "Große Propagandaaktion der N.S.D.A.P.," *Der völkische Beobachter* (Berlin), 4 May 1934: 1.

13. "Einheitliches Theaterrecht," *Der völkische Beobachter* (Berlin), 17 May 1934: 8.

14. "'Kunst darf nicht kommandiert werden.' Aus der Begründung des Theatergesetzes," *Der völkische Beobachter* (Berlin), 24 May 1934: 6.

15. "Dresden feiert den Führer," *Der völkische Beobachter* (Berlin), 29 May 1934: 1.

16. The official agenda had Hitler leaving at the 11:00 P.M. intermission to appear at a city hall reception, but he decided to stay to the end (at 1:30 A.M). *Tristan*, after all, was his favorite opera—he saw it repeatedly during his Vienna years and completed a scene design in 1925. One design is in Joachim C. Fest, *Hitler*, tr. Richard and Clara Winston (New York, 1973): after 564.

17. "The Führer's outrage burst out before one picture: 'The man belongs in prison!'"; "Der dritte Dresdner Tag," *Dresdner Anzeiger*, 30 May 1934: 2. The exhibit, the seventh of its kind, opened in September 1933; 207 paintings, sculptures, watercolors, and etchings were displayed to popular ridicule (minors could attend only on specially guided tours). These exhibits prefigured the more famous Munich exhibition of 1937. See Stephanie Barron ed., *"Degenerate Art": The Fate of the Avant-Garde in Nazi Germany* (New York, 1991): 100–101. Hildegard Brenner includes a review of the exhibit in her *Kunstpolitik des Nationalsozialismus* (Reinbeck bei Hamburg, 1963): 175–77.

18. Goebbels, "Triumph Richard Wagners; Feierliche Eröffnung der Reichs-Theaterfestwoche," *Der völkische Beobachter* (Berlin), 29 May 1934: 5.

19. In January 1934, as the new Reichsdramaturg, Schlösser delivered a speech ("Vom kommenden Volksschauspiel" ["Concerning the Coming Volk Drama"]) that was subsequently published in the press and as the *Thingspiel* chapter of his *Das Volk und seine Bühne* (Berlin, 1935). Schlösser argued that the new *Volk* drama would come from National Socialist holidays or from German history viewed through the lens of National Socialism: "Would not the theme of history, advanced into the light of our natural and legitimate myth of Blood and Honor, reveal a totally new concept? . . . Now through the national revolution, the entire world, once again, is given to us for a second time" (61).

20. See Glen W. Gadberry, "The *Stedingers*: Nazi Festival Drama of the Destruction of a People," *Theatre History Studies* 10 (1990): 105–26. Goebbels issued a more explicit directive on 30 January 1941: "It is forbidden to pit one national group against another, one city against another, or one part of the *Reich* or *Volk* against another, even if done in a seemingly well-intentioned manner. Every aspect of public life must be directed toward the unity of the *Volk*." Boguslaw Drewniak, *Das Theater im NS-Staat: Szenarium deutscher Zeitgeschichte, 1933–1945* (Düsseldorf, 1983): 229.

21. Joseph Goebbels, "Das deutsche Theater im neuen Reich," *Der völkische Beobachter* (Berlin), 1 June 1934: 2. Reprinted 2 June 1934: 2.

22. Goebbels's laboratory was the experimental *Thingspiel* (literally, "play of Volk judgment"). It was an open-air, choric theatre form envisioned and set in motion by Third Reich playwrights and the Reichsdramaturg. It was a supposedly new form intended to revive the German stage. Goebbels was nominal head and patron of the program; the relationship was republicized in May: "Reichsminister Dr. Goebbels Schirmherr der Thingarbeit," *Der völkische Beobachter* (Berlin), 23 May 1934: 6. His comments about "legitimate" theatre experiment at the Festival only a few days later must be viewed in this context. See Henning Eichberg, "The Nazi *Thingspiel*: Theater for the Masses in Fascism and Proletarian Culture," *New German Critique* 11 (Spring 1977): 133–150.

23. Goebbels studied history, philology, history of art, and literature and earned a Ph.D. in 1922. His dissertation was titled "Wilhelm von Schütz als Dramatiker. Ein Beitrag zur Geschichte des Dramas der Romantischen Schule." In the

1920s it disappeared from the Heidelberg library. It was in Heidelberg that Goebbels wrote his novel *Michael* and two plays, *Blutsaat* ("Blood Seed") and *Der Wanderer*.

24. In *Mein Kampf,* Hitler used *Kitsch* to describe the products of Weimar Jewry: "The fact that nine-tenths of all literary filth, artistic Kitsch, and theatrical nonsense is attributable to a people who constitute one-one hundredth of the country's population is simply not to be denied"; in Wayne Kvam, "The Nazification of Max Reinhardt's Deutsches Theater Berlin," *Theatre Journal* 40, no. 3 (Oct. 1988): 361. In 1934 Goebbels applied the term to German, Party-approved writers.

25. The Nazis frequently praised Schiller as one of "the first National Socialists." See Joseph Wulf, *Theater und Film im Dritten Reich: Eine Dokumentation* (Gütersloh, 1964): 188, and Kvam, "Nazification," 363ff.

26. "Reichstheater-Festspiele in Dresden," *Berliner Börsenzeitung,* evening ed., 20 Jan. 1934, and "Dr. Goebbels in der Dresdner Staatsoper," *Dresdner neueste Nachrichten,* 28 Jan. 1934, Dresden Staatsarchiv, Collection 1392/2, nos. 124 and 168.

27. A remarkable 268 plays premiered in 1933, plus 32 foreign plays in translation; 52 others had been printed. In 1934 there were 294 German premieres, 27 foreign, and 37 book dramas. The figures include Austrian and Swiss premieres—in 1934, 27 premiered in Vienna and Basel. From Wilhelm Frels, "Die deutsche dramatische Produktion 1934," *Die neue Literatur* 36, no. 6 (June 1935): 325, 331. Wilhelm von Schramm observed in 1935 that new plays were not wanting in the new Germany—just good ones. Schramm, "Praktische Dramaturgie: Erfahrungen im Bühnenvertrieb," *Deutsche Allgemeine Zeitung* (Berlin, Reichs-Ausgabe), 27 Jan. 1935: 5.

28. Rosenberg first met Eckart in 1918 and published articles in Eckart's *Auf gut Deutsch* and subsequent *Völkischer Beobachter*. When Eckart retired in 1923, Rosenberg became chief editor. In 1927, he published the first authoritative collection and commentary on the author, *Dietrich Eckart, Ein Vermächtnis* (Munich, 1928). He dedicated the volume to "one of the best of the German *Volk*," and wrote that it was to record "in *which* ranks Dietrich Eckart had fought for a German future" (Rosenberg, *Eckart,* 7). He had also used his Militant League for German Culture to wage the unsuccessful battle to have Eckart's plays produced during the "Jewish-dominated" Weimar Republic; Hermann Wanderscheck, *Deutsche Dramatik der Gegenwart* (Berlin, 1938): 47. At a memorial service, on the sixty-sixth anniversary of Eckart's birth and two months before Dresden, Rosenberg again lauded his former editor; Rosenberg said, " 'Der Name Dietrich Eckart unlöslich mit dem neuen Deutschland verbunden.' Dietrich-Eckart-Gedächtnis-Feier in München," *Der völkische Beobachter* (Berlin), 24 March 1934: 2.

29. George Mosse, *The Crisis of German Ideology: Intellectual Origins of the Third Reich* (New York, 1964): 26.

30. Adolf Hitler, *Hitler's Secret Conversations, 1941–1944,* tr. Norman Cameron and R. H. Stevens (New York, 1953): 260–61, night of 19–20 Feb. 1942: "The first show I went to after the First World War was *Peer Gynt,* which I saw with Dietrich Eckart, at the Staatliche Schauspielhaus. In Berlin the play was always given in Eckart's translation. At Munich, on the other hand, it was in a Jewish translation," i.e., by Christian Morgenstern. See Fest, *Hitler,* 139ff.

31. Rosenberg, *Eckart*, 39: *Peer*'s stage "impression was so strong, that even theatre directors of the race with 'sagging lips' performed the Eckart version of 'Peer Gynt,' for the sake of its racial success." Many theatres continued to use the older translations, by Ludwig Passarge (the authorized translator) and Christian Morgenstern.

32. Ibsen in Edmund Gosse, *Henrik Ibsen* (New York, 1908): 103. Ibsen repeatedly objected to critics making *Peer* a commentary on contemporary social problems: "They have discovered much more satire in *Peer Gynt* than was intended by me. Why can they not read the book as a poem?" (Gosse, *Ibsen*, 104).

33. David E. R. George, *Henrik Ibsen in Deutschland. Reception und Revision*, tr. Heinz Arnold and Bernd Glasenapp (Göttingen, 1968): 70–71.

34. Stage interpretation might have developed racial stereotypes; the subhuman trolls, for example, as George suggests, might have been played as stereotyped Jews, but that did not seem to be the case. If it were so racist, the adaptation would not have been so popular, under the Kaiser or the Weimar Republic.

35. Mosse, *Crisis*, 26–27.

36. Gerhart Göhler, "Ausklang der Reichstheaterfestwoche," *Frankfurter Zeitung* (Reichsausgabe), 12 June 1934: 9.

37. Hermann Dannecker, "Reichs-Theaterwoche in Dresden: Das Schauspiel," *Der völkische Beobachter* (Munich), 6 June 1934: 8.

38. Kurt Arnold Findeisen, "'Peer Gynt' in Dietrich Eckarts Übersetzung," *Der völkische Beobachter* (Berlin), 31 May 1934: 5.

39. Dannecker, "Reichs-Theaterwoche," 8, and Findeisen, "'Peer Gynt,' " 5.

40. From Joseph Goebbels, *The Early Goebbels Diaries, 1925–1926*, ed. Helmut Heiber, tr. Oliver Watson (New York, 1963): 54.

Yesterday *Peer Gynt* with Karl Kaufmann. Aase's death out of this world. I thought of my mother and could have wept. How soon life passes, and we have gladdened hearts so rarely. Solveig's lullaby. I can't get Grieg's tune out of my head. On the whole the performance was a little too virile. In Ibsen's mind, soul and reason dwell closely together. Hence he often appears to be brutal and boorish—perhaps also trite. The words are sometimes shameless and common. But the music is chaste like nature's youngest child. (entry 15 Dec. 1925)

Most versions used Edvard Grieg's music.

41. Hans Knudsen, "Was lehrt uns die Reichs-Theaterwoche?" *Berliner Lokal-Anzeiger*, 8 June 1934, Dresden Staatsarchiv, Collection 1392/2, no. 407.

42. Rainer Schlösser, "Die Sendung des deutschen Bühnenschriftstellers der Gegenwart," *Der völkische Beobachter* (Berlin), 7 June 1934: 5.

43. Dr. Hz. St., "Die Reichs-Theaterwoche. Ihre leistung und ihr Ertrag," *Dresdner neueste Nachrichten*, 5 May 1934, Dresden Staatsarchiv, Collection 1392/2, no. 397.

44. Alfred Rosenberg, *Das politische Tagebuch Alfred Rosenbergs aus den Jahren 1934/35 und 1939/40*, ed. Hans-Günther Seraphim (Göttingen, 1956): 30.

45. The accord was signed on 6 June 1934. It formalized an earlier linkage: on 14 April a spectator organization was created within Strength Through Joy and governed and led by the German Stage Alliance. That agreement was signed by Claus Selzner for the Labor Front and Walter Stang for the Alliance; "Abkommen

zwischen 'Kraft durch Freude' und 'Deutsche Bühne,'" *Der völkische Beobachter* (Berlin), 17 April 1934: 1. Goebbels may have seen this accord as a threat and hence laid the groundwork to intervene in such organizations with his Unified Theatre Law.

46. When Edmund Kiss' extreme anti-Christian and racist *Wittekind* (a drama that agreed quite nicely with Rosenberg's *Mythus*) was produced in Hagen in 1935, it met the protests of the Church and Party moderates. The NS-Kulturgemeinde purchased most of the subsequent performances, assuring full houses and ideologic education. The play received a longer run than it would have without this Rosenberg subsidy. Edmund Kiss, *Wittekind; Trauerspiel in vier Aufzügen* (Leipzig, 1935); see NN, "Neues Tendenz-Drama um Wittekind. Zustimmung und Protest bei der Uraufführung in Hagen," *Germania* (Berlin), 29 Jan. 1935: 9.

47. As ideologist, Rosenberg demanded an ideolgically pure text; he was not a man of the theatre and did not understood how performance and imagination could shape ideas or contemporary events. Goebbels, with a literary background, preferred near-perfect technical production of legitimate drama to serve German propaganda, including Hinrichs's *Die Stedinge, Spiel vom Untergang eines Volkes* (premiered 27 May 1934 at "Stedings Ehre," Altenesch) and Hans Hermann Wilhelm's *Ulrich von Hutten* (6 July 1934 at Wartburg-Waldbühne, Eisenach). Hinrichs's play was subsequently published (Oldenburg i. O.: Rudolf Schwarz, 1935).

48. Hitler, cited in Drewniak, *Theater im NS-Staat*, 44.

10

Collaboration or Survival, 1933–1938: Reassessing the Role of the *Jüdischer Kulturbund*

Rebecca Rovit

It is unusual for theatre scholars to acquire updated reassessments by eyewitnesses who survived events long documented in history books. When those experiences date back to Nazi Germany and the witnesses are German Jewish theatre artists and musicians, some of whom worked in Berlin even after the outbreak of World War II, one must recognize the value that such extraordinary testimony may lend to already recorded history. The almost inconceivable phenomenon of a legitimate theatre organized and managed by unemployed Jewish artists for Jews, yet approved and supervised by the Nazis, prompts provocative questions about the nature of artistic and political collaboration under extreme circumstances. The present reevaluation of the *Jüdischer Kulturbund* (Jewish Cultural Organization) by its surviving members attests to the flexibility of fact and its reinterpretation.[1]

A dialogue thought to have been solely within the historian's domain was revived in 1992, when Berlin's Akademie der Künste presented newly acquired information from the personal archives of ex-Kulturbund members in an exhibition that also included recently filmed interviews with some of the artists.[2] Then, in a symbolic reunion in April, fifty-nine years after the Nazis ruled that non-Aryans must be "removed" from the cultural sector, a group of German-Jewish artists gathered in the reunified city (and former center of the Kulturbund activities) to discuss their past participation in the Kulturbund. The group of artists, who either went into exile before the war or survived concentration camps and the underground, were divided in their opinions on the Jewish cultural association. Their basic point of contention, which questioned the ultimate function of the Jewish Kulturbund and its theatre, renewed a familiar dispute from the 1930s. As stated in its by-laws, the Kulturbund's primary obligations to its community had been to provide employment and to present challenging cultural events for its Jewish members.[3]

The principal founders of the Kulturbund, stage director Kurt Baumann and musicologist Dr. Kurt Singer, developed the plan for a Berlin cultural circle whose theatre, music, and lecture program would be subsidized through member subscriptions. Membership entitled one to attend three events a month—either a play or an opera, a concert, and a lecture of one's choice. The proposed repertoire focused on European classic playwrights (Molière, Shakespeare, Ibsen, Shaw, Pirandello), including Germans (Goethe, Schiller, Kleist, Grabbe, Hauptmann). It also featured plays based on biblical Jewish themes, such as Hebbel's *Judith*, or by Jewish authors such as Schnitzler and Beer-Hoffmann. Another category was reserved for Jewish plays from Palestine and East Europe. Singer projected that the organization's tasks would serve social, ethical, and intellectual purposes: to provide work and the will to live, to promote pride and unity among Jews, and to teach and to learn through art.[4]

The association, originally called the Cultural Organization of German Jewry, sought to uphold German-Jewish art in Nazi Germany but had to make many concessions, including a name change.[5] The conditions prescribed by the government restricted the organization's autonomy and its freedoms. Only Jews could be members and attend events. Only the Jewish press could advertise and report on the cultural offerings. And the programming would be subject to strict censorship. This meant that many of the proposed German plays were forbidden. With each year, the organization directors felt increased pressure to produce "Jewish" culture. And by 1938, not one musical or theatrical work by non-Jewish Germans or Austrians was performable.[6]

Baumann has claimed that after 1936, the Bund's existence "was based ever more on the fact that the Nazis were using us as a counterpropaganda against the growing pressure of foreign public opinion."[7] In fact, once the government centralized all regional cultural circles under the *Reichsverband der Jüdischen Kulturbünde* (1935), officials did refer to the Berlin-directed association as an example of their humanitarian *Judenpolitik*.[8] But through centralization, the Nazis could better control and limit the activities of the Jewish artists. Indeed, the complex of regulations imposed on the German Jews' personal and artistic lives threatened them with both physical isolation and the spectre of spiritual ghettoization.[9]

Were the artists merely pawns of the Gestapo, ghettoized in a perverse parody of theatre? Or was the theatre a breath of fresh air that liberated

Jewish actors and audiences from the stifling atmosphere of Nazi oppression? Did the theatre uphold high standards of performance and give young artists a chance to practice their craft, as some suggest? Or did this privileged work cause those young artists to compromise their ideals by their collaboration with the enemy?[10]

These questions—long debated—reemerged in light of the recent exhibition and its accompanying publications, which presented a new emphasis on the individuals who participated in and represented the Kulturbund. And the remarkable face-to-face meeting of Bund members (now in their eighties and nineties) shifted the focus from plain historical fact to the complexity of live human beings who once sought to pursue their artistic careers under extreme circumstances and now reflected upon the choices they made. Their conflicting perspectives complicate the task for the historian accustomed to recording facts with precision and accuracy. For the scholar who studies documents in order to clarify them, the voices in the present express contradiction about the past.

"It was a grotesque plan.... We were figures on the Nazi chessboard," insisted Kulturbund actor Bert Bernd in an interview. Others felt differently, "It was not a ghetto theatre!" "Theater was our salvation; we had blinders on, which was probably a good thing."[11] For Camilla Spira, self-protection motivated her decisions to cooperate, first within the Kulturbund, and later on the concentration camp stage at Westerbork, where she acted for her life: "I was a talent who never reflected; only the acting counted. I wanted to bring people comfort and to pull myself out of misfortune."[12] And at the academy round-table discussion, Ruth Anselm-Herzog defended her role as actress: "Where could I have gone as a young person? Above all, I wanted to be in the theatre. It gave me time to develop my skills. Besides, we could not imagine what the Germans had in store for us."[13]

Anselm-Herzog's view was echoed by other artists who had used the Kulturbund for artistic and economic security. Such security brought with it a liberated sense of self for some of the artists. Several actors have suggested their joy at having been on stage, lifted above the realities of their situation. As one actress put it, "I was happy to be in my element. When one was on stage, you didn't feel it was 'ghetto' theatre."[14] Herbert Freeden, the most vocal historical witness, has advanced the notion that performances of the classics provided actors with a "door to freedom" and strengthened their mental resistance to possible ghettoization.[15] At the academy discussion, however, he criticized the notion of apparent artistic and economic freedoms by describing the "dangerous illusion" afforded by the outlook that one might profit from an institution whose employment hindered emigration and, ultimately, safety. The discussion's moderator also argued along these lines, referring to the Kulturbund as a "catastrophic misunderstanding, in which Jews had been abused for the Nazi cause."[16] It has been suggested, however, that the Jewish leaders also had some occasion to exercise what little power they had to manipulate Nazi officials.[17]

But the Kulturbund reunion ended on a note of compromise that stressed an essential human response to adversity. Conceding to ex-members who felt that acting had liberated them from the everyday hardships, even Freeden acknowledged that their productions offered solace to actors and theatregoers: "It is true that people emerged from their loneliness and fear to laugh together for a few hours."[18]

The recent research unveiled at the Akademie der Künste has humanized the Kulturbund theatre and thereby revealed the contradictions of its former players. Documentation of the arts during the Third Reich characteristically stresses the systematic bureaucratization of art, which subordinated the individual artist to the collective ideology of the Reich. Within the *Reichkulturkammer* (Reich culture chamber) and its various sub-chambers for the arts, paragraphs of official laws dehumanized, excluded, limited, and proclaimed both art and artist as culturally acceptable or subversive. In its aim to discriminate, the Nazi theatre chamber emphasized "otherness" by reducing individuals and their work to such labels as "Bolshevik," "degenerate," or "judaized."

Given this historical context, it was probably fitting that the Kulturbund board chose to open the first theatre season in October 1933 with Lessing's *Nathan the Wise*. The play's Jewish protagonist advocates the idea that humanity precedes any religious label, whether Christian or Jew.[19] The eighteenth-century message of equality among men reflected an enlightened Germany where assimilated Jews and Christians had lived together and shared stages and auditoriums. In 1933, the majority of Berlin's Jews were still assimilated, but they were losing their rights because they were Jews. An all-Jewish performance of *Nathan the Wise* may have been a plea for tolerance, but it may also have been a calculated attempt to please all the segments of the prospective audience, which included Nazi officials and Zionist Jews.

For the Kulturbund also came under pressure from the community it wanted to serve. The theatre's representatives were aware that the Zionist minority within the Jewish community might disapprove of any concessions made by the assimilationists. While the Zionists favored cultural events with Hebrew or Yiddish sources, Baumann remembers the reactions of the majority, who were cultivated within the German humanist tradition; as he put it, they would not go "voluntarily into the ghetto" of a Jewish cultural club.[20] He suggests that Lessing's play, with its Jewish theme and German author, was chosen as the "only *one* work that was suited to depict our new situation."[21]

A former Bund actress has suggested that some of her former colleagues fooled themselves about their situation and the extent to which they might be deceived of their identity as Germans. "That's the irony. These German

Jews believed in Germany and identified with the nation."[22] But Anselm-Herzog's retrospective remarks stem from historical hindsight. On the day of the Lessing premiere, Kulturbund Dramaturg Julius Bab truly believed what he stressed as the identity of those actively involved in the theatre and the community at large: "We will create a Jewish stage, which, at the same time, will be a German one; it will stem from these double roots of being, which nourish us German Jews, and from which we cannot be severed."[23]

The Kulturbund's central document—its *Aufruf*, or invitation to join—also encouraged fellow German Jews to uphold their identity, which to many may have felt more German than Jewish. Its call to prospective members asserted that the organization's goals did not mean a return to the ghetto where Jews were once cut off from the world; instead the goals reinforced a desire to lead an "intellectual life open to the human ideals which we have learned from the German classics." In addition, artists were called upon to develop what they felt connected them with "the being and spirit of Judaism."[24]

Such a notion of a separatist Jewish cultural organization appealed to the Nazis as they moved to purge their own art of Jewish elements. Indeed, they envisaged the Kulturbund as a showcase of Jewish art for Jews. But the Jewish theatre founders, who truly sought to integrate the spirit of Judaism into their work, faced a problem in determining what exactly *was* Jewish culture. Such Jewish newspapers as the *Israelitisches Familienblatt* and particularly the *Jüdische Rundschau* sought to define that culture by attempting to strengthen Jewish consciousness among readers. The day after Hitler took power, the *Jüdische Rundschau* advised Jews that the time for conformity and self-denial was over; in order to preserve one's sense of dignity for the present and the future, one must have faith in the Jewish spirit.[25]

Even before the *Nathan* premiere, the newspaper demanded that the production must reflect the contemporary situation of the Jew, instead of "spinning a world of illusions around German Jews." The editorship had no objection to the choice of the play as long as the production was not intended as a political assimilationist statement; in other words, the editors were concerned about the attitude of the producers, not the play's content.[26] Kurt Singer responded to the newspaper's pique in an open letter. He defended the theatre's motives for choosing to stage *Nathan* by claiming that Nathan's notion of tolerance should also be practiced among Jews (i.e., Berlin's assimilationists and Zionists). The *Kulturbund* practiced art, not politics, Singer assured his readers.[27]

But politics did play a role in determining the cultural season. In light of the laws against Jewish artists and the censorship of their work, it was vital not only to feature Jewish playwrights, but also to stage the dramatic content in such a way as to foster a Jewish experience among spectators. Further, the Kulturbund needed to gain Zionist support. Thus it may have been to appease both the Zionist contingent and the Nazi censor that the staged *Nathan the Wise* provided audiences with a Jewish milieu. In fact, the *Jüdische Rundschau* graciously reported the success with which the director "underscored Jewish needs." Not only did Nathan appear onstage humming Hassidic songs, but his first words were a Hebrew blessing. His religiosity was apparent several times in the production as he murmured Hebrew and prayed in his home, which featured a visible menorah. The *Kulturbund*'s ending to the play emphasized Nathan's exclusion from the group by depriving him of Lessing's directed "all around embraces." The ending, however, succeeded in depicting "Jewish fate."[28]

Although the newspaper declared "rich applause" for the *Nathan* production, not everyone agreed with the interpretation.[29] The majority of the public did not readily identify with such a representation of Jewishness. Nor were the audiences transported to a Jewish experience by subsequent plays from the alien East European *schtetl*: *Sonkin and the Jackpot* (1934) in Jewish costume, for example, or *The Golem* (1937). Arthur Eloesser admitted that the audience may not have understood the cabalistic nuances of Halper Leiwik's *Golem*. Still, he claimed that the audience responded with pride at the artistic success that was so "innerly Jewish."[30] Biblical themes as in Stefan Zweig's drama about the destruction of Jerusalem, *Jeremias* (1934), were not nearly as successful with audiences as light comedies and Shakespeare's dramas. The audience's lack of enthusiasm for specifically Jewish fare showed at the box office, with monthly lows, for example, in the 1936–37 season when the only Jewish opera was offered, *Joseph in Egypt*.[31]

Bab had suggested that Jewish themes eventually would be synthesized into play production. So too might specifically Jewish subtleties of gesture, rhythm, or intonation color a performance. But the result would merely be a "Jewish-toned German cultural theatre."[32] Freeden recently restated the difficulty of shaping an exclusively Jewish culture for the Kulturbund actors and audiences: "One had to offer something that did not exist, to someone who did not want it."[33] That something, at least on stage, appeared to be some kind of external suggestion of Jewish culture. But the intended recipients of this culture were German Jewish audiences: who preferred to see champagne bottles rather than menorahs on stage, tuxedos rather than caftans, and low-cut necklines instead of women's head coverings.[34]

The Kulturbund actors themselves found it difficult, first, to restrict their repertory to mostly non-German plays and, second, to emphasize Jewish customs on stage. These actors relied on the spoken and written word to produce their art. They had incorporated the great roles of the German stage into their repertoires. And because their art was tied so intrinsically to their German language, it was more difficult for them to emigrate than for musicians or painters. Thus many Jewish actors who had not been invited to work abroad stayed in Germany and sought work in the regional cultural circles, in spite of the censors that limited their expression.[35] Several, such as Camilla Spira, left Germany only to return before World War II: "We wanted to be German and to live here. I would have preferred to perform German plays," she conceded.[36]

In late 1936, the German Ministry for Propaganda could claim a virtual monopoly on German culture and a victory over all non-Aryan elements that tried to pollute it. Commissar Hans Hinkel, responsible for Jewish cultural affairs, boasted that the Reichskulturkammer was completely free of Jews. Meanwhile, Germany had used the Olympics as an occasion to make the world aware of its liberal program for Jews (even inviting foreign guests to Kulturbund performances). Hinkel, in fact, seemed proud of his collaboration with the Kulturbund as he reported on the theatre's success. "Our work could hardly be called barbaric," he declared, restating his 1933 goal, which had been to "nurture the Jewish spirit and allow for the production of Jewish art."[37] But those Jews who belonged to the Kulturbund were faced with worsening circumstances. Less than a month after the Olympics, they sought desperately to clarify their aims at a national conference for all their regional branches. The September meeting centered on the problem of Jewish content.[38] Hinkel's presence at the three-day conference, and that of delegates from various Jewish organizations, indicates that the Kulturbund had to answer to and appease several very different factions.

The assembled speakers grappled with the persistent question of what constituted Jewish content, and how that content might be related to culture. Rabbi Joachim Prinz appealed to ethnic pride, attributing a "national-pedagogic" objective to the choice of theatre content. Content does not determine culture, he preached. Instead, it was the cultural representative, or Jew, who must define his culture. But Prinz recognized that the German language complicated the ability of German Jews to realize Jewish culture. Because many Jews were unable to define their culture as Jewish, the Jewish theatre must adopt a fundamental teaching role in shaping Jewish culture.[39]

Prinz thus cast the actor in the primary role of teacher. Ideally, once the proper plays were chosen, the actor-cum-teacher would interpret the Jewish lessons to the audience. This assumes that the actors would be well versed in Hebrew, possibly Yiddish, and in the historical aspects of Judaism. But we know that the Kulturbund actors were not thus equipped. Prinz was also aware of this; he called for actors to go beyond the library to learn about Judaism. But besides admitting that German Jewish actors could not train in Palestine or East Europe, he offered little practical help in schooling the Jewish actor in Germany.

Fritz Wisten's speech, however, indicated some practical means for the education of the Jewish actor. Like Prinz, he suggested that the actor was the best harbinger of future Jewish cultural work, "because we want to be Jews and through our art, contribute to the education of a proud class of free Jews!"⁴⁰ Wisten's strategy for the actor was more immediately realizable than Prinz's plan. First, actors must overcome psychological inhibitions about feeling declassé. For Wisten, this would mean coming to terms with the fact that their co-actors and audience were all Jews, as were many of the available roles. He also targeted the next generation of actors as the new missionaries—those whose special training would incorporate mandatory Hebrew classes and the practice of Yiddish intonation. But the present actors were not to be excluded. Their training would come not in the form of lectures or fantasy trips to Palestine. Rather, Judaism would be imparted to them through work-group discussions with enthusiastic guides whose excitement would inspire the actors. By familiarizing actors with the Jewish world of mysticism, they would gain insight into the soul of Judaism and thereby into their own souls.

Kurt Singer's closing remarks reinforced the idea that actors must be trained in new ways. But he warned against creating utopias. Too many theoretical demands on the actors, he believed, would inhibit their performance: "The actor must feel; he must acknowledge things he has not yet learned intuitively."⁴¹ Nevertheless, Singer announced that pedagogical work for actors would be necessary for performances of East European Jewish plays. And lectures would be arranged to prepare the audiences. By 1935, Berlin already had three Jewish schools where citizens could attend lectures on Jewish art, history, and philosophy.⁴²

The persistence with which Jewish leaders proselytized Jewish culture may seem perverse, especially given the programs established by Nazis to spread their own Nazi culture. Besides idealizing the Aryan, Nazi art also caricatured the Jew—both on and off the stage. The Jewish community's attempts at organizing methods of "Jewish" actor training and audience response appeared to be more molded by the Nazis than by themselves.

By the time the Kulturbund conference on Jewish content took place, Goebbels had already instituted the national inculcation of *völkish* values through art. With theatre as a didactic means to strengthen national identity, actors of the Reich participated vigorously. They attended ideological training institutes to learn the differences between the old bourgeois theatre tradition and the new one. And through such schooling, cultural directors led the fight to renew German theatre in the spirit of the new political order.⁴³

The new German order in theatre proposed that actors be chosen to represent group values onstage. For the Nazis, this premise was based on the principle of race. The ideological lessons could best be imparted by the purest representatives of the race, trained in their mission. The Kulturbund conference reflected an unfortunate parody of this—at least in theory—as speakers considered ways to propagandize Jewish culture. The suggestions of how Jewish actors might learn to act "Jewish" recall the distorted caricatures of Jews by Nazi propaganda. In spite of the Torahs painted on scenic backdrops, the side curls pasted to costume wigs, and the Hebrew and Yiddish expressions grafted onto speeches, the Jews of the Kulturbund remained Jews who did not know how to represent themselves as Jews onstage. As Gronius states in his discussion of the Kulturbund's token "Jewish" play, "One wanted to put on the 'correct' shirt and was already stuck in a straitjacket."[44]

For the Nazis, race became not only the standard for choosing representative actors, but also the determinant for the proper onstage portrayal. Because enthusiasts of Nazi theatre believed that the process of acting depended on inner attributes such as blood, they insisted that the actor in performance could best embody "the racial soul and racial values" of the Volk.[45] This theorist, Wilhelm von Schramm, was, of course, referring to supposed biological phenomena that, like ideological training, prove that onstage segregation should be practiced. He argued that while the *Habimah* Yiddish theatre expressed its Judaism through its elemental energies, so too could the blood-Germans best express their theatre. In sum, he concluded that it would be unnatural for any of "that [Jewish] race who has neither the appearance, nor the myth of the blood" to play the ideal figures of German or Nordic drama.[46]

The German Jew Arnold Zweig also described the need for a "biological group representation" on the German stage. Referring to the significant Mediterranean heritage of the Jews, Zweig focused on "an overlooked group of European citizens," often characterizing the Jewish actor in terms almost as exotic as Schramm's.[47] Zweig attributed the Jew's onstage agility, for example, to mystical, magical energies that elicited impulses "more violent and mercurial in the Jew than in the Southern German or Russian."[48] While Zweig's intent was not to politicize the theatre and its acting process for ideological purposes, like Schramm he attempted to feature the Jew and Jewish artistic characteristics as separate from his European, specifically German, counterparts.

The major difference between the authors lies in their motives for writing. Certainly, the Nazi theatre and Germany's Jewish theatre promoted their separate groups of artists for very different reasons. The Nazi theatre was subject to a political system that strove to purify its country and its art. While Schramm advocated a new theatre for the Nazi nation, Zweig called attention to the contributions Jews had made to German theatre and then tried to promote solidarity against the threat to Jewish art. In 1927, Zweig had already sensed an audience anti-Semitism that hindered the presentation of a Jew as a serious model or "group representative" (*Volksperson*) symbolizing the past and present.[49] Zweig's discussion of the Jewish play anticipated by some ten years the Kulturbund artists who also sought solidarity in what defined them in their exclusion.[50]

In its attempts to define culture for its audiences, the Kulturbund replicated, in part, the Nazi organization of both Nazi and Jewish culture. By all accounts, the efforts to impose pedagogical purposes onto its Kulturbund theatre agenda failed to produce a stronger sense of Jewish culture.[51] The demand for objectives for artists to consciously create "Jewish" works and instill Jewish awareness in audiences could hardly be fulfilled. True artistic creativity cannot be forced; if the artist or spectator remains indifferent to or even resists an imposed cultural experience, then the attempt to organize culture fails.

This fact renews the nagging question of how far artists collaborated in or resisted their situation in the Kulturbund. That the Jewish theatre even existed is a fact of collaboration, both artistic and political. In order to establish any ground for themselves, the Kulturbund artists had to consult with Nazis such as Hinkel. Likewise, within the Jewish community, the Zionists became collaborators in an enterprise whose purpose was to include all Jews. Their acceptance of censors and their tolerance of Gestapo visitors had been the preconditions of the alliance between the artists and the authorities. But given the historical conditions for the actor at the Kulturbund, some kind of arrangement with the Nazis was obviously necessary.

Did the artist benefit from this curious collaboration? One cannot weight the factor of opportunism for the Jewish actors as heavily as that for their "Aryan" counterparts. The "virtuosos" who conformed without opposition to the Nazi system played the political role assigned them as perfectly as their stage roles.[52] Unlike the Kulturbund actors who joined the theatre for basic survival, the great actors of the Third Reich were bought with material means, special privileges, and recognition—and without much difficulty.[53] The Jewish artists seemed genuinely to strive at first for art's sake, relishing the chance to perform the classics, but it is also true that there was the possibility of personal benefits and institutional leverage in their acquiescence to the Nazi theatre arrangement.[54]

One Jewish actress recalls how privilege and collaboration were combined after the theatre was closed in 1941. Instead of being sent to work in factories, the Kulturbund artists, who "had priority," wrote up lists of Jews to be picked up by the Gestapo. This would delay the collaborators' own deportation. The actress speaks of her actor-husband's list making, but not her own. She does recount, however, how her role as an actress had unexpectedly spared her sister and her sister's children from deportation. A Gestapo officer whose job had been to check in on Kulturbund performances agreed to grant her plea for their lives because, as he put it, "I saw you in many roles."[55]

Whether it was collaboration or survival, the Jewish artists worked within the parameters given them. It can be argued, however, that some tenuous forms of resistance also existed within the Kulturbund. The artists clung to their double roots of German and Jew. While they appeared to conform to the demands made on them to produce Jewish art, their audiences withstood conversion, largely indifferent to staged Jewish lore. After decades of trying to assess and understand the Kulturbund phenomenon, Herbert Freeden has honed an explanation for his one-time theatre's inability to organize culture. While the theatre had accepted its duty to provide Jewish content for its members, the association had always opposed being cut off from European culture. To be separated from the traditions of Western humanism would have meant a cultural and intellectual ghettoization for the members. So, according to Freeden, "in its stubborn refusal to give up its bond to Europe and to deny its intellectual tradition, the *Kulturbund* became a moral reservoir of strength for German Jews, and ... an element of spiritual resistance."[56]

Regardless of censorship, the Nazis could not control the spiritual, intellectual aspects of the theatre's work. The ability to perform great European works such as Priestley and Schnitzler on stage offered a "window to the world" through which to escape.[57] For Freeden, such resistance does not usually win physical freedom with it or even manifest itself in overt opposition, but Baumann referred to their organization as a kind of "spiritual underground movement," able to "blackmail" even the Nazis.[58] He claims that such unexpected triumphs made the founding of a Jewish Kulturbund and its continuation in that critical time "worthwhile."[59]

It is true that after 1938, the Kulturbund lost the control it had maintained earlier. After *Kristallnacht* the theatre was ordered to continue. Many performers who could emigrate did so. The interview responses and recent remarks by ex-members show their distaste at the direction that their theatre took after 1938. Referring to the "absurdity" and "grotesquerie" of the Nazi-steered events, one actor asked, "How could we play after *Kristallnacht?*" But some members did play.[60]

The Kulturbund could hardly be successful as an institution that was eventually forced to exist. Gronius calls it a "schizophrenic organization," unable to work because its basis for existence was the misery of the Jews. In the shadow of destruction, delay was its biggest success. Without any real freedom to make decisions, he believes, the Kulturbund can not be identified with either collaboration or heroic resistance.[61] Given the fate of Germany's Jews, how can one imagine that a Jewish theatre under the Nazis could produce anything positive? One is inclined to agree with Gronius, until one hears the voices and sees the faces of those individuals who recall moments of personal achievement on the Kulturbund stage.

Something did endure for these men and women who survived what many of their co-stars did not. These artists do not refer to themselves as victims or heroes. Their words merely express a sense of dignity and toughness as they look back on their lives and their art. They do not regret. As a group of individuals their attitude is not unlike one advocated by a writer whose editorial on the fate of the artists appeared shortly before the Kulturbund was founded: "We will hold on tightly to spirit. That is Jewish.

We will not become dulled; we will not become bitter. We will not become vindictive. We will persevere in the space left to us, with the means left us. The spirit cannot be blocked."[62] These words not only express the will to continue art production, but also suggest a means of self-protection.[63] Surely, the performers communicated such spiritual defiance to their audiences as well. The Kulturbund must have been meaningful psychologically, morally, and intellectually for all those involved as a way of preserving their sense of self and heightening their quality of life—at least temporarily. The gathering of former artists from the Kulturbund who together looked back on their lives allows us to consider how the human spirit may prevail—albeit with extreme fragility—even in the most extreme of circumstances.

NOTES

1. Herbert Freeden, the primary historian of the Kulturbund, was also a member and dramaturg for the theatre. He has provided what is still the most comprehensive history of the Kulturbund, *Jüdisches Theater in Nazi Deutschland* (Tübingen, 1964; Frankfurt/Main, 1985). The book was preceded by the only article Freeden has published in English, "Theatre Under a Swastika," *Leo Baeck Institute Yearbook* 1 (1956): 142–62. Freeden has written an array of articles that, for the most part, are derived from his 1964 book. It is essential to recognize Freeden's role as an active participant of the Kulturbund who seeks to recall the facts of his place within the theatre and to understand the theatre's role in history. Because of his membership in the organization he writes about, he may lack the critical objectivity toward his topic that other historians have (cf. Cochavi, Dahm, Gadberry, Zortmann, below); still, Freeden's writing is a necessary historical guide to the Kulturbund. For insight into the controversy about Jewish culture and the press see his *Jüdische Presse im Dritten Reich* (Frankfurt/Main, 1987; English translation 1993) and "Vom geistigen Widerstand der deutschen Juden: ein Kapitel jüdischer Selbstbehauptung in den Jahren 1933 bis 1938," in *Widerstand und Exil 1933–1945* (Bonn, 1986): 47–59. His most recent reinterpretations on the *Kulturbund* include an autobiography (1991) and a summary of his ideas in "Jüdischer Kulturbund ohne jüdische Kultur," in *Geschlossene Vorstellung: Der jüdische Kulturbund in Deutschland 1933–1941* (Berlin, 1992): 55–66.

2. The Academy of the Arts (Berlin-West) began its archives on the Kulturbund in 1963 when it acquired the correspondence and writings of Julius Bab, responsible for the Kulturbund lecture series from 1933 to his emigration in 1938. But it was not until 1986 that the collection expanded with donated material from the family of actor and director Fritz Wisten. Wisten's tenure at the Kulturbund lasted until 1941. In 1990, the academy hosted an exhibit on Wisten. In 1988, Henryk M. Broder and Eike Geisler sought to piece together information on the last years of the Kulturbund and its members. In their film, *Es waren wirklich Sternstunden* (produced by Bayrischer Rundfunk and Sender Freies Berlin), the researchers interviewed ex-members who had survived. Broder and Geisel, convinced that there were still other Bund artists alive who might bear witness to the past, gained the sponsorship of the academy and a government subsidy to pursue their search. The result has been the archival addition of donated photos, letters,

and reports from members of the Kulturbund. Most recently, the academy held the 1992 exhibition and published a substantial catalogue with replications of primary documents as well as interpretive essays. See *Geschlossene Vorstellung* (Berlin, 1992). Broder and Geisel edited a book which incorporates the memories of the ex-Kulturbund members they interviewed on film in 1988. See Eike Geisel and Henryk Broder, *Premiere und Pogrom: Der Jüdische Kulturbund 1933–1941, Texte und Bilder* (Berlin, 1992).

3. *Geschlossene Vorstellung*, Doc. 3: 221–22 (Fritz Wisten archives, 74/86/2002). The paragraph literally pledges to "nuture the artistic and scientific interests of the Jewish population and to provide work for Jewish artists and scientists."

4. "Um die Tätigkeit des Kulturbundes," *Die jüdische Rundschau* (Berlin), 8 August 1933: 405. The newspaper was Zionist in perspective. In the *Philo-lexikon: Handbuch des jüdischen Wissens* (Berlin, 1937), the Kulturbund is referred to as a "non-partisan" association with an independent theatre (and opera) where the "cultural strengths of German Jews have been brought together to create work for Jewish artists" (405).

5. The name change is an interesting example of how the term *German Jew* could be interpreted as subversive. The change officially took place after the Nürnberg Laws were passed in September 1935. But the debate between Kurt Singer and the authorities began as early as 1934, when the president of the Berlin police suggested in a letter to cultural senator Hans Hinkel (who oversaw the Kulturbund activities) that the Kulturbund Jews wanted to "form a national minority" in Germany (16 Jan. 1934, Doc. 5). See the series of documents in *Geschlossene Vorstellung*, 223–30. The Prussian court ruled against the inclusion of *German* in the organization's title on 9 July 1934 because the title was "misleading": "there are only Jews, not German Jews, French Jews, or Polish Jews" (Doc. 9: 225).

6. Besides Freeden, *Jüdisches Theater*, see Volker Dahm's extensive treatment of the Kulturbund activities: "Kulturelles und geistiges Leben," in *Die Juden in Deutschland 1933–1945*, ed. Wolfgang Benz (Munich, 1989). Factual overviews of the Jewish theatre are presented in English in Glen W. Gadberry, "Nazi Germany's Jewish Theatre," *Theatre Survey* 21, no. 1 (May 1980): 15–32, and Bruce H. Zortmann, "Theatre in Isolation: The *Jüdischer Kulturbund* of Nazi Germany," *Educational Theatre Journal* 24, no. 2 (1972): 159–68. Gadberry provides details on the repertory and government censorship, 19–20.

7. Monika Richarz, ed., *Jewish Life in Germany: Memoirs from Three Centuries*, tr. Stella P. and Sidney Rosenfeld (Bloomington, IN., 1991): 383. Julius Bab had said virtually the same thing in 1950, when he referred to the Kulturbund as "perhaps a regrettable mistake." Bab's notion was that the Nazis merely "tolerated" the cultural association to demonstrate abroad their tolerance for Jews. Excerpts from Julius Bab archives in *Geschlossene Vorstellung*, 341–57.

8. Dahm, "Kulturelles," 110–11.

9. Freeden, "Vom geistigen Widerstand," 52.

10. Baumann refers to the "first-class" cultural offerings of the Kulturbund in an excerpt from his 1977 memoirs, document 74, *Geschlossene Vorstellung*, 353. Several artists interviewed in Broder and Geisel's 1988 film hold similar views. Dahm reports that with the emigration of the top German-Jewish stars the Kulturbund had to hire lesser-known actors and artists from the provinces for the ensem-

ble and orchestra ("Kulturelles," 90). Jörg W. Gronius questions the true quality of the Bund's productions, suggesting that the Jewish press was biased toward the Kulturbund. He refers specifically to productions after 1938 as clear instances where the artists had to compromise artistic ideals to succumb to Nazi regulations; in *Geschlossene Vorstellung*, 86–88. After 1938, the choice of plays was reduced each season, and the proportion of comedies and fluff exceeded serious drama.

11. Bert Bernd, Ernst Lenart, and Martin Brandt in Broder and Geisel, *Sternstunden*.

12. In Daniela Pogade, "Atempause oder künstlerisches Ghetto?" *Berliner Zeitung*, 25/26 Jan. 1992: 17.

13. In Mariam Niroumand, "Freiheitshauch und tödliche Illusion," *Berliner Zeitung*, 4/5 April 1992: 66.

14. Leni Steinberg in Broder and Geisel, *Sternstunden*.

15. Cf. notes 1 and 6, above. Freeden offers some new angles for scholars. Chapter 5 of *Die jüdische Presse* provides a useful view of the cultural controversy and the role of the Jewish newspapers during the Nazi period. His provocative essay "Vom geistigen Widerstand," on the question of spiritual or mental resistance, continues an idea only hinted at in his *Jüdisches Theater in Nazi Deutschland*. In addition, his interview responses are consistent with this idea of freedom (in Broder and Geisel, *Sternstunden*).

16. Henryk M. Broder, "Selbstbehauptung in der Sackgasse," *Berliner Zeitung*, 27 Jan. 1992: 25.

17. Kurt Baumann has indicated the Kulturbund's own powers of manipulation, referring to Kristallnacht (1938), when the theatre was ordered to perform. The Bund leaders agreed only upon the release of two hundred artists and intellectuals from camps. Even after his emigration in 1939, Baumann adhered to his conviction that it had been correct to found the Kulturbund (1977); in *Geschlossene Vorstellung*, 353.

18. Niroumand, "Freiheitshauch," 66.

19. In act 2, scene 5, Nathan asks the Christian templar, "Are we Christian and Jew before we are man?"

20. Richarz, *Jewish Life*, 379.

21. Ibid., 381.

22. Anselm-Herzog in Broder and Geisel, *Sternstunden*.

23. This citation is from Bab's entry in the accompaniment to the first issue of the Kulturbund's *Monatsblätter*, 1 Oct. 1933; in *Geschlossene Vorstellung*, 239–40. Bab queries whether Jewish plays exist and whether a Jewish theatre will be created. He pledges to turn to plays of Jewish and East European origins. But he also claims a commitment to great German and other European playwrights.

24. The document, which was featured at the Akademie der Künste exhibition, has been reproduced in *Geschlossene Vorstellung*, 44–45.

25. "Regierung Hitler," *Die jüdische Rundschau* (Berlin), 31 Jan. 1933: 1.

26. Editorial, *Die jüdische Rundschau* (Berlin), 25 July 1933: 365.

27. "Um die Tätigkeit," 405.

28. Review of *Nathan der Weise*, *Die jüdische Rundschau* (Berlin), 4 Oct. 1933: 624.

29. Gronius cites the disapproval of the *Israelitisches Familienblatt* (11 Oct. 1933); the newspaper would have preferred to see the play staged as Lessing had meant it to be played. In *Geschlossene Vorstellung*, 69.

30. Wisten's production of *The Golem* appeared to be spectacular in setting, costume, and lighting. Eloesser's report on the audience's "enthusiastic acknowledgement" of the production suggests his own captivation: "The audience kept quite still at the end of each act, which was the correct attitude given this abduction into speculative and mystical depths. But at the end, the tension broke into a storm of applause." Arthur Eloesser, review of *The Golem, Die jüdische Rundschau* (Berlin), 12 Oct. 1937: 3. Photographs of the production also appear on this page.

31. Freeden, *Jüdische Presse*, 97, and "Jüdischer Kulturbund," 63.

32. Bab in *Geschlossene Vorstellung*, 240.

33. Freeden, "Jüdischer Kulturbund," 66.

34. Gronius in *Geschlossene Vorstellung*, 75.

35. See Dahm, "Kulturelles," 90. Besides great directors such as Max Reinhardt and Leopold Jessner, star performers Elizabeth Bergner, Ernst Deutsch, and Max Pohl had all emigrated to perform abroad.

36. In Pogade, "Atempause," 17. Camilla Spira was known in Berlin musical reviews before 1933. Thereafter, she acted primarily in the Kulturbund's *Kleinkunstbühne*, which was the stage for musical comedy and cabaret. She still lives in Berlin. Kurt Singer also left Germany for the United States After the events of November 1938, he returned not to Germany but to Holland, where he lived and worked until his transport to Theresienstadt. His cabarettist, Max Ehrlich, left Holland for Berlin in 1935, went to the United States in 1937, and then returned to Berlin.

37. Hans Hinkel in *Geschlossene Vorstellung*, 302. Hinkel cites Kurt Singer, who supposedly had referred to the artists' loyalty to the theatre's endeavors. Singer is quoted as having said that there had never been an incident in which authorities had to intervene.

38. The conference's speakers and their speeches are documented in the Akademie der Künste Fritz Wisten archives. The documents are reproduced in *Geschlossene Vorstellung*, 266–97.

39. Prinz in *Geschlossene Vorstellung*, 273–79.

40. Wisten in *Geschlossene Vorstellung*, 282.

41. Singer in *Geschlossene Vorstellung*, 294. His speech was on 7 September 1936. He announced that actor training and discussion would begin with rehearsals of Bistritzky's *Schabatai Zwi* (premiered 3 November 1936).

42. Freeden, *Jüdische Presse*, 105–6, n. 35. The lectures were poorly attended; the visitors tended to be elderly Jews who had little urge to learn more about Judaism. Freeden repeats this claim in "Jüdischer Kulturbund," 60–62. It should be pointed out, however, that an amateur theatre, independent of the Kulturbund, sprang into existence in 1936. The Theaterstudio, sponsored by the Berlin Zionist organization, featured Jewish plays in Yiddish; see Dahm, "Kulturelles," 158, 173.

43. Boguslaw Drewniak, *Das Theater im NS-Staat: Szenarium deutscher Zeitgeschichte, 1933–1945* (Düsseldorf, 1983): 24.

44. *Geschlossene Vorstellung*, 73.

45. Wilhelm Andreas von Schramm, *Neubau des deutschen Theaters* (Berlin, 1934): 59.

46. Ibid., 59–60.

47. Arnold Zweig, *Juden auf der deutschen Bühne* (Berlin, 1927): 28.

48. Ibid., 141–42.

49. Ibid., 263.

50. Arnold Zweig wrote several Jewish plays. In his book he advocated that Jewish plays be written and performed in a "time like this that screams for the detoxification of Jews and non-Jews" (*Juden*, 267). He emigrated from Germany in 1933, which is why he was not part of the Kulturbund. He should not be confused with the Austrian Jew Stefan Zweig, whose plays were part of the Kulturbund repertory.

51. Freeden, "Jüdischer Kulturbund," 65–66.

52. Drewniak, *Theater*, 46, 146–47.

53. Drewniak discusses the role of the government strategy to persuade actors and directors to disseminate the Party line. Referring to the lack of opposition among theatre artists, he claims, "It is shocking how most actors and directors lacked a specific standpoint" (*Theater*, 146).

54. At the (West) Berlin Document Center, among the items related to Hinkel and the Kulturbund are two letters from Werner Levie (a later head of the Kulturbund) to Hinkel, 3 February and 6 May 1939. They suggest Levie's advantageous position as Jewish supervisor of the national association. The first is a request on behalf of an actor with multiple sclerosis to be allowed to remain in the Reich. The second regards the emigration plans of Levie's wife. Levie requests that Hinkel contact furniture movers so that the emigration may proceed.

55. This example of random help by the Gestapo stems from a 1986 interview with Steffi Ronau-Walter, formerly Hinzelmann, in *Geschlossene Vorstellung*, 356–57. She now lives in the United States.

56. Freeden, "Jüdischer Kulturbund," 65–66.

57. Freeden in Broder and Geisel, *Sternstunden*; Camilla Spira in Pogade, "Atempause," 17.

58. See note 17, above.

59. Richarz, *Jewish Life*, 385.

60. Martin Brandt in Broder and Geisel, *Sternstunden*. It is an ironic twist of fate that Brandt emigrated to the United States and became a leading film actor whose speciality was Nazis. Of course, not all of Brandt's colleagues emigrated. Eike Geisel describes a continuation of the Kulturbund in 1941 Amsterdam and traces the deportation of members after 1942 to the concentration camp stages of Theresienstadt and Westerbork. See "Da Capo in Holland" in *Geschlossene Vorstellung*, 189–214.

One cannot help but think of Joshua Sobol's play, *Ghetto*, which is based on the Vilna Ghetto Theatre troupe's last season of performances in 1942 before the Nazis ordered the total liquidation of the Jews from the ghetto. Sobol's use of primary documents from the ghetto allows him to shape dramatic characters who voice similar sentiments to these real-life former Kulturbund artists.

61. In *Geschlossene Vorstellung*, 94.

62. Moritz Goldstein, "Kulturghetto?" *Die jüdische Rundschau* (Berlin), 28 July 1933: 373.

63. See Bruno Bettelheim, "Owners of Their Faces," in *Surviving the Holocaust* (London, 1986): 97–103. He stresses the importance of maintaining one's self-respect in order to survive: "Even the worst mistreatment by the SS failed to extinguish the will to live—that is, as long as one could muster the wish to go on and maintain one's self-respect" (97).

11

The Final Chapter: Theatre in the Concentration Camps of Nazi Germany

Michael Patterson
with material by Louise Stafford-Charles

The repressive cultural policy of the Third Reich was at its strongest in those situations where denial of artistic freedom coincided with the complete removal of basic human liberties—in the concentration camps of Nazi Germany. These institutions of horror were established in the peace years, but, except for an intensification of the suffering and destruction of the inmates, the war did not have the same immediate effect on the camps as it had on most civilian institutions. The war against the Jews and dissidents had already broken out in 1933; for them there were no peace years. The account that follows will of necessity stretch beyond the declared confines of this anthology to include the hideous epilogue of theatre in the shadow of the Holocaust. In more senses than one, it is the final chapter of Nazi cultural policy.

Many Jewish and left-wing theatre workers fled into exile in the 1930s. Reinhardt, despite having been invited to become an "honorary Aryan," remained in Austria until the threat of the Anschluß, then, like the more fortunate, made his way to the United States, which provided a home for some of the leading German theatre and cinema figures of the day, notably Bertolt Brecht, Marlene Dietrich, Peter Lorre, Ernst Toller, and Erwin Piscator. There had even been a proposal by Goebbels that Piscator should be invited, through the mediation of Edward Gordon Craig, to return to Germany from his initial exile in Moscow to form a propaganda theatre for the Nazis, which suggests either extreme obtuseness on the part of Goebbels or political ambivalence on the part of Piscator, or both. Other German theatre practitioners were less fortunate: seeking refuge in Holland, they found themselves trapped within the confines of the Reich shortly after the outbreak of war. The actor Kurt Gerron refused Marlene Dietrich's invitation to come to the United States, relying on his First World War decoration to keep him safe from arrest. By 1944 he had perished in the gas chambers of Auschwitz.

Those theatre practitioners who found themselves in Nazi concentration camps did not abandon their calling. That theatre continued to be pursued so vigorously in the deadening circumstances of the concentration camps is remarkable in itself. In the so-called First World, with its high technology and culture of constant entertainment, serious theatre-going is now the activity of a cultural minority, and so it is easy to forget what a basic need theatre fulfills. But where societies are in a state of crisis or change, theatre remains a vital means of expressing the aspirations and the apprehensions of society. This may occur during a period of revolutionary change, as in the vigorous popular theatre in parts of Latin America, or in times of acute deprivation. In *The Empty Space* Peter Brook records how, despite the devastation of war, theatre was brought alive in the ruins of postwar Germany:

> In the burnt-out shell of the Hamburg Opera only the stage itself remained—but an audience assembled on it whilst against a back wall on a wafer-thin set singers climbed up and down to perform *The Barber of Seville*, because nothing would stop them doing so. In a tiny attic fifty people crammed together while in the inches of remaining space a handful of the best actors resolutely continued to practise their art. In a ruined Düsseldorf, a minor Offenbach about smugglers and bandits filled the theatre with delight. There was nothing to discuss, nothing to analyse—in Germany that winter, as in London a few years before, the theatre was responding to a hunger. What, however, was this hunger? Was it a hunger for the invisible, a hunger for a reality deeper than the fullest form of everyday life—or was it a hunger for the missing things in life, a hunger, in fact, for buffers against reality?[1]

The question of the actual function of theatre in such a context is one to which we must return. There can, though, hardly be a greater testimony to the human need to make theatre than the work that was created by the internees of the concentration camps of Nazi Germany from the *Machtübernahme* (seizure of power) until the process of extermination destroyed all human endeavour. That men and women living degraded lives, daily coping with hunger, sickness, and brutality, and with death as the only probable release could find the time and energy to perform theatre is not only evidence of the extraordinary resilience of the human spirit, but also witness to the transformational power of theatre to give shape to the terrors that surround humankind—experienced here with particular acuteness.

Theatre in the Nazi concentration camps took a wide variety of forms. Apart from the extermination camps that now so vividly occupy our minds with their haunting images of victims' shoes and spectacles, there were the "model camps," which the Red Cross was invited to visit. In these, extraordinarily, even operas were mounted, and we know of productions of *The Marriage of Figaro*, *The Magic Flute*, *Tosca*, *Aida*, *Carmen*, *Die Fledermaus*, *La Bohème*, and *The Bartered Bride*. These were most certainly staged less for the sake of the prisoners than for the entertainment of the guards and as a reassurance to the outside world that the quality of life was being maintained.

Similarly, after the outbreak of war, in Malines in Belgium, where prisoners of French, German, Flemish, and Dutch origins were interned, the SS arranged for those who had been theatre performers to present "variety shows" in the camp yard on Saturdays and Sundays. Following these performances reports would appear in the Belgian press to present a better picture of camp life and to diminish rumours of German atrocities. Even in the less-favored camps the SS attempted to preserve some level of normality. They encouraged sports for those who were strong enough to participate, including football, handball, volleyball, and—in an ironic mockery of the internees' physical degeneration—boxing. In some camps radio music was played on the public address system. In May 1941 the Buchenwald SS equipped a hall as a cinema. In the evenings the prisoners filed in to see old films, and during the day they witnessed public hangings in the same hall. In 1942 and 1943 Mauthausen, Buchenwald, and Auschwitz opened brothels (restricted to "Aryan" prisoners in the case of Mauthausen). The authorities also turned a blind eye to some of the clandestine libraries set up in the camps.

Predictably, then, even when they were not attempting to reassure the outside world of the humanity of their camps, the guards encouraged or condoned theatrical activities. This attitude must have contained a fair amount of cruel cynicism, rather in the manner of the Pip Simmons Theatre Group creation *An die Musik*, in which, in one harrowing scene, the performers, representing camp inmates, are required by the "guards" to tell virulently anti-Semitic jokes and are beaten up if the audience does not find them funny.

On New Year's 1938 the camp commandant at Buchenwald ordered the inmates to give a week of "humorous" presentations. One of the prisoners had been compere at a Berlin music hall, and he was chosen to discover talent, finally selecting fifteen fellow prisoners. It was a dark irony to wander among his pale, malnourished friends looking for those who could make the inmates laugh because their German warders had demanded seasonal humour. Other prisoners constructed a rough theatre for this show by tearing down the partitions of a large barrack and creating a stage along one of its walls. A few lights were hung and some crude scenery produced. The production included jugglers, acrobats, dancers, magicians, and musicians. The comedy sketches satirized camp conditions and even made fun of the SS officials. However, in the tradition of the authorized critique of the court jester, such satire was tolerated as an opportunity to release and express tensions that might otherwise have surfaced in the form of riots and rebellion.

An even more sinister case of the SS encouraging theatrical activity occurred in Theresienstadt, whose Jewish ghetto initially, as part of the *Stadtverschönerung* (town improvement), boasted a fine Jewish library brought from the Jewish community center in Prague and also possessed a simple theatre. Here the first commandant of the camp, Dr. Friederich Seidel, a possible model for the sinister doctor in Rolf Hochhuth's *The Deputy*, developed a fascination for Jewish culture, not from any sympathy but from a disgusted curiosity about beings he regarded as *Untermenschen*, "similar to the entomologist's curiosity about insects," as one survivor put it.[2] Seidel therefore permitted Jewish music and plays to be performed, although these of course were banned in the rest of the Reich.

In Theresienstadt theatre that was specifically Jewish could take place, but only with the approval of the authorities. In particular, Karl Schwenk, a Czechoslovakian Jew who had been a former theatre director, won Seidel's trust by his magnificent stagings of classics such as Rostand's *Cyrano de Bergerac*, Molière's *Georges Dandin*, and Gogol's *The Marriage*, all designed by Frantisek Zelenka, formerly of the National Theatre in Prague. Having established his credentials with these noncontroversial pieces, Schwenk was permitted to move on to more satirical and overtly Jewish pieces, earning himself the title "The Aristophanes of Theresienstadt." Perhaps his most memorable production was that of *The Last Cyclist*. This piece was described by the historian Nora Levin as

> based on the old saying that "Jews and cyclists are responsible for all misfortunes." The plot is an allegory of Hitler-Europe, but with a happy ending. All cyclists and those who cannot prove that their ancestors had been pedestrians for six generations are deported to a horrible island by lunatic rulers of a mythical country. One cyclist—the last—escapes deportation and is first exhibited in a zoo. Everything can be blamed on him. In the end, however, he prevails, and the rule of the lunatics is defeated.[3]

Schwenk's piece clearly served two functions: first, to satirize the ridiculous racial laws of the Third Reich (reminiscent of Charlie Chaplin's *Great Dictator*, in which the Führer wishes to eliminate all people with brown hair), and second, to hold out the hope that one day sanity might prevail.

The tragedy is that very few of those who defiantly celebrated their Jewishness by performing and attending *The Last Cyclist* lived to experience the defeat of the lunatics.

The same sense of defeating a vicious oppressor occurs in the children's theatre, which was produced in some internment centers. An original children's opera, *Brundibar* was staged at Theresienstadt with music by Hans Krasa and text by Adolf Hoffmeister, and directed and designed by Frantisek Zelenka. It dealt with the children's hatred of a wicked organ-grinder who refuses to let them sing for money in order to buy food. Friendly animals advise the children to band together to fight the evil Brundibar, who is finally defeated:

> Beat your drum,
> We have won, . . .
> We did not give in!
> We are not afraid.[4]

In sharing in the defeat of the mythical Brundibar the children could feel for once that their situation was not entirely hopeless.

Other theatrical offerings were clearly designed above all to give the Jewish players and their audience a sense of solidarity amid adversity, just as Mordecai Gebirtig's song "Our Town is Burning," which commemorated a massacre in Poland in 1938, was frequently sung. Thus Sholom Aleichem's *Teyve the Milkman*, now better known as *Fiddler on the Roof*, was performed, as was the Yiddish classic *Both Kuni Lemels*. One theatrical evening staged at the Monowitz infirmary for Jewish doctors included a lecture on the contribution of Yiddish theatre to European theatre, again asserting the value of Jewish culture.

Even well into the war years the SS could be persuaded to permit the occasional theatrical offering. In the summer of 1943 in Dachau, Viktor Matejka, later to become Vienna's Councilor for Cultural Affairs, negotiated to allow the production of a parodistic piece of Grand Guignol entitled *Bloody Night at Horror Castle, or Sir Adolar's Bride Ride and Its Gruesome End*. Written by a Viennese journalist, Rudolf Kalmar, on the back of discarded typed paper, the melodramatic violence and blood letting of the piece were a thinly disguised attack on the cruelty of the SS guards, who, however, seemed to miss the point as they tolerated its being performed on six successive weekends. The actor performing Sir Adolar, Erwin Geschonneck, who survived to become a well-known actor in East Germany, accounted for the success of the piece thus: "It was not possible without humour. Humour made us strong. It could pull people out of lethargy, keep them on their feet."[5]

Later still, between July 1943 and June 1944, in the Dutch transit camp of Westerbork six revues were staged with the approval of the authorities.

They were written and composed by Willy Rosen and Erich Ziegler, two leading figures of Berlin cabaret who had sought a haven from German oppression in the Netherlands. The star of the first three revues was Camilla Spira, who had achieved colossal fame in the operetta *The White Horse Inn* more than a decade earlier. Indeed, such was her success that it no doubt contributed to her becoming reclassified as "Aryan" and so escaping from Westerbork. It appears that, in common with much of the officially permitted theatrical activities, the content of these revues was fairly anodyne. A Dutch journalist noted in his diary: "The revue was a mixture of antiquated sketches and mild ridicule of the conditions and circumstances prevailing at the camp. Not a single sharp word, not a single harsh word, but a little gentle irony in the passing, avoiding the main issues. A compromise."[6]

Except for some mild fun about roll calls and overcrowding many of the numbers were purely escapist, including trivial sexism in a scene with schoolgirls wearing very short skirts and in the sentimentality of a nineteenth-century "postcoach idyll." From some surviving photographs, reproduced in Peter Jelavich's fascinating *Berlin Cabaret*, it can be seen that sets and costumes were quite elaborate, and it is known that the SS commandant, Konrad Gemmeker, made considerable sums available for what became fairly described as "the best cabaret in Holland."

The official encouragement of such entertainment created a moral dilemma for the inmates. The wood for the Westerbork stage had been taken from a local synagogue and the barrier used to herd incoming prisoners together during the day was used at night as a piece of decor. Some prisoners stayed away in disgust. Others, despite their ambivalent feelings, went along to seek relief from the misery of their daily existence and to forget, if they could, the likely fate awaiting them. As one of the inmates recorded in July 1943, "It is a complete madhouse here; we shall have to feel ashamed of it for three hundred years. . . . The . . . hall full. People laughed until they cried—oh yes, cried. . . . Kormann told me about it, adding, 'This whole business is slowly driving me to the edge of despair.'"[7] It was an extreme case of the situation faced by many political playwrights and theatre workers in the twentieth century, from Brecht and Piscator to any socialist dramatist who has written for television or Hollywood—the question of how much to compromise one's integrity in order to gain access to the public.

Perhaps the saddest case of a great talent having to compromise with the Nazis was that of Kurt Gerron. This leading actor, who had played Tiger Brown at the premiere of *The Threepenny Opera* and Marlene Dietrich's boss in *The Blue Angel*, arrived in Theresienstadt in January 1944. Like many others, he had hoped to remain secure in Holland and now found himself incarcerated but wooed by the commandant, who was proud to have such a star in his camp. At first Gerron was obliged to give a one-man show for the benefit of the SS and was then required to stage a lavish revue, *Karussell*

("Carousel"), which was performed over fifty times, mainly in the summer of 1944. The music was composed by Martin Roman, the leader of the camp jazz band, and the sets were designed, as with Schwenk's stylish productions, by Frantisek Zelenka. Once again the content was mainly escapist, although it is amusing to consider that it was probably only in Theresienstadt that songs from *The Threepenny Opera* were still sung—a sobering reflection too on the harmlessness of Brecht's supposedly subversive lyrics. Some cabaret numbers, however, did attempt to alleviate despair and encourage solidarity, as in one of the humorous songs, which described a newly arrived lady of some wealth who expected to be able to arrange food, clothes, and accommodation to her liking.

Ironically, the performers of the cabaret did enjoy some of the privileges satirized in this song. They had private sleeping quarters, a better diet, and above all, a delay in transportation to the extermination camps. The worst example of having to compromise occurred when Gerron was told that he would have to direct a Nazi propaganda film, *Der Führer schenkt den Juden eine Stadt* ("The Führer Gives the Jews a Town"). Filmed in August and September 1944, it purported to show the luxurious life-style of the Jews in Theresienstadt, enjoying the relaxed entertainment of Gerron's cabaret while young Germans sacrificed their lives to protect the Fatherland. The reality of the filming was somewhat different, however: "'Whoever looks into the camera, makes faces or speaks into the camera, will be arrested immediately.' Bathed in sweat, Gerron urged us, implored us, begged for discipline, for us to follow orders absolutely. He cracked jokes and made despairing efforts. 'Please, no incidents, don't provoke any use of force!'"[8]

The reality of camp life—and death—was also very different, and in addition to the officially sanctioned performances were the more numerous, more spontaneous, and usually clandestine performances in which inmates could truly express their feelings and fears. These could take many forms. In an internment camp near Riga a group of women organized a satirical puppet show. They made the puppets out of the material of their striped uniforms, sewn together with thread picked from their scarves. A bench with blankets served as an improvised puppet theatre. There must have been some satisfaction in using the outward manifestation of their oppression, their camp uniforms, as a means of escape into the world of fantasy.

Some satirical pieces were performed only once in order to avoid reprisals from the camp authorities. Such was the case with *Roar China*, performed at the Polish camp of Czestochowa, which was originally run not by the SS but by the Wehrmacht. This piece, adapted from Soviet propaganda and containing echoes of Brecht's *The Measures Taken*, dealt with the exploitation of Chinese coolies by Western powers. Goldfarb summarizes the plot as follows: "When a Chinese boatman kills an American businessman in self-defense, retributions are demanded, including the execution of three innocent coolies. The final scene depicts the successful beginnings of a revolt by the oppressed."⁹ The parallels between the exploited Chinese and the Jewish slave laborers in Czestochowa are obvious.

Much more common than the full-length play was the cabaret format. The cabaret had enjoyed a vigorous tradition in German and Austrian cities, counting Wedekind and Brecht among its exponents, and had thrived on its satirical content. It was hardly surprising, therefore, that secret theatrical performances in the concentration camps were often in the form of cabarets. The cabaret had the further advantage of being popular, incorporating song and dance, and therefore appealed to internees from different classes and backgrounds; it was also, by its nature, very topical, and had the obvious practical value of being divided into brief "turns," which required less preparation than a full-length drama and which could be easily interrupted, perhaps by an approaching German guard, without ruining the flow of the piece.

It seems that such shows were staged simply. The Yiddish actor and theatre historian Yonas Turkov reported: "Instead of a stage a table was used, on which . . . actors stood and gave their recitals. The program consisted of songs and recitations . . . and humorous sketches."¹⁰ Curt Daniel also gave a brief, almost contemporary account of such a performance at Buchenwald:

> The first item was always the singing of the Buchenwald song by the group. . . . Next came a humorous monologue of an imaginary conversation between the drunken camp leader and the equally drunken leader of the German labor front, Robert Ley. . . . This would be followed by more political songs. The most important item would be a short play for three players, lasting some twenty minutes, a mixture of comedy and satire attacking the administration of the camp and the blood-soaked system which maintained it.¹¹

In Dachau, Fritz Grünbaum, who had over three decades established an international reputation as a cabaret artist and comedian, regularly delighted inmates with his wit. Just two weeks before his death, on New Year's Eve 1940, he still managed to gather his failing strength to raise one last laugh: "To be honest, I don't give a damn about my life. I wouldn't mind leaving the whole mess right this moment. The problem is, I might go to heaven."¹²

Given the context in which these actors had to perform, it would be an impertinence to attempt to assess the aesthetic quality of their work. Certainly, of the official productions at Theresienstadt, Mirko Tuma could write: "These performances were no makeshift events, but subtle professional productions."¹³ However, the clandestine cabaret performances were staged not to display talent or to provide aesthetic pleasure, but as a means of bringing together into a communal experience those who had been stripped of everything except their racial identity and their suffering.

In answer then to the question posed by Brook—"What . . . was this hunger?"—we may surmise that the hunger for theatre was different in the different contexts of camp life. In the professional productions at Theresienstadt and other model camps, it may well have been that theatre served in large measure as a form of escape from the harsh realities of everyday existence in the camp, as is suggested by the euphoric endings of *The Last Cyclist* and *Brundibar*.

NOTES

1. Peter Brook, *The Empty Space* (London, 1988): 49.
2. Mirko Tuma, "Memories of Theresienstadt," *Performing Arts Journal* 1, no. 2 (Fall 1976): 15.
3. Noral Levin, *The Holocaust: The Destruction of European Jewry 1933–1945* (New York, 1968): 485.
4. Alvin Goldfarb, "Theatrical Activities in the Nazi Concentration Camps," *Performing Arts Journal* 1, no. 2 (Fall 1976): 8.
5. Volker Kühn, "The Last Laugh," *The Guardian* (Manchester) 17 May 1991, n.p.
6. Peter Jelavich, *Berlin Cabaret* (Cambridge, MA, 1993): 264. The final chapter of Jelavich's book offers an interesting and well-researched account of the destiny of Berlin cabaret performers in the Third Reich.
7. Ibid., 268.
8. Alice Randt, "Die Schleuse; drei Jahre Theresienstadt," unpublished manuscript, cited in Jelavich, *Berlin Cabaret*, 281.
9. Goldfarb, "Theatrical Activities," 9. (*Brülle China* ["Roar China"] by Soviet playwright Sergei Tretiakov had been staged by Meyerhold and, as adapted by Leo Lania, had its German premiere at the Schauspielhaus Frankfurt 9 November 1929, directed by Fritz Peter Buch. The camp production was inspired by that earlier revolutionary docudrama. Cf. Bruno Reifenberg's 1929 review in Günther Rühle, *Theater für die Republik* [Frankfurt am Main, 1967]: 991–94.—.*Ed*]
10. Yonas Turkov, "Teater un kontsertn in di getos un kontsentratsye lagern," *Yidisher Teater in Yirope . . . Poyln* (New York, 1968): 502.
11. Curt Daniel, "The Freest Theatre in the Reich: In the German Concentration Camps," *Theatre Arts* 25 (Nov. 1941): 806. The chorus of the Buchenwald song translates roughly as "Keep going, comrade, don't lose heart/The will to live is in our blood/And faith, yes faith, is in our soul."
12. Kühn, "The Last Laugh," n. p.
13. Tuma, "Memories," 17.

Bibliography

"Abkommen zwischen 'Kraft durch Freude' und 'Deutsche Bühne.' " *Der völkische Beobachter* (Berlin), 17 April 1934: 1.
Adler, H. G. *Theresienstadt 1941–1945: das Antlitz einer Zwangsgemeinschaft*.Tübingen: J. D. B. Mohr, 1955.
"Adolf Hitlers Staatsbesuch in Dresden." *Der völkische Beobachter* (Berlin), 31 May 1934: 1.
Ahleff, Eberhard, ed. *Das dritte Reich*. Hannover: Fackelträger, 1970.
Ahrens, Gerhard, ed. *Das Theater des deutschen Regisseurs Jürgen Fehling*. Berlin: Quadriga, 1987.
Allen, William S. *The Nazi Seizure of Power: The Experience of a Single German Town, 1922–1945*. Rev. ed. New York: Franklin Watts, 1984.
Alth, Minna von, ed. *Burgtheater, 1776–1976. Aufführungen und Besetzungen von zweihundert Jahren*. 2 vols. Vienna: Überreuter, 1979.
"Anordnung." *Der völkische Beobachter* (Berlin), 28/29 May 1933: 2.
August, Wolf-Eberhard. "Die Stellung der Schauspieler im Dritten Reich." Ph.D. diss. University of Cologne, 1973.
Barron, Stephanie, ed. *"Degenerate Art": The Fate of the Avant-Garde in Nazi Germany*. New York: Harry N. Abrams, 1991.
Bartetzky, Dieter. *Zwischen Zucht und Ekstase; zur Theatralik von NS-Architektur*. Berlin: Mann, 1985.
Becker, Ernest. *The Denial of Death*. New York: Free Press, 1973.
Benjamin, Walter. "The Work of Art in the Era of Mechanical Reproduction." In *Illuminations: Essays and Relflections*. Ed. Hannah Arendt, tr. Harry Zohn. New York: Schocken Books, 1968.

Bethge, Friedrich. *Reims*. Berlin: Langen-Müller, 1934.
Bettelheim, Bruno. "Owners of Their Faces." In *Surviving the Holocaust*. London: Flamingo, 1986: 97–103.
Biedrzynski, Richard. *Schauspieler, Regisseure, Intendanten*. Heidelberg: Hüthig, 1944.
Bleuel, Hans-Peter. *Strength Through Joy*. Tr. Maxwell Brownjohn. London: Secker and Warburg, 1973.
Boelcke, W. A. *Kriegspropaganda 1938–41. Geheime Ministerkonferenzen im Reichpropagandaministerium*. Stuttgart: Deutsche Verlags-Anstalt, 1966.
Brandt, Rolf. "'Die Räuber' im Theater der Nation." *Berliner Lokal-Anzeiger*, 19 January 1934: n. p.
Brenner, Hildegard. "Die Kunst im politischen Machtkampf der Jahre 1933/34." *Vierteljahrsheft für Zeitgeschichte* 10, no. 1 (January 1962): 17–42.
———. *Die Kunstpolitik des Nationalsozialismus*. Reinbek bei Hamburg: Rowohlt, 1963.
Brinkmann, Joachim, ed. *Festschrift für Heinz Hilpert*. Göttingen: Drückerei- und Verlagsgesellschaft, 1960.
Broder, Henryk M. "Selbstbehauptung in der Sackgasse." *Berliner Zeitung*, 27 January 1992: 25.
Broder, Henryk M., and Eike Geisel. *Es waren wirklich Sternstunden*. Film. Bayrischer Rundfunk/Sender Freies Berlin, 1988.
Brockett, Oscar G., and Robert F. Findlay. *Century of Innovation*. Englewood Cliffs, NJ: Prentice Hall, 1973.
Brook, Peter. *The Empty Space*. London: Atheneum, 1988.
Cadigan, Rufus, J. "Richard Billinger, Hanns Johst, and Eberhard W. Möller: Three Representative National Socialist Playwrights." Ph.D. diss. University of Kansas, 1979.
Carlé, Wolfgang. *Kinder wie die Zeit vergeht*. Berlin: Henschel, 1987.
Carlé, Wolfgang, and Heinrich Martens. "Berlin am Zirkus 1; Eine Geschichte des Friedrichstadt-Palastes." *BZ am Abend* (Berlin), no. 24 (January-February 1976). Clipping file, Berlin Akademie der Künste.
Cochavi, Yehoyakim. "Georg Kareski's Nomination as Head of the Kulturbund. The Gestapo's First Attempt—and Last Failure—to Impose a Jewish Leadership." *Leo Baeck Institute Yearbook* 34 (1989): 227–246.
———. "Kultur und Bildungsarbeit der deutschen Juden 1933–1941: Antwort auf die Verfolgung durch das NS Regime." *Neue Sammlung* 26, no. 3 (1986): 396–407.
"Culture Chamber Ousts Jews." *New York Times*, 4 September 1935: 14.
Dahm, Volker. "Kulturelles und geistiges Leben." In *Die Juden in Deutschland 1933–1945*, ed. Wolfgang Benz. Munich: C. H. Beck, 1989.
Daniel, Curt. "The Freest Theater in the Reich: In the German Concentration Camps." *Theatre Arts* 25 (November 1941): 801–7.
Dannecker, Hermann. "Reichs-Theaterwoche in Dresden: Das Schauspiel." *Der völkische Beobachter* (Munich), 6 June 1934: 8.
Daube, Otto, ed. *Amtlicher Führer durch die Richard-Wagner-Festwoche, Detmold 1937*. Detmold: Ernst Schnelle, 1937.
Davies, Cecil W. *Theatre for the People*. Austin, TX: Texas University Press, 1977.
"Deutsche Reichsbank." Document #3566. Bundesarchiv, Abteilung Potsdam.

"Das deutsche Theater im neuen Reich. Reichsminister Dr. Goebbels vor den Mitglieder des Deutschen Bühnenvereins." *Der völkische Beobachter* (Berlin), 1 June 1934: 2.
Deutschland Erwacht. Werden, Kampf und Sieg der NSDAP. Hamburg-Bahrenfeld: Cigaretten-Bilderdienst, 1933.
Diebold, Bernhard. "Dreierlei Kunst. Drei dramatische Beispiele." *Frankfurter Zeitung* (Reichsausgabe), 11 February 1933: 9.
Dietzenschmidt, Anton. "Eröffnung mit 'Ein Sommernachtstraum.' " N. p., 17 September 1934. Clipping file, Berlin Akademie der Künste.
———. " 'Peer Gynt' im Theater des Volkes." N. p. 6 March 1936. Clipping file, Berlin Akademie der Künste.
———. " 'Wallenstein' im Theater des Volkes." N. p., 12 November 1934. Clipping file, Berlin Akademie der Künste.
Dillmann, Michael. *Heinz Hilpert: Leben und Werk*. Berlin: Akademie der Künste, 1990.
"Dr. Goebbels in der Dresdner Staatsoper." *Dresdner Neueste Nachrichten*, 28 January 1934. Dresden Staatsarchiv, Collection 1392/2, no. 168.
"Dr. Ley und Alfred Rosenberg bei der Deutschen Bühne." *Der völkische Beobachter* (Berlin), 7 June 1934: 4.
"Dresden feiert den Führer." *Der völkische Beobachter* (Berlin), 29 May 1934: 1.
Drewniak, Boguslaw. *Das Theater im NS-Staat: Szenarium deutscher Zeitgeschichte, 1933–1945*. Düsseldorf: Droste, 1983.
Drews, Berta. *Heinrich George*. Hamburg: Rowohlt, 1959.
Drews, Wolfgang. *Festgabe für Heinz Hilpert*. Göttingen: Drückerei- und Verlagsgesellschaft, 1965.
"Der dritte Dresdner Tag." *Dresdner Anzeiger*, 30 May 1934: 2.
Dussel, Konrad. *Ein neues, ein heroisches Theater?* Bonn: Bouvier, 1988.
Editorial. *Die jüdische Rundschau* (Berlin), 25 July 1933: 365.
Eichberg, Henning. "The Nazi *Thingspiel*: Theater for the Masses in Fascism and Proletarian Culture." *New German Critique* 11 (Spring 1977): 133–50.
"Eingliederung der RKK in die Deutsche Arbeitsfront." *Der völkische Beobachter* (Berlin), 13 February 1934: 1.
"Einheitliches Theaterrecht." *Der völkische Beobachter* (Berlin), 17 May 1934: 8.
Eloesser, Arthur. Review of *The Golem*. *Die jüdische Rundschau* (Berlin), 12 October 1937: 3.
Elwood, William R. "The War Conscience on the Berlin Stage." *Quarterly Journal of Speech* 53, no. 4 (December 1967): 378–79.
Engelmann, Bernt. *In Hitler's Germany: Daily Life in the Third Reich*. Tr. Krishna Winston. New York: Schocken, 1986.
"Eröffnung der historischen Theaterschau Dresdens." *Der völkische Beobachter* (Berlin), 30 May 1934: 5.
Esslin, Martin. *Anatomy of Drama*. New York: Hill and Wang, 1977.
———. Introduction to *The Enthusiasts*, by Robert Musil. New York: Performing Arts, 1983.
F [Emil Fechter]. "Kleines Volksstück." *Deutsche Allgemeine Zeitung* (Berlin), 25 January 1933: 4.
Fehling, Jürgen. *Die Magie des Theaters*. Hannover: Friedrich, 1965.

Fest, Joachim C. *The Face of the Third Reich: Portraits of the Nazi Leadership.* Tr. Michael Bullock. New York: Pantheon Books, 1970.

———. *Hitler.* Tr. Richard and Clara Winston. New York: Harcourt Brace Jovanovich, 1973.

"Die Festsitzung der Reichskulturkammer in der Staatsoper." *Der völkische Beobachter* (Berlin), 3 May 1934: 9.

Findeisen, Kurt Arnold. " 'Peer Gynt' in Dietrich Eckarts Übersetzung." *Der völkische Beobachter* (Berlin), 31 May 1934: 5.

Freeden, Herbert. *Die jüdische Presse im Dritten Reich.* Frankfurt/Main: Jüdischer Verlag bei Athenäum, 1987.

———. "Jüdischer Kulturbund ohne jüdische Kultur." In *Geschlossene Vorstellung: Der jüdische Kulturbund in Deutschland 1933–1941.* Akademie der Künste. Berlin: Edition Heinrich, 1992: 55–66.

———. *Jüdisches Theater in Nazideutschland.* Tübingen: J. D. B. Mohr, 1964; Frankfurt/Main: Ullstein, 1985.

———. "Kultur 'nur für Juden': Kulturkampf in der jüdischen Presse in Nazi-Deutschland." In *Die Juden im nationalsozialistischen Deutschland,* ed. Arnold Pauker. Tübingen: J. C. B. Mohr, 1986: 258–271.

———. "Theater Under a Swastika." *Leo Baeck Institute Yearbook* 1 (1956): 142–62.

———. "Vom geistigen Widerstand der deutschen Juden: ein Kapitel jüdischer Selbstbehauptung in den Jahren 1933 bis 1938." In *Widerstand und Exil 1933–1945.* Bonn: Bundeszentrale für politische Bildung, 1986: 47–59.

Frels, Wilhelm. "Die deutsche dramatische Produktion 1934." *Die neue Literatur* 36, no. 6 (June 1935): 325–32.

Freydank, Ruth. *Theater in Berlin, Von den Anfängen bis 1945.* Berlin: Argon, 1988.

Friedrichs, Axel, ed. *Die nationalsozialistische Revolution 1933.* Berlin: Junker und Dünnhaupt, 1935 and 1937.

Fuchs, Elinor. *Plays of the Holocaust.* New York: Theatre Communications Group, 1987.

"Der Führer dankt seinen hervorragendsten Mitkämpfern." *Der völkische Beobachter* (Berlin), 2 January 1934: 2.

Gadberry, Glen W. "Dramatic Contraries: The Paine Histories of Hanns Johst and Howard Fast." *Text and Presentation* 9 (1989): 61–72.

———. "Nazi Germany's Jewish Theatre." *Theatre Survey* 21, no. 1 (May 1980): 15–32.

———. "The *Stedingers*: Nazi Festival Drama of the Destruction of a People." *Theatre History Studies* 10 (1990): 105–26.

———. "The Theatre of the Third Reich: Issues and Concerns." In *Nordic Theatre Studies*—Special International Issue: New Directions in Theatre Research. Proceedings of the XIth FIRT/IFTR Congress, Stockholm, 1989, ed. Willmar Sauter. Copenhagen: Munksgaard, 1990: 75–78.

Garten, H. F. *Modern German Drama.* 2nd ed. London: Methuen, 1964.

Geehr, Richard. *Karl Lueger, Mayor of Fin de Siècle Vienna.* Detroit: Wayne State University Press, 1990.

Geehr, Richard, John Heineman, and Gerald Herman. "Wien 1910: An Example of Nazi Anti-Semitism." *Film and History* 15, no. 3 (September 1985): 50–65.

Geisel, Eike, and H. M. Broder. *Premiere und Pogrom: Der jüdische Kulturbund 1933–1941, Texte und Bilder.* Berlin: Siedler, 1992.

George, David E. R. *Henrik Ibsen in Deutschland. Rezeption und Revision.* Tr. Heinz Arnold and Bernd Glasenapp. Göttingen: Vandenhoeck und Ruprecht, 1968.
Geschlossene Vorstellung: Der jüdische Kulturbund in Deutschland 1933–1941. Akademie der Künste. Berlin: Edition Heinrich, 1992.
Goebbels, Joseph. "Das deutsche Theater im neuen Reich." *Der völkische Beobachter* (Berlin), 1 June 1934: 2.
———. *The Early Goebbels Diaries, 1925–1926.* Ed. Helmut Heiber, tr. Oliver Watson. New York: Praeger, 1963.
———. *Goebbels-Reden.* Vol 1. Ed. Helmut Heiber. Düsseldorf: Droste, 1971.
———. " 'Hier gilt's der Kunst!' Zur Tagung der Reichskammer der bildenden Kunst." *Der völkische Beobachter* (Berlin), 3/4 June 1934: 5.
———. "Rede des Propagandaministers vor den Theaterleitern, 8. Mai 1933." *Das deutsche Drama in Geschichte und Gegenwart* 5 (1933): 28–40.
———. "Rede des Reichspropagandaministers Dr. Goebbels vor den deutschen Theaterleitern." In *Die nationalsozialistische Revolution 1933,* ed. Axel Friedrichs. Berlin: Junker and Dünnhaupt, 1938: 286–300.
———. "Triumph Richard Wagners; Feierliche Eröffnung der Reichs-Theaterfestwoche." *Der völkische Beobachter* (Berlin), 29 May 1934: 5.
Goertz, Heinrich. *Gustav Gründgens.* Reinbek: Rowohlt, 1965.
Goetz, Wolfgang. *Werner Krauß.* Hamburg: Hoffmann und Campe, 1954.
Göhler, Gerhart. "Ausklang der Reichstheaterfestwoche." *Frankfurter Zeitung* (Reichsausgabe), 12 June 1934: 9.
Goldfarb, Alvin. "Theatrical Activities in the Nazi Concentration Camps." *Performing Arts Journal* 1, no. 2 (Fall 1976): 3–11.
Goldstein, Moritz. "Kulturghetto?" *Die jüdische Rundschau* (Berlin), 28 July 1933: 373.
Gordon, Sarah. *Hitler, Germans and the "Jewish Question."* Princeton, NJ: Princeton University Press, 1984.
Gosse, Edmund. *Henrik Ibsen.* New York: Scribner's, 1908.
Graff, Sigmund. *The Endless Road.* Ed. and tr. Graham Rawson. London: George Allen and Unwin, 1930.
———. "Die endlose Straße im Berliner Osten." *Neue Preußische Zeitung* (Berlin), 15 November 1933: 10.
———. *Erinnerungen eines Bühnenautors: 1900–1945. Von SM zu NS.* Munich: Welsermuhle, 1963.
———. *Über das Soldatische.* Berlin: Nibelungen, 1943.
———. *Unvergesslicher Krieg: Ein Buch vom deutschen Schicksal.* Leipzig: Breitkopf and Härtel, 1936.
———. "Der Weg zu 'Endlose Straße.'" *Neue Preußische Zeitung* (Berlin), 17 November 1933: 6.
Graff, Sigmund, and Carl Ernst Hintze. *Die endlose Straße. Ein Frontstück in vier Bildern.* In *Von der Republik zur Diktatur: 1925–1933,* vol. 2 of *Zeit und Theater,* ed. Günther Rühle. Frankfurt: Propyläen, 1972: 699–767.
"Große Propagandaaktion der N.S.D.A.P." *Der völkische Beobachter* (Berlin), 4 May 1934: 1.
Grosshans, Henry. *Hitler and the Artists.* New York: Holmes & Meier, 1983.

Grunberger, Richard. *A Social History of the Third Reich*. London: Weidenfeld and Nicolson, 1971.
"Grußworte zur Reichs-Theaterwoche." *Der völkische Beobachter* (Berlin), 29 May 1934: 5.
Haan, Christa. "Werner Krauß und das Burgtheater." Diss. University of Vienna, 1970.
Hamilton, Richard F. *Who Voted for Hitler?* Princeton, NJ: Princeton University Press, 1982.
Heilborn, Ernst. "Schieberkomödie." *Frankfurter Zeitung* (Reichsausgabe), 2 February 1933: 10.
Herschkowitz, Annie. "Symbiosis as a Driving Force in the Creative Process." In *Pictures at an Exhibition: Selected Essays on Art and Art Therapy*, ed. Andrea Gilroy and Tessa Dalley. London and New York: Tavistock/Routledge, 1989.
Hesse, Otto Ernst. "Großes Zaubertheater." *Berliner Zeitung am Mittag*, 6 March 1936: n. p.
Hinz, Berthold. *Art in the Third Reich*. Tr. Robert and Rita Kimber. New York: Pantheon, 1979.
Hitler, Adolf. "Adolf Hitlers Rede auf der Kulturtagung der NSDAP. am 1. September [1933]." In *Die nationalsozialistische Revolution 1933*, ed. Axel Friedrichs. Berlin: Junker and Dünnhaupt, 1935: 281–90.
———. *Hitler: Reden und Proklamationen 1932–1945*. Vol 1. Part 2. Ed. Max Domarus. Munich: Süddeutsche, 1965.
———. *Hitler: Speeches and Proclamations 1932–1945, The Chronicle of a Dictatorship*. Vol 1. *1932–1934*. Ed. Max Domarus, tr. Mary Fran Gilbert. Wauconda, IL: Bolchazy-Carducci, 1990.
———. *Hitler's Secret Conversations, 1941–1944*. Tr. Norman Cameron and R. H. Stevens. New York: Farrar, Straus and Young, 1953.
———. *Mein Kampf*. Munich: Zentralverlag der NSDAP, 1927.
———. *Mein Kampf*. 123–124th ed. Munich: Zentralverlag der NSDAP, 1935.
———. *Mein Kampf*. Ed. and tr. John Chamberlain, et al. New York: Rynal & Hitchcock, 1939.
———. *Mein Kampf*. Tr. Ralph Mannheim. Boston: Houghton Miflin, 1962.
Hitler kämpft und siegt in Lippe 1933. Detmold: N.S. Verlag Lippische Staatszeitung, 1934.
Huder, Walter. "Zur Ausstellung, Filmretrospective und Konferenz." In *Theater im Exil 1933–1945*, ed. Lothar Schirmer. Berlin: Akademie der Künste, 1979.
Huesmann, Heinrich. *Welttheater Reinhardt*. Munich: Prestel, 1983.
Hull, David Stewart. *Film in the Third Reich*. New York: Simon and Schuster, 1969.
Ihering, Herbert. "'Die lustigen Weiber von Windsor.' Theater des Volkes." N. p., 4 February 1935. Clipping file, Berlin Akademie der Künste.
———. *Regie*. Berlin: Hugo, 1943.
———. "Zwei Regisseuren, zwei Welten." *Theater heute* 6, no. 3 (1965): 18–20.
Jelavich, Peter. *Berlin Cabaret*. Cambridge, MA: Harvard University Press, 1993.
J-r. "Die lustigen Weiber von Windsor." N. p., 5 February 1935. Clipping file, Berlin Akademie der Künste.
"Der Jude im Kulturschaffen." *Die jüdische Rundschau* (Berlin), 21 July 1933: 353.

"Juden und deutsches Kunstleben." *Die jüdische Rundschau* (Berlin), 7 April 1933: 139.
Jürgen Fehling der Regisseur. Berlin: Akademie der Künste, 1978.
K., P. "Falstaff in Nöten." N. p., 4 February 1935. Clipping file, Berlin Akademie der Künste.
"Der Kampfbund für Deutsche Kultur schafft die 'Deutsche Bühne.' " *Der völkische Beobachter* (Berlin), 16/17/18 April 1933: 1.
" 'Kampf durch Freude!' Die große Kundgebung der Deutschen Arbeitsfront." *Der völkische Beobachter* (Berlin), 29 November 1933: 2.
Kershaw, Ian. *Der Hitler-Mythus: Volksmeinung und Propaganda im Dritten Reich*. Stuttgart: Deutsche Verlagsanstalt, 1980.
Ketelsen, Uwe-Karsten. *Vom heroischen Sein und völkischen Tod*. Bonn: Bouvier, 1970.
Kiss, Edmund. *Wittekind; Trauerspiel in vier Aufzügen*. Leipzig: Koehler and Amelang, 1935.
Knudsen, Hans. "Was lehrt uns die Reichs-Theaterwoche?" *Berliner Lokal-Anzeiger*, 8 June 1934. Dresden Staatsarchiv, Collection 1392/2, no. 407.
Krafft, Erich. "Das neue Theater des Volkes." N. p., 19 January 1934. Clipping file, Berlin Akademie der Künste.
Krauß, Werner. *Das Schauspiel meines Lebens*. Ed. Hans Weigel. Stuttgart: Henry Goverts, 1958.
———. Telegram to Adolf Hitler, 17 June 1939. Berlin Document Center.
Kühlken, Edda. *Die Klassiker-Inszenierungen von Gustaf Gründgens*. Meisenheim: Hain, 1972.
Kühn, Volker. "The Last Laugh." *The Guardian* (Manchester), 17 May 1991: n.p.
"Künftig einheitliche Regelung bei Verboten von Theateraufführungen." *Der völkische Beobachter* (Berlin), 31 January 1934: 6.
"'Kunst darf nicht kommandiert werden.' Aus der Begründung des Theatergesetzes." *Der völkische Beobachter* (Berlin), 24 May 1934: 6.
Kvam, Wayne. "The Nazification of Max Reinhardt's Deutsches Theater Berlin." *Theatre Journal* 40, no. 3 (October 1988): 357–74.
Langer, Lawrence L. *The Holocaust and the Literary Imagination*. New Haven, CT: Yale University Press, 1975.
Laubinger, Otto. "Ein Jahr Aufbauarbeit." *Deutsches Bühnen-Jahrbuch* 46 (1935): 1–8.
Levin, Nora. *The Holocaust: The Destruction of European Jewry, 1933–1945*. New York: Schocken, 1968.
Ley, Robert. *Wir alle helfen dem Führer*. Munich: Eher, 1937.
Lichberg, Heinz von. "Eröffnung des Theaters der Nation in Berlin: 'Die Räuber' im Großen Schauspielhaus." *Der völkische Beobachter* (Berlin), 20 January 1934: 9.
Loewenberg, Peter. *Decoding the Past: The Psychohistorical Approach*. New York: Knopf, 1983.
Luft, Friedrich. *Gustaf Gründgens*. Berlin: Rembrandt, 1959.
Lukács, Georg. *Die Zerstörung der Vernunft*. Berlin: Aufbau, 1954.
Mann, Klaus. *Mephisto*. Hamburg: Rowohlt, 1981.
Melchinger, Siegfried. "Struktur, Klima, Personen." *Theater heute* 11, no. 10 (1970): 3–7.

Meyer, Alfred. "Das Kampfjahr 1932 und der Landtagswahlkampf in Lippe im Januar 1933." In *Hitler kämpft und siegt in Lippe 1933*. Detmold: N.S. Verlag Lippische Staatszeitung, 1934.
Möhrke. "Götz von Berlichingen." N. p., n. d. Clipping file, Berlin Akademie der Künste.
Möller, Eberhard Wolfgang. *Das Frankenburger Würfelspiel*. Berlin: Langen-Müller, 1937.
_____. *Panamaskandal*. Berlin: Langen-Müller, 1936.
_____. *Rothschild siegt bei Waterloo*. Berlin: Langen-Müller, 1934.
_____. *Der Sturz des Ministers*. Berlin: Langen-Müller, 1937.
_____. *Der Untergang Karthagos*. Berlin: Langen-Müller, 1938.
_____. *Volk und König*. Berlin: Langen-Müller, 1935.
Morgenroth, F. " 'Die endlose Straße.' Festaufführung in der 'Plaza.' " *Neue Preußische Zeitung* (Berlin), 19 November 1933: 8.
Mosse, George. *The Crisis of German Ideology; Intellectual Origins of the Third Reich*. New York: Grosset & Dunlap, 1964.
_____. *Masses and Man: Nationalist and Fascist Perceptions of Reality*. New York: Fertig, 1980.
_____. *The Nationalization of the Masses*. New York: Fertig, 1975.
_____. *Nazism: A Historical and Comparative Analysis of National Socialism*. New Brunswick, NJ: Transaction, 1978.
Mosse, George L., ed. *Nazi Culture*. New York: Grosset & Dunlop, 1966.
Mühr, Alfred. *Großes Theater. Begegnungen mit Gustaf Gründgens*. Berlin: Oswald Arnold, 1950.
_____. *Mephisto ohne Maske: Gustaf Gründgens, Legende und Wahrheit*. Munich: Langen-Müller, 1981.
_____. *Die Welt des Schauspielers Werner Krauß*. Berlin: Brunnen/Karl Winckler, 1928.
_____. *Werner Krauß, Das Schicksal auf der Bühne*. Berlin: Frundsberg, 1933.
Müller-Scheld, Wilhelm. "Der nationale Aufbruch." In *Frankfurter Theater Almanach*, vol. 17 (Frankfurt/Main: 1933): 18–19.
"Nazis Order Jews Ousted from Stage." *New York Times*, 6 March 1934: 28.
Niroumand, Mariam. "Freiheitshauch und tödliche Illusion." *Berliner Zeitung*, 4/5 April 1992: 66.
Overesch, Manfred, ed. "Das Dritte Reich, 1933–1939." Part I of *Chronik deutscher Zeitgeschichte: Politik—Wirtschaft—Kultur*, vol. 2. Düsseldorf: Droste, 1982.
NN. "Neues Tendenz-Drama um Wittekind. Zustimmung und Protest bei der Uraufführung in Hagen." *Germania* (Berlin), 29 January 1935: 9.
Noakes, J., and G. Pridham, eds. *Nazism 1919–1945*. Vol. 2, *State, Economy and Society 1933–1939, a Documentary Reader*. Exeter: University of Exeter, 1984.
Nolte, Ernst. *Three Faces of Fascism*. Tr. Leila Vennewitz. New York: New American Library, 1969.
P., H. "'Die Räuber' im Großen Schauspielhaus." N. p., n. d. Clipping file, Berlin Akademie der Künste.
Patterson, Michael. *The Revolution in German Theatre: 1900–1933*. London: Routledge and Kegan Paul, 1981.

Peters, Hans Georg. *Vom Hoftheater zum Landestheater: Die Detmolder Bühne von 1825 bis 1969*. Detmold: Landesverband Lippe, 1972.
Petley, Julian. *Capital and Culture: German Cinema 1933–1945*. London: British Film Institute, 1979.
Peukert, Detlev J. K. *Inside Nazi Germany: Conformity, Opposition, and Racism in Everyday Life*. Tr. Richard Deveson. New Haven, CT: Yale University Press, 1987.
Pfeiffer, Herbert. "Eine Sommernachtstraum-Revue." *12–Uhr-Blatt* (Berlin), 17 September 1934: n. p.
———. "Wallenstein." *12–Uhr-Blatt* (Berlin), 12 November 1934: n. p.
Philo-lexikon: Handbuch des jüdischen Wissens. Berlin: 1937.
Poche, Klaus, and Hans Ludwig. "Von der Markthalle zum Weltstadtvarieté." N. p., no. 7 (n. d.): 38. Clipping file, Berlin Akademie der Künste.
Pogade, Daniela. "Atempause oder künstlerisches Ghetto?" *Berliner Zeitung*, 25/26 January 1992: 17.
Pois, Robert A. "German Expressionism in the Plastic Arts and Naziism: A Confrontation of Idealists." *German Life and Letters* 21, no. 3 (April 1968): 204–14.
———. "Jewish Treason Against the Laws of Life: Nazi Religiosity and Bourgeois Fantasy." In *Towards the Holocaust: The Social and Economic Collapse of the Weimar Republic*, ed. Michael N. Dobkowski and Isidor Wallimann. Westport, CT: Greenwood, 1983: 343–76.
———. *National Socialism and the Religion of Nature*. New York: St. Martins Press, 1968.
"Die preußische Theater." *Frankfurter Zeitung* (Reichsausgabe), 8 May 1933: 2.
Proctor, Robert N. *Racial Hygiene: Medicine Under the Nazis*. Cambridge, MA: Harvard University, 1988.
Rainalter, Erwin H. "Im Theater des Volkes 'Götz von Berlichingen.'" *Der völkische Beobachter* (Berlin), 21 November 1935: 6.
"Regierung Hitler." *Die jüdische Rundschau* (Berlin), 31 January 1933: 1.
"Reichsminister Dr. Goebbels Shirmherr der Thingarbeit." *Der völkische Beobachter* (Berlin), 23 May 1934: 6.
"Reichsministerium für Volksaufklärung und Propaganda." Document #296, Film #6436. Bundesarchiv, Abteilung Potsdam.
"Reichstheater-Festspiele in Dresden." *Berliner Börsenzeitung*, evening ed., 20 January 1934. Dresden Staatsarchiv, Collection 1392/2, no. 124.
Reimann, Viktor. *Dr. Joseph Goebbels*. Munich: Molden, 1971.
Reinhardt, Gottfried. *The Genius, A Memoir of Max Reinhardt by his Son*. New York: Alfred A. Knopf, 1971.
Reinhardt, Max. *Schriften*. Ed. Hugo Fetting. Berlin: Henschel, 1974.
Review of *Nathan der Weise*. *Die jüdische Rundschau* (Berlin), 4 October 1933: 624.
Richarz, Monika, ed. *Jewish Life in Germany: Memoirs from Three Centuries*. Tr. Stella P. and Sidney Rosenfeld. Bloomington, IN: Indiana University Press, 1991.
Riess, Curt. *Gustaf Gründgens: die Klassische Biographie des grossen Künstler*. Hamburg: Hoffmann and Kampe, 1965.
Rischbieter, Henning, ed. *The Encyclopedia of World Theater*. New York: Scribner's, 1977.

---. *Gründgens*. Hannover: Friedrich, 1963.
Ritchie, James MacPherson. *German Literature under National Socialism*.Totowa, NJ: Barnes and Noble, 1983.
Rosenberg, Alfred. *Dietrich Eckart, Ein Vermächtnis*. Munich: F. Eher, 1928.
---. *Letzte Aufzeichnungen*. Göttingen: Plesse, 1955.
---. *Memoirs of Alfred Rosenberg*. Ed. Serge Lang and Ernst von Schenck, tr. Eric Posselt. New York: Ziff-Davis, 1949.
---. *The Myth of the Twentieth Century*. Tr. Vivian Bird. Torrance, CA: Noontide, 1982.
---. *Der Mythus des 20. Jahrhunderts*. 87–90th ed. Munich: Hoheneichen, 1935.
---. "'Der Name Dietrich Eckart unlöslich mit dem neuen Deutschland verbunden.' Dietrich-Eckart-Gedächtnis-Feier in München." *Der völkische Beobachter* (Berlin), 24 March 1934: 2.
---. *Das politische Tagebuch Alfred Rosenbergs aus den Jahren 1934/35 und 1939/40*. Ed. Hans-Günther Seraphim. Göttingen: Musterschmidt, 1956.
---. *Selected Writings*. Ed. Robert Pois. London: Jonathan Cape, 1970.
Rouse, John. *Brecht and the West German Theatre: The Practice and Politics of Interpretation*. Ann Arbor, MI: University of Michigan Press, 1989.
Rühle, Günther. *Theater für die Republik, im Spiegel der Kritik: 1917–1933*. Frankfurt am Main: Fischer, 1967.
---. *Zeit und Theater*. vols. 1–3. Berlin: Propyläen, 1974.
Schlösser, Rainer. "Aufführung von Kriegsstücken." *Die Deutsche Bühne: Amtliches Blatt des Deutschen Bühnenvereins* 26, no. 5 (23 April 1934): 89.
---. "Die Sendung des deutschen Bühnenschriftstellers der Gegenwart." *Der völkische Beobachter* (Berlin), 7 June 1934: 5.
---. *Das Volk und seine Bühne; Bemerkungen zum Aufbau des deutschen Theaters*. Berlin: Langen, 1935.
Schoenbaum, David. *Hitler's Social Revolution: Class and Status in Nazi Germany, 1933–1939*. New York: Doubleday, 1967.
Schramm, Wilhelm von. *Neubau des deutschen Theaters*. Berlin: Schlieffen,1934.
---. "Praktische Dramaturgie: Erfahrungen im Bühnenvertrieb." *Deutsche Allgemeine Zeitung* (Berlin, Reichs-Ausgabe), 27 January 1935: 5.
Shirer, William L. *Berlin Diary: The Journal of a Foreign Correspondent*. New York: Penguin, 1979.
Sironneau, Jean-Pierre. *Sécularization et religions politiques*. New York: Mouton, 1982.
Smelser, Ronald. *Robert Ley, Hitler's Labor Front Leader*. New York: Berg,1988.
"'Sommernachtstraum' im Theater des Volkes." N. p., 17 September 1934. Clipping file, Berlin Akademie der Künste.
St., Dr. Hz. "Die Reichs-Theaterwoche. Ihre Leistung und ihr Ertrag." *Dresdner neueste Nachrichten*, 5 May 1934. Dresden Staatsarchiv, Collection 1392/2, no. 397.
Stachura, Peter D. "Who Were the Nazis?" *European Studies Review* 11, no. 3(1981): 293–324.
Stege, Fritz. "Die Bühnenmusik." *Der völkische Beobachter* (Berlin), 18 September 1934: 5.
Stern, Fritz. "The Political Consequences of the Unpolitical German." *History* 3 (1960): 104–34.

Stern, J. P. *Hitler: The Führer and the People*. Berkeley: University of California Press, 1975.
Sternaux, Ludwig. "Irregang und Läuterung 'Peer Gynt' im Theater des Volkes." N. p. 6 March 1936. Clipping file, Berlin Akademie der Künste.
Stollmann, Rainer. "Fascist Politics as a Total Work of Art." Tr. Ronald L. Smith. *New German Critique* 14 (1978): 41–60.
Taylor, Ronald. *Literature and Society in Germany, 1918–1945*. Totowa, NJ: Barnes and Noble, 1980.
"Texts of Verdicts of the International Military Tribunal in Trial of German War Leaders." *New York Times*, 2 October 1946: 22.
"Theaterbesprechung bei Reichsminister Dr. Goebbels." *Der völkische Beobachter* (Berlin), 12 April 1934: 5.
"Theaterschau in Dresden." *Der völkische Beobachter* (Berlin), 27/28 May 1934: 5.
Theweleit, Klaus. Vol. 1. *Male Fantasies*. Tr. Stephen Conway. Minneapolis: Minnesota University Press, 1987.
Trask, Claire. "*Richard III* Adorns a Berlin Stage." *New York Times*, 7 May 1937: n. p.
Trotha, Thilo v. "Heroische Sachlichkeit: Gedanken über einen neuen Stil." *Der völkische Beobachter* (Berlin), 14 March 1934: 5.
Tuma, Mirko. "Memories of Theresienstadt." *Performing Arts Journal* 1, no. 2 (Fall 1976): 12–17.
Turkov, Yonas. "Teater un kontsertn in di getos un kontsentratsye lagern." In *Yidisher Teater in Yirope . . . Poyln*. New York: Knight, 1968.
Turner, Henry Ashby, Jr. *German Big Business and the Rise of Hitler*. New York: Oxford University Press, 1985.
"Um die Tätigkeit des Kulturbundes." *Die jüdische Rundschau* (Berlin), 8 August 1933: 405.
Van Zandt Moyer, Laurence. "The *Kraft durch Freude* Movement in Nazi Germany: 1933–1939." Ph.D. diss. Northwestern University, 1967.
"Verpflichtung und Aufgabe der deutschen Theater." *Deutsches Bühnen-Jahrbuch*. Berlin: Genossenschaft Deutscher Bühnen-Anhörigen, 1943: 1ff.
W., C. "Falstaff: Heinrich George." N. p. 5 February 1935. Clipping file, Berlin Akademie der Künste.
———. " 'Wallenstein' im Theater des Volkes." N. p. 13 November 1934. Clipping file, Berlin Akademie der Künste.
Waite, Robert G. L. *The Psychopathic God: Adolf Hitler*. New York: New American Library, 1977.
Wanderscheck, Hermann. *Deutsche Dramatik der Gegenwart*. Berlin: Bong, 1938.
———. *Dramaturgische Appassionata*. Leipzig: Max Beck, 1944.
Wardetzky, Jutta. *Theaterpolitik in faschistischen Deutschland*. Berlin: Henschel, 1983.
Weichardt. "Peer Gynt." N. p., n. d. Clipping file, Berlin Akademie der Künste.
Weise, Gerhart. "Dietrich Eckarts 'Peer Gynt.'" *12–Uhr-Blatt* (Berlin), 6 March 1936: n. p.
"Weitere Briefe des Führers an alte Mitkämpfer." *Der völkische Beobachter* (Berlin), 3 January 1934: 1.
Welch, David. *Propaganda and the German Cinema 1933–1945*. Oxford: Clarendon, 1983.
Willett, John. *The Theatre of the Weimar Republic*. New York: Holmes & Meier, 1988.
Winnicott, D. W. *Playing and Reality*. London: Tavistock Publications, 1971.

Wulf, Josef. *Theater und Film im Dritten Reich; Eine Dokumentation.* Gütersloh: Sigbert Mohn, 1964.
Wüst, H. Th. "Ein Nationaltheater in Frankfurt." In *Frankfurter Theater Almanach*, vol. 17 (1933): 35.
Young, James E. *Writing and the Holocaust: Narrative and the Consequences of Interpretation.* Bloomington, IN: Indiana University Press, 1988.
Zortmann, Bruce H. "Theater in Isolation: The *Jüdischer Kulturbund* of Nazi Germany." *Educational Theatre Journal* 24, no. 2 (1972): 159–68.
Zum Jubiläum des Landestheaters: 150 Jahre Theater in Detmold. Detmold: Landestheater Detmold, 1975.
Zweig, Arnold. *Juden auf der deutschen Bühne.* Berlin: Welt, 1927.

Index

Aeschylus, *Oresteia* (Vollmöller adaptation), 104–5
Amann, Max, 12
Arent, Benno von, 109–10, 115
Artists: and Jewish theatre, 141, 143, 150; as politically (in)dependent, 80, 85, 97–99, 106; and theatre in concentration camps, 162–63

Baumann, Kurt, 142, 144, 151
Becker, Emil, 34, 35
Bethge, Friedrich, *Reims*, 48
Billinger, Richard, *Lob des Landes*, 6
Blunck, Hans Friedrich, 11
Blut und Boden (Blood and Soil), 6, 10, 22, 57; as "biological mysticism," 22, 24–25; in Jewish context, 148–49; as "racial soul," 149
Brahm, Otto, 75
Brecht, Bertolt, 80, 81, 82; *Threepenny Opera*, 162–63
Brügmann, Walther, 108–16, 123
Buch, Walter, 15 n.29

Burte, Hermann, on Shakespeare, 44 n.17

Cabaret, revue at concentration camps, 161–65
Censorship, 7, 9–11, 79, 123–25, 142; Detmold, 43; and *Die endlose Straße*, 51–52
Communists, 7–8; performance at Großes Schauspielhaus, 105
Concentration camp performances, 157–65
Cremers, Paul Joseph: *Marneschlacht*, 6; *Richelieu*, 42–43
Criticism, 19–21, 43, 83; undermining national art policy, 124
Cultural Bolshevism, 3, 21, 76, 82, 86, 105

Dada, 3, 21
"Decadent Art" exhibits, 21, 126, 136 n.17
Dorsch, Käthe, 81, 94, 99

Eckart, Dietrich, 3–4; Bühne (Berlin), 69; *Peer Gynt* adaptation, 114, 130–32; Prize (Hamburg), 51
Engel, Erich, 80
Erler, Otto, *Zar Peter*, 130
Esslin, Martin, 24–27, 76
Expressionism, 21, 110, 134 n.2

Fehling, Jürgen, 80–87
Feuchtwanger, Lion, *Jud Süß*, 95
Fodor, László, *Kuß vor dem Spiegel*, 7
Forster, Friedrich, *Alle gegen einen—einer für alle*, 39
Freut euch des Lebens, revue, 114–15
Fronterlebnis, Frontstück (front-line war experience, play), 48–63; given special status, 52
Führerprinzip (leadership principle), 75
Führerrat der Vereinigten Deutsche Kultur und Kunst Verbände (Führer's Council of United German Culture and Arts Organizations), 20
Furtwängler, Wilhelm, 9, 94

George, Heinrich, 108–12
Gerron, Kurt, 158, 162–63
Gleichschaltung (political synchronization), 77, 78
Goebbels, Joseph, 8–12, 29 n.15, 77–87, 93–97; academic career, 136 n.23; on art, 9, 22, 77–78, 106, 121–34; as author, 81; forbids art criticism, 20, 83; and Großes Schauspielhaus, 106–16; on Hitler, 78–79; *Michael*, 57; on Schiller, 39, 83–84, 128; on Wagner, 126. *See also* Reichsministerium für Propaganda und Volksaufklärung
Goethe, Johann Wolfgang von: *Egmont*, 85; *Faust*, 81; *Götz von Berlichingen*, 108
Göring, Hermann, 15 n.29; at Staatstheater, 79–87, 106; takes control of Prussian theatres, 9; and Werner Krauß, 94, 95, 97

Grabbe, Christian Dietrich, 34, 82; Grabbe Festival in Detmold, 40. *See also* Johst, *Der Einsame*
Graff, Sigmund: *Die endlose Straße* (with Carl Ernst Hintze), 49–63, 130; *Die Heimkehr des Matthias Bruck*, 39, 54
Großes Schauspielhaus (Berlin), 103–16
Gründgens, Gustaf, 79–87, 94

Hauptmann, Gerhart, 88 n.10; *Vor Sonnenuntergang*, 100 n.21
Hegel, Georg, 23
Heimkehrer Drama (homecoming dramas), 39, 54, 65–66
Hermannsdenkmal, 35
Hess, Rudolf, 8–9, 11
Heuser, Annelies, 81
Hilpert, Heinz, 80–87, 94
Himmler, Heinrich, 12
Hindenburg, Paul von, 8
Hinkel, Hans, 12, 147
Hinrichs, August: *Krach um Iolanthe*, 36–37; *Die Stedinge*, 127
Hintze, Carl Ernst, *Die endlose Straße* (with Sigmund Graff), 49–63
Hitler, Adolf, 7–8, 11–12; as artist, 3, 78–79, 81, 121–22; on the Aryan, 75–76; on "decadent" art, 21, 76, 126; and Dietrich Eckart, 137 n.30; at Dresden theatre festival, 125–26; and film, 28; on Jews, 4, 10; *Mein Kampf*, 2–4, 21; at Nürnberg, 10, 24, 54; as orator, 26–27; preferred art(ists), 3, 31 n.36, 136 n.16; as spiritual Führer, 26–27; as symbolic dramatic character, Figure in Black Armor, 70, Gustav Wasa 39, Hasdrubal, 72, Schlageter, 36; on theatre, 3, 21, 78, 134; on the Volk community, 18–19
Hoffmeister, Adolf, *Brundibar*, 161
Homosexuality, 64 n.27; and Gründgens, 82, 88 n.44; and male bonding in war, 57–58
Hornsteiner, Ludwig, 112, 113–14

Horvath, Ödön von, *Glaube Liebe Hoffnung*, 85

Ibsen, Henrik, 3; *Peer Gynt* (in Eckart adaptation), 113–14, 130–32
Iffland Ring, 99

Jessner, Leopold, 75, 76–77
Jews, Judaism, as characters, Baat Baal, 72, in *Jud Süß*, 95–96, Rothschild, 66–68, Shylock, 37, 95–96; cultural identity, 146–50; forced retirement, 8, 15 n.30; supposed domination of the German stage, 4, 7, 9, 14 n.18, 52; Zionism, 144–46, 150, 155 n.42. *See also* Kulturbund Deutscher Juden
Johst, Hanns, 11, 37, 40; *Der Einsame*, 41; *Schlageter*, 36; *Thomas Paine*, 5–6, 41
Jud Süß (film), 92, 95, 96

Kaiser, Georg, *Das Los des Ossian Balvesen*, 85
Kallir, Alfred (pseud. for Ernst Lach), *Nr. 51 "Badendes Mädchen,"* 6–7
Kalmar, Rudolf, *Bloody Night at Horror Castle*, 161
Kampfbund deutscher Kultur (Militant League for German Culture), 8, 76
Kiss, Edmund, *Wittekind*, 139 n.46
Kitsch: and Third Reich art, 110, 127–28; and Weimar art, 137 n.24
Klucke, Walther, *Einsidel*, 49
Kolbenheyer, Erwin: *Die Brücke*, 42; *Heroische Leidenschaften*, 63 n.13, 130
Kraft durch Freude (Strength Through Joy), 11, 138 n.45; in Detmold, 38, 40, 79; and Theater des Volkes, 106–16. *See also* Ley, Robert.
Krauß, Werner, 82, 84, 91–99, 112; as Richard III, 86, 87
Kube, Wilhelm, *Totila* 40–41
Külb, Karl, *Narren des Ruhms*, 7
Kulturbund Deutscher Juden (Cultural Union of German Jewry), 11, 141–52

Kyser, Hans, *Es brennt an der Grenze*, 37

Langenbeck, Curt, *Hochverräter*, 42
Last Cyclist, 160
Laubinger, Otto, 11, 94, 97, 125, 132
Leiwik, Halper, *The Golem*, 146, 155 n.30
Lessing, Gotthold: *Minna von Barnhelm*, 84; *Nathan der Weise*, 144, 145–46
Ley, Robert, 11, 106–7, 122, 123; satirized at Buchenwald, 164
Lüger, Karl, 4

Machtergreifung (Nazi Seizure of Power), 1, 49, 77
Mann, Klaus, 81; *Mephisto*, 89 n.44
Mannheim, Lucie, 81, 88 n.27
Martin, Karl-Heinz, 80
Military Analogies in Art, 20–21
Möller, Eberhard Wolfgang, 65–74; *Douaumont*, 65–66; *Frankenburger Würfelspiel*, 69–70; *Kalifornische Tragödie*, 65–66; *Panamaskandal*, 68–69; *Rothschild siegt bei Waterloo*, 40, 66–68; *Sturz des Ministers*, 70–71; *Untergang Karthagos*, 71–72; *Volk und König*, 68
Mühlfeldt, Karl von, *Was uns fehlt? Arbeit!*, 6
Müller, Traugott, 86
Müller-Scheld, Wilhelm, 21
Mussolini, Benito, *Hundert Tage* (with Giavaccino Forzano), 94

National Socialism: anti-intellectual, 19–20; art ideals, 3–6, 20–23; as secular religion, 18–20, 24–25, 27; as theatre, 27–28
Neher, Caspar, 81
NS-Kulturgemeinde (National Socialist Cultural Community), 79, 133–34

Operetta, 115–16
Ortner, Eugen, *Aufbruch aus Österreich*, 6

Paust, Otto, *Weg in den Morgen*, 48–49
Piscator, Erwin, 75, 80, 105, 157
Poelzig, Hans, 104, 107–8, 115

Race and acting, 148–49
Rauschning, Hermann, 22
Reichkulturkammern (National Culture Chambers), 10–11, 20, 144; Theaterkammer, 78
Reichsministerium für Propaganda und Volksaufklärung (Propaganda Ministry), 8, 77–78
Reichstheaterfesten (National Theatre Festivals), 22, 121–34
Reichstheatergesetz (National Theatre Law), 77
Reichsverband Deutsche Bühne (National German Stage Alliance), 8, 125
Reichsverband Deutscher Schriftsteller (National Association of German Authors), 6
Reinhardt, Max, 75, 80–81, 92–93, 95, 96, 157; casting style, 116 n.5; at the Großes Schauspielhaus, 103–5; surrenders Berlin theatres, 10
Röhm, Ernst, 12, 58, 126
Rosenberg, Alfred, 8–10, 12, 22, 29 n.15, 83, 127; and Dietrich Eckart, 131– 32, 137 n.28; forms the NS-Kulturgemeinde, 133–34; on Gerhart Hauptmann, 88, n.10; on Goebbles, 133; *Mythus des 20. Jahrhunderts*, 76; as Nazi Ideologue, 122–23; on Weimar theatre, 13 n.11
Rotter, Alfred and Fritz, 7

Schiller, Johann Friedrich von: *Don Carlos*, 83–84; *Die Räuber*, 109; *Wallenstein*, 110–11; *Wilhelm Tell*, 98
Schirach, Baldur von, 15 n.29
Schlösser, Rainer: and *Die endlose Straße*, 51–53; on Grabbe, 40; on history plays, 127, 136 n.19; named Reichsdramaturg, 10; program, 78, 83
Scholarship: on Jewish Theatre, 141–44; on Third Reich Theatre, 2, 91, 98

Schönherr, Karl, *Glaube und Heimat*, 37
Schütte, Ernst, 81
Schwarz, Franz X., 11–12
Schwenk, Karl, 160
Seldte, Franz, 15 n.29
Shakespeare, William, 76–77; *As You Like It*, 83; *King Lear*, 84; *Merchant of Venice*, 37, 95–96; *Merry Wives of Windsor*, 111–12; *Midsummer Night's Dream*, 109–10, 118 n.37; Nazi respect for, 37, 122; productions in Detmold, 34, 37; *Richard III*, 85–86, 87; *Winter's Tale*, 83
Shaw, George Bernard, 94; *Apple Cart*, 84; *Don Juan in Hell*, 99; *Pygmalion*, 84; support of Hitler, 84
Singer, Kurt, 142, 146, 148, 155 nn.36, 37
Sobol, Joshua, *Ghetto*, 156 n.60
Sonnemann, Emmy, 36, 82, 84
Spira, Camilla, 143, 147, 162
Strauß, Richard, 94, 126
Sturm, Eduard, 111
Subsidy, 8, 10, 78–79

Thing, Thingspiel (play of *Volk* judgment), 28, 69–70, 136 n.22
Toller, Ernst and Erich Weinert, *Trotz alledem!*, 105
Tretiakov, Sergei, *Brülle China*, 163–64
Trotha, Thilo von, 122, 135 n.3
Truppe 31, *Wer ist der Dümmste?*, 13 n.16

Volksgemeinschaft (national folk community), 17–28, 108, 110; in history plays, 127, 136 n.20; in *Peer Gynt*, 131

Wagner, Richard, 126; *Tristan und Isolde*, 126, 136 n.16; Wagner Festival in Detmold, 39–40
Wedekind, Frank, 92
Weichert, Richard, 108, 110
Will-Rasing, Otto, 35
Winnicott, Donald, definition of play, 26–27
Wisten, Fritz, 147–48, 152 n.2

Zelenka, Frantisek, 160, 161, 163
Zindler, Rudolf, 115–16

Zuckmayer, Carl, 94
Zweig, Arnold, 149

About the Editor and Contributors

RUFUS J. CADIGAN has taught English in Libya with the Peace Corps and theatre at the University of Kansas and Ottawa University. He is currently professor of theatre at Rockford College. In addition to his interest in modern German theatre, he is a director and playwright.

RON ENGLE is Chester Fritz Distinguished Professor of Theatre Arts at the University of North Dakota, and founding editor of *Theatre History Studies*. His books include *Shakespeare Festivals and Companies: An International Guide* (edited with Daniel Watermeier and Felicia Londré) and *The American Stage: Social and Economic Issues from the Colonial Period to the Present* (edited with Tice Miller). He was visting professor in the Institut für Theaterwissenschaft at Munich University in 1989.

WILLIAM R. ELWOOD is Dean of Graduate Studies at Emerson College in Boston. He was formerly chair of the Department of Theatre & Drama at the University of Wisconsin-Madison, where he taught theatre history and dramatic literature. He held two Fulbright-Hays Grants for study at the Freie Universität in Berlin and at Ludwig Maximilian Universität in Munich. His major research interest is in German expressionism. His most recent publications include "Eugene O'Neill's *Dynamo* and the Expressionist Canon," *Eugene O'Neill in China*, Greenwood Press, 1992.

About the Editor and Contributors

GLEN W. GADBERRY is Associate Professor of Theatre at the University of Minnesota—Twin Cities. His research focus is the German-language theatre of the late 19th to mid 20th century. He has written many articles on the theatre and drama of the Third Reich. He is currently working on a book on the theatre of Agnes Straub.

WILLIAM GRANGE chaired the department of Performing Arts at Marquette University in Milwaukee, where he currently is associate professor, teaching courses in theatre history, drama analysis, and drama theory. He has written essays appearing in scholarly journals, *Theatre Survey, New England Theatre Journal, Essays in Theatre* among them. He has also written reviews for *Theatre Journal, Western European Stages, 19th Century Theatre Research*, and many others. He is currently at work on a book-length study titled *Comedy in the Weimar Republic*.

MICHAEL PATTERSON, after serving as Lecturer in Drama at the University of Ulster, Coleraine, is currently Head of the Department of Visual and Performing Arts at De Montfort University, Leicester. His research into German theatre has led to important articles and books, including *German Theatre Today: Post-War Theatre in West and East Germany, Austria and Northern Switzerland* (1976), *The Revolution in German Theatre, 1900–1933* (1981), *Peter Stein, Germany's Leading Theatre Director* (1982), and *The First German Theatre: Schiller, Goethe, Kleist, and Büchner in Performance* (1990).

ROBERT A. POIS has taught at the University of Colorado at Boulder since 1965, and is a Professor of History. Areas of interest include philosophy of history, with emphases upon historicism and psychohistory, Weimar Germany, National Socialist Germany, German Expressionism in the plastic arts, and World War I. He has published, or is about to, in these fields.

REBECCA ROVIT, most recently a Visiting Assistant Professor at Indiana University, is a theatre historian whose essays on issues in German theatre performance—past and present—have appeared in such journals as *American Theatre, TDR*, and *Contemporary Theatre Review*. Her present research on the *Kulturbund* is being sponsored by a grant from the Memorial Foundation for Jewish Culture.

YVONNE SHAFER has taught at several universities in America including the University of California at Santa Barbara and the University of Colorado at Boulder. She has also taught and lectured in China, Belgium, Norway, and Germany. Her writing includes books on Ibsen, articles for national and international theatre journals, and articles and reviews for the *New York Times* and other newspapers.

WILLIAM SONNEGA is an Assistant Professor in the Department of Speech-Theater at St. Olaf College where he teaches theatre history, playwriting, and media studies. His articles on twentieth-century German and American theatre appear in *Theatre Studies, Theatre History Studies, Text & Presentation,* and *TDR*. His plays have been staged Off-Broadway and at regional and university theaters in the United States.

ISBN 0-313-29516-6

9 780313 295164

90000>

EAN

HARDCOVER BAR CODE